DESTINATION SHANGHAI

PAUL FRENCH was born, and is currently based in London, but has also lived and worked in Shanghai for many years. After a career as a widely published analyst and commentator on China he is now a full-time author, scriptwriter and historian focusing on China and Asia in the first half of the twentieth century. He has written a number of books, including a history of foreign correspondents in China and a biography of the legendary Shanghai adman, journalist and adventurer Carl Crow.

His recent book *Midnight in Peking* was a *New York Times* Bestseller, a BBC Radio 4 Book of the Week, a Mystery Writers of America Edgar award winner for Best Fact Crime and a Crime Writers' Association (UK) Dagger award for non-fiction. His most recent work, *City of Devils: A Shanghai Noir* focuses on the dance-halls, casinos and cabarets of wartime Shanghai. Both *Midnight in Peking* and *City of Devils* have been optioned by Kudos.

French is also a regular contributor and book reviewer for publications including *The Literary Hub*, the *Financial Times Weekend*, the *South China Morning Post Magazine*, *Crime Reads* and *Real Crime*. He also occasionally works in radio drama with productions including *Death at the Airport: The Plot Against Kim Jong-nam* for BBC Radio 4.

Praise for *Midnight in Peking*

'A fascinating tale of life and death in a city on the brink of all-out war.'
— *Time*

'He resurrects a period that was filled with glitter as well as evil, but was never, as readers will appreciate, known for being dull.'
— *The Economist*

'The most talked-about read in town this year.'
— *New Yorker*

'A crime story set among sweeping events is reminiscent of Graham Greene, particularly *The Third Man*, while French's terse, tightly-focussed style has rightly been compared to Chandler. *Midnight in Peking* deserves a place alongside both these masters.'
— *The Independent* (UK)

'It is the storytelling flair that marks *Midnight in Peking* so highly above the run-of-the-mill true crime stories: with its false leads and twists, it sucks the reader in like the best fiction.'
— *The Scotsman*

'The shocking true tale, combined with prose you can't drag yourself away from, makes *Midnight in Peking* a work of non-fiction as compulsive as any bestselling crime novel.'
— *Sunday Express* (UK)

'One of the best portraits of between-the-wars China that has yet been written.'
— *Wall Street Journal*

Praise for *City of Devils*

'It's hard to go wrong with dope, decadence, and the demimonde . . . French recounts all this with great energy and brio.'
— Gary Krist, *The New York Times Book Review*

'Wonderfully atmospheric . . . French's two-fisted prose makes this deep noir history unforgettable.'
— *Publishers Weekly* (starred review)

'Nothing lasts forever: In 1930s Shanghai, the no-holds-barred gangster scene was run by an American ex-Navyman and a Jewish man who'd fled Vienna. Their milieu – and its end – comes alive.'
— Carolyn Kellogg, *Los Angeles Times*

'A tale of flash and noir demands a voice to match; fortunately, French combines the skills of a scholar with the soul of Dashiell Hammett.'
— Boris Kachka, *Vulture*

'Move over Weimar: Paul French's *City of Devils*, a history of glam and seedy interwar Shanghai's refugees and criminals, is nostalgic noir at its best.'
— *New York Magazine*

'The story is brought alive by Mr French's Shanghai-noir telling, which echoes Dashiell Hammett and James Ellroy. He grips his reader to the end.'
— *The Economist*

'French's louche and moodily lit recreation of Shanghai is thrillingly done. This atmospheric survey hangs on the zoot-suited shoulders of the two leads. French's story chops and changes between Jack and Joe as they make their wayward ways east until fates and hardscrabble fortunes collide in the dive bars and dancehalls of Shanghai's Blood Alley.'
— Laura Freeman, *The Times* (UK)

'A story with the dark resonance of James Ellroy's novel *L.A. Confidential* and the seedy glamour of Alan Furst's between-the-wars mysteries . . . Reader advisory: By the time you are done with this extraordinary book, you will believe in devils, too.'
— Mary Ann Gwinn, *Newsday*

Also by Paul French

City of Devils: A Shanghai Noir
Midnight in Peking: How the Murder of a Young
    Englishwoman Haunted the Last Days of Old Peking
The Badlands: Decadent Playground of Old Peking
Bloody Saturday: Shanghai's Darkest Day
Supreme Leader: The Making of Kim Jong-un
Betrayal in Paris: How the Treaty of Versailles
    Led to China's Long Revolution
The Old Shanghai A–Z
Through the Looking Glass:
    China's Foreign Journalists from Opium Wars to Mao
Carl Crow – A Tough Old China Hand:
    The Life, Times, and Adventures of an American in Shanghai
North Korea: The Paranoid Peninsula – A Modern History
Murders of Old China (an Audible Original)

DESTINATION SHANGHAI

by

Paul French

BLACKSMITH BOOKS

DESTINATION SHANGHAI

ISBN 978-988-77927-5-8 (paperback)
Text and photographs © 2019 Paul French unless otherwise noted

Published by Blacksmith Books
Unit 26, 19/F, Block B, Wah Lok Industrial Centre,
31–35 Shan Mei St, Fo Tan, Hong Kong
www.blacksmithbooks.com

Typeset in Adobe Garamond by Alan Sargent
Printed in Hong Kong

First printing 2019

Once again for A.V.W.

Contents

Introduction

The eighteen pieces contained in this collection cover the true experiences of a range of foreigners who, for one reason or another, came to Shanghai in the twentieth century. The earliest story is set in 1906 and the latest in 1977. Together their stories reflect the multitude of experiences and interactions foreigners had with the city. For most to hear the cry 'Destination Shanghai' was an exciting adventure, but for others it heralded the start of a life in exile, for some an attempt to escape their past.

They include the then famous and still well known such as the playwright Eugene O'Neill, the movie stars Douglas Fairbanks and Mary Pickford, and the poet Langston Hughes. Others were famous once but have since fallen from the public eye – the 'Charlie Chan' actor Warner Oland, the Broadway comic actress Lyda Roberti, the American vaudeville star Irene West. Others were known only to those living in the city at the time – the thief and swindler Elly Widler, or the cabaret dancer Terese Rudolph.

For most foreigners Shanghai was a place of escape or distraction of one sort or another – Eugene O'Neill sought refuge from the pressures of fame, the author Penelope Fitzgerald the sadness of widowhood, Lyda Roberti's family the Bolsheviks, Berlin silent movie star Lily Flohr the Nazis. O'Neill and Fitzgerald stayed only briefly; Roberti and Flohr longer but all eventually moved on – O'Neill and Fitzgerald to reawakened creativity; Roberti to stardom in Hollywood; Flohr to a safe retirement in Australia.

But these are not all stories with a happy ending. Eliza Shapera was trafficked to Shanghai from her home in Europe, forced into prostitution and murdered in her slum lodgings in 1907. The American conman C.C. Julian ended his Shanghai adventure overdosing in the Astor House Hotel.

All these stories show us various aspects of life in Shanghai. Douglas Fairbanks and Mary Pickford came to sell American talking-picture technology to Asia's most advanced and largest movie making city; the young Australian singer and dancer Bobby Broadhurst to see the Far East's most lavish nightlife capital. The city's politics attracted others – the left-wing journalist Arthur Ransome, the writer André Malraux and an assortment of foreign communists who saw China as the next revolutionary centre. Some just washed up by chance – the future bestselling author Louis L'Amour as a merchant seaman; others, like the occultist Aleister Crowley, on a last-minute whim.

Whatever forces or reason brought these men and women to Shanghai they encountered an incredible city – modern, challenging, full of opportunities and pitfalls, a place to conquer or submit to. They came from different countries, at different moments to encounter very different Shanghais. But they all at some point heard the call 'Destination Shanghai'.

Paul French – September 2018

A note on names and spellings

Names in this book reflect the spellings most commonly used in the first half of the twentieth century. Hence Peking and not Beijing; Nanking and not Nanjing. Where Chinese people were commonly known by Western names to foreign audiences these are used, rather than the Pinyin romanisations. Additionally I have used the best known variations of some Chinese names rather than their more modern variants, such as Sun Yat-sen rather than Sun Zhongshan or Chiang Kai-shek as opposed to Jiang Jieshi.

I have also used the former, pre-war road and district names of the International Settlement and French Concession within the text. A list of these roads and their current names, as well as the names of Chinese cities and Shanghai districts both before and after 1949 are added as an appendix at the end of the book.

As the writer, sojourner and one-time 'Shanghailander' (foreign resident of the city) Emily Hahn once commented when tackling the question of rendering Chinese into English, 'This writer has done her best but knows it is not good enough, and meekly bends her head before the inevitable storm.'

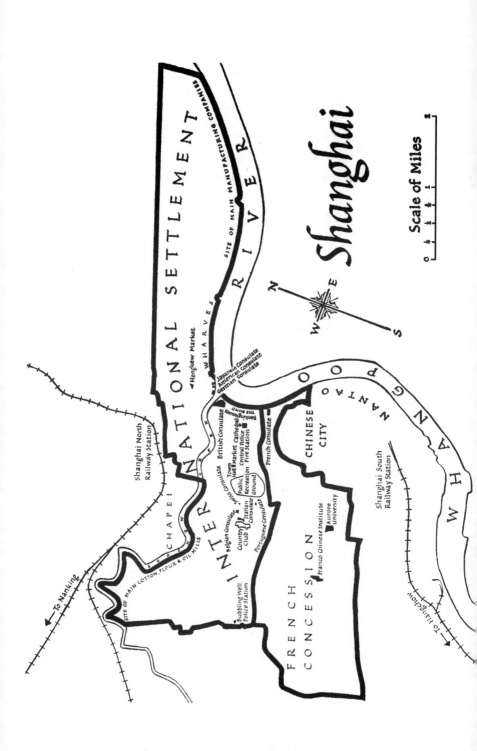

Shanghai

INTERNATIONAL SETTLEMENT

SITE OF MAIN MANUFACTURING COMPANIES

WHARVES

Hongkew Market

HUANGPOO RIVER

Scale of Miles

N
W E
S

Japanese Consulate
American Consulate
German Consulate

THE BUND
Bank Houses
British Consulate
Town Hall Market Cathedral
Swiss Consulate
Central Police Fire Station
Public Recreation Ground
French Consulate

Belgian Consulate
Country Italian Consulate
Club
Portuguese Consulate

CHINESE CITY

NANTAO

Shanghai North Railway Station

CHAPEI

To Nanking

SITE OF MAIN COTTON, FLOUR & OIL MILLS

Bubbling Well Police Station

FRENCH CONCESSION

Franco Chinese Institute
Aurore University

Shanghai South Railway Station

WHANGPOO

To Hangchow

How America's Most Famous Playwright Went to Shanghai, Fooled Everyone and had a High Old Time of It: Eugene O'Neill (1928)

'I have found more snoops and gossips per square inch in Shanghai than there is in any New England town.'

Part One – O'Neill is missing!

The best of times; the worst of times

In 1928 Eugene O'Neill was arguably America's most prominent and famous playwright. His experimental and highly controversial play *Strange Interlude* was a sell-out on Broadway with the veteran actors Tom Powers and Lynn Fontanne in the lead roles.[1] The play was a marathon – nine acts, lasting five hours starting at 5.30 PM, finishing at 11 PM with an hour's interval at 7.30 PM for dinner to be served! Published in book form, *Strange Interlude* hit the bestseller lists where the Modern Library's collection of O'Neill's plays, including *The Emperor Jones* and *The Straw*, were already listed. Outside New York, readings of *Strange Interlude* (or at least portions of it) were organised in hotels, bookshops and among local literary circles. A lavish production of O'Neill's *Marco Millions* (a satire on Marco Polo), starring Alfred Lunt, was settled in for a seemingly long run at the Guild Theater downtown.[2] Around the country numerous repertory theatres were performing O'Neill's earlier plays to full houses. His fame had spread overseas – his 1925 play *Lazarus Laughed* (which requires over a hundred actors) was being performed to packed houses at the Moscow Art Theatre, directed by the legendary Vladimir Nemirovich-Danchenko, while another production was opened to acclaim at Frankfurt's Shauspielhaus theatre. O'Neill's *The Hairy Ape* was running at London's *avant-garde* Gate Theatre before moving to the Festival Theatre at Cambridge. While London's more stuffy theatre critics were less fulsome in their praise of O'Neill than those in New York, the Oxford University Dramatic Society declared themselves fans and

1   At the John Golden Theatre on West 58th Street.
2   After its New York run *Marco Millions* was to be taken on tour across the United States by the Theater Guild, which specialised in staging supposedly non-commercial plays.

performed his one-act play *Where the Cross is Made*. Despite the critics, the Gate found O'Neill to be box-office gold and moved from *The Hairy Ape* straight to a production of his 1924 play about segregation, *All God's Chillun Got Wings*.

The man himself was most sought after. He chaired a prestigious dinner in honour of The Provincetown Players, the experimental theatre that first performed his work and made *The Hairy Ape* a success, at which his table for the night included such luminaries as the poet Edna St Vincent Millay and Paul Robeson (who had made the role of Brutus Jones in O'Neill's *The Emperor Jones* his own on the New York and London stage). He found himself elected chairman of the Ibsen Memorial Committee formed to erect a statue to the Norwegian dramatist in New York. In May 1928 O'Neill was awarded a Pulitzer Prize for *Strange Interlude* (his third Pulitzer after wins in 1920 for *Beyond the Horizon* and 1922 for *Anna Christie*). He also collected a cheque for us$1,000 (worth us$15,000 in 2018 money) that came with it. Newspapers reporting the prize described O'Neill as 'America's greatest dramatist'. In October it was announced that his new play *Dynamo* would be produced on Broadway the following year.

Shortly after this announcement, Eugene O'Neill dropped out of sight, sparking a media hunt for the man, fears for his safety, his mental health, and column inches of rumour, speculation and false leads as to his whereabouts. The reporters hot on the O'Neill story soon found their trail stretching a long, long way from Broadway – all the way to the China coast where the Yangtze River meets the East China Sea and the International Settlement of Shanghai. There, in a hotel sickbed, O'Neill was said to be critically ill and in the throes of a nervous breakdown. America's most notorious playwright, burnt out, had fled the United States to escape his fame and find privacy.

In fact the press corps hadn't got much right at all, apart from that the playwright Eugene O'Neill had been in Shanghai, had not been in the best of health and had stayed for a while at the Astor House Hotel. That was just the tip of the iceberg.

The other life

Despite his much-publicised run of success in 1928 with what the newspapers described as 'morbid yet fascinating dramas', O'Neill was a highly troubled man. His popularity as a playwright not withstanding, he was fated to suffer with depression, accentuated by alcoholism. His condition led him to shun the limelight, avoid the newspapers and isolate himself and, as witnessed by his sudden flight to Shanghai, he would go to extraordinary lengths to achieve this.

Hotels were a central part of O'Neill's life – he was born in one; would hide out in one in Shanghai to escape his notoriety, and eventually die in one. Eugene Gladstone O'Neill was born, in 1888, in the Barrett House Hotel on Broadway, close to 43rd Street on Longacre Square (that soon became far better known as Times Square). His father was an Irish Catholic immigrant actor and his mother was also of Irish descent. His father was a chronic alcoholic and his mother suffered from various mental illnesses her whole life. O'Neill spent a year at Princeton, before being thrown out for unspecified reasons. He then opted for a life at sea. On-board ship he fell into drinking accompanied by bouts of melancholy; nevertheless developing a deep love for the oceans, which would become, like depression, a recurring theme in his dramas. Both his parents, and his older brother Jamie, died within quick succession of each other; his brother also succumbing to alcoholism.

In 1912 O'Neill was admitted to a sanatorium for tuberculosis (a condition worsened by his drinking). It was while confined that he decided on the life of a dramatist. His time in the sanatorium would later provide him with background for his best-known work, *Long Day's Journey Into Night*. In 1914 he attended classes in dramatic technique at Harvard, but dropped out and never completed the course. He gravitated towards New York's Bohemian enclave of Greenwich Village and its vibrant literary scene. While at sea he had joined the Industrial Workers of the World, the 'Wobblies', a radical syndicalist union, and in Greenwich Village moved once more in radical circles. He was friends with the socialist journalist John Reed who would eventually travel to the newly founded Soviet

Union. He also had a brief romantic relationship with Reed's equally fiery socialist wife, Louise Bryant.

In 1916 he arrived in Provincetown with 'a trunk full of plays'[3] to join the highly innovative and experimental Provincetown Players theatre collective in Cape Cod. He soon became their de facto in-house playwright, with his work performed both in Provincetown and at the Players' theatre space on Greenwich Village's MacDougall Street. He had some success and several plays moved to Broadway. Nineteen twenty was his breakthrough year with the success of *Beyond the Horizon*, a story of a seafaring family, which garnered him his initial Pulitzer Prize for his first full-length work. *The Emperor Jones*, a play about the occupation of Haiti (a big issue in that year's presidential election) played on Broadway, as did *Anna Christie* (a prostitute seeking redemption tale), which scooped O'Neill a second Pulitzer in 1922. *Desire Under the Elms*, an attempt to transport Greek tragedy to a rural New England setting, was a hit while his plays *The Great God Brown* and *Lazarus Laughed* made use of Japanese Noh theatre techniques and the Greek Chorus respectively. By 1928, and the success of *Strange Interlude* on Broadway, his reputation was assured – three Pulitzers, a string of Broadway hits, his work performed in repertory across the country and increasingly appreciated internationally.

But O'Neill's personal life was more problematic. In 1909 he had married Kathleen Jenkins, a more-or-less conventional young woman from a good family, and had a son, Eugene O'Neill Jr. However, the marriage had failed by 1912. O'Neill met the British-born pulp fiction writer Agnes Boulton in 1917 in the Golden Swan Saloon, better known as 'The Hell Hole', in Greenwich Village. They married six months later and had two children – Shane in 1919 and Oona in 1925. O'Neill's work was earning him good money by this point, and Boulton herself was a successful popular writer, allowing them to buy 'Spithead', an estate on Bermuda's Great Sound – a 6,000 square foot property boasting a spacious harbour-side terrace and its own dock. At Spithead O'Neill worked

3   Quoted in Michael Manheim, *The Cambridge Companion to Eugene O'Neill*, (Cambridge: Cambridge University Press, 2008).

happily with his dog Finn MacCool at his feet, but slid back into alcoholism. In 1928, the year when O'Neill was enjoying so much acclaim and success, the marriage to Agnes fell apart.

A major reason for the marriage's failure was Carlotta Monterey, an actress from San Francisco. O'Neill and Monterey had first met back in 1922 when she appeared in a Broadway production of *The Hairy Ape*. Born Hazel Neilson Taasinge in 1888, she had won a 'Miss California' competition and then journeyed to London to study under the famous actor and theatre manager Sir Herbert Beerbohm Tree, who had recently founded the Royal Academy of Dramatic Art. She returned to America just before the outbreak of World War One and took the stage name Carlotta Monterey. While she had appeared in a number of Broadway plays before *The Hairy Ape,* her acting was not nearly as admired as her looks that won seemingly universal praise from the critics.

The relationship between Monterey and O'Neill began in 1926 and Agnes appears to have become aware of it in early 1928 – retaining the Provincetown attorney Harry Weinberger to begin divorce proceedings. Monterey had previously married a well-known caricaturist Ralph Burton, whose work epitomised early 1920s Manhattan and regularly appeared in *Vanity Fair, The New Yorker, Collier's* and *Harper's Bazaar*, among other fashionable magazines. She divorced Barton, himself a manic-depressive, in 1926 around the time she took up with O'Neill.[4] Effectively Monterey exited a relationship with one extremely talented and creative manic-depressive of some wealth and fame to immediately enter another relationship with an extremely talented and creative depressive who had achieved wealth and fame.

It was in June 1928 that Agnes announced publicly she was seeking to divorce O'Neill. She told the press that she was travelling to either Reno or Mexico to obtain a quickie divorce and that all matters – financial and paternal – between her and her husband had been sorted out through their lawyer (getting a double payday;

---

4   Barton committed suicide, shooting himself through the right temple, in
    May 1931 in his Manhattan penthouse. His suicide note said he feared a
    worsening of his manic-depression and had irrevocably 'lost the only woman
    I ever loved'. This is generally taken to mean Carlotta Monterey.

Weinberger was also O'Neill's attorney). She intended to seek the divorce on grounds of desertion and was living in seclusion in a Park Avenue hotel in Manhattan. Monterey was not cited in the petition. As the newspapers reported, her husband was abroad, 'his exact whereabouts unknown'.[5]

Leading Shanghai a merry dance

Eugene O'Neill was in Shanghai. He had managed to stay incognito in the city for about a month before the city's press corps discovered that the famous playwright was in town and one of the strangest pursuits of a celebrity by the media began. The hunt came to involve the Shanghai Municipal Police (SMP), Shanghailander society doctors, one of the International Settlement's best known hostesses, as well as journalists from as far afield as Hong Kong and Manila.

On December 10th, 1928 the press reported that O'Neill was in a Shanghai sanatorium with a recurrence of his former lung condition. His situation was reported as having turned 'critical after Mr O'Neill had been ill for some time'.[6] The report had reached London from the offices of the Japanese news agency, the Nippon Denpo, which supplied news dispatches to the British newspapers, as well as the new American news service, United Press, from its Shanghai branch office. Though the Nippon Denpo had a reputation for rather sensationalising its wire stories there was no reason to doubt the substance.

The newspaper rumour mill went into immediate overdrive. A day later several American newspapers reported that O'Neill had simply suffered a case of sunstroke while in Asia but was now 'pronounced cured'.[7] Perhaps this was true – the newspapers reported variously that O'Neill had come down with sunstroke

5   'Eugene O'Neill's Second Wife is Divorce Seeker', *News-Review* (Roseburg, Oregon), June 21, 1928.

6   'Eugene O'Neill Ill in Shanghai London Hears', *Reading Times* (Pennsylvania), December 10, 1928.

7   'Cured of Sunstroke', *Woodland Daily Democrat* (California), December 11, 1928.

during stopovers in either Colombo, Singapore or Saigon, where he was rumoured to have also caught a bad cold that had developed into full-blown influenza. The same day several newspapers had a somewhat different story. O'Neill had apparently suffered 'a slight nervous breakdown and bronchitis occasioned by the strain of travel and overwork.' The playwright, the reports said, had been prescribed a week in bed to ensure his full recovery.[8] In the more detailed reports a name was first heard that, as the hunt for O'Neill intensified and became decidedly stranger, would be constantly mentioned – Dr Alexander Renner, described as 'an Austrian nerve specialist resident in Shanghai'.

In Shanghai itself the local English-language China Coast newspapers, the legion of stringers for foreign papers and news services including the Associated Press, United Press, the Trans-Pacific News Service and Reuters, as well as the resident foreign Shanghailander population, became consumed by the story. Shanghai was a city that craved celebrity, loved visits by important personages and generated vast amounts of gossip as to what those celebrities thought of the city and, given Shanghai's growing reputation as a world sin capital, what they got up to while they sojourned in town. Shanghainese and Shanghailander both were obsessed by the modern, the new, the in-vogue. Those that represented those worlds were treated as honoured guests and their every movement closely watched and reported on. They were also monitored – especially if they were perceived to have left-wing proclivities. The SMP and its political section, Special Branch, were also to take an interest in Eugene O'Neill's covert visit to their city.

In December 1928 in smart Shanghailander homes O'Neill was a major topic of gossip – where he was, who he was with, and why he was in the International Settlement, consumed the dinner party chat of the swankier sort hosted by the city's '400', the wealthiest and most influential foreigners in town.

And then O'Neill vanished again. . . .

8   'Eugene O'Neill Recovering', various reports including *Brooklyn Daily Eagle*, December 10, 1928.

It transpired, as told in a small story in the local *North-China Daily News*, that O'Neill was staying in the Settlement's Astor House Hotel and had been there for a month or so laid up in his sick bed, it was believed since early November.

The recently appointed Manager, Mr H.O. 'Henry' Wasser, oversaw the Astor, located at the junction of the Whangpoo River and the Soochow Creek, just across from the famous Bund. The hotel was technically in Shanghai's Hongkew district at the northern end of the Garden Bridge that crossed the creek. The Astor had been founded as a boarding house and existed in one form or another since the 1840s, not long after the opening of Shanghai as a foreign-administered treaty port in the wake of the Opium Wars. The incarnation of the Astor building in which Eugene O'Neill lodged had been completed in 1911, boasting a 500-seat dining room and a grand, sprung dance floor. It termed itself the 'Waldorf Astoria of the Orient' boasting that all its 211 rooms had twenty-four-hour hot water, telephones and 'the finest service in the world'.

As soon as the news got out that O'Neill was resident at the Astor House the local newspapers besieged the hotel lobby seeking interviews with the famous playwright. He gave none despite their entreaties. Then, on December 13th, it was announced that O'Neill

Astor House Hotel

had risen from his sickbed at the hotel and disappeared leaving a letter with his doctor, Alexander Renner, who claimed to have been treating him there in his room.

The letter, in O'Neill's own handwriting, was delivered to Dr Renner, who subsequently released it to the waiting journalists in Henry Wasser's crowded lobby. In the letter O'Neill claimed that he had vacated his hotel room and left Shanghai immediately, that his bronchitis cough was gone and his nerves returning to normal. The letter was dated December 11th – O'Neill had at least a day's head start on his pursuers. The playwright claimed that there had been numerous persons at the hotel seeking to interview him and inquire into his personal circumstances and that they had become a nuisance. He stated that he had come to Shanghai for peace and to work. He claimed, rather with tongue in cheek, that Shanghai's 'wholesome virtues' made the city no place in which to accomplish any serious writing, even if he were completely well physically. The letter expressed apologies to Dr Renner for his hasty departure and continued:

> *I came to China seeking peace and quiet and hoping that here at least people would mind their business and allow me to mind mine. But I have found more snoops and gossips per square inch than there is in any New England town of a 1,000 inhabitants. This does not apply to American newspaper correspondents, who have been most decent, carrying out their duties in a most gentlemanly manner.*
>
> *I am going to Honolulu and then to Tahiti, if Honolulu adopts the same attitude as Shanghai – that I am a politician whose life must be public. At any rate, I will find peace and solitude to work in if I have to go to the South Pole.*
>
> *I expect to be in the pink of condition in the shortest time.*[9]

---

9   Letter extracts and quotes from 'Eugene O'Neill Disappears', *Oakland Tribune*, December 13, 1928.

As soon as the assembled journalists heard the contents of the letter they set to work. No steamers had left Shanghai for Honolulu on the 11th, the date of O'Neill's letter indicating he was leaving immediately. The Associated Press speculated that perhaps O'Neill had boarded a Japanese tramp steamer and would then take a transpacific liner from Japan to Hawaii. Stringers were posted at Japanese ports but nobody matching O'Neill's description was sighted at Tokyo, Kobe or Yokohama. Meanwhile the United Press stringer, probably due to a disingenuous comment from the Astor's Henry Wasser, speculated that O'Neill had actually gone in the other direction from his letter's stated intent and was *en route* south to the British Crown Colony of Hong Kong.[10] A gaggle of expectant Hong Kong-based stringers for the UP and AP gathered at the docks in the British colony waiting for the *President Monroe* to arrive from Shanghai, a Dollar Line steamship on the round-the-world service that connected through to Marseille and New York. It berthed on time but O'Neill was not among the passengers. Still, the stringers got another couple of column inches (and another small payday) the following morning out of reporting that the missing playwright was not aboard and had not come to Hong Kong at all.[11] A Chinese newspaper, joining in the fun, suggested that perhaps bandits had captured him. Other stringers wrote that O'Neill was now missing again and, despite his letter stating he was in full recovery, that he was actually still 'critically ill'.[12]

Shanghai was an easy city in which to disappear quickly, but also a very tricky one in which to remain anonymous for long. It was big, the fourth or fifth largest city in the world with a population, estimated in the city's 1928 census, at nearly three million, but less than 50,000 of those were foreigners. Shanghailander society was close knit; most people were only a remove or two from everyone else through the networks of large foreign trading companies (the *hongs*), members' clubs, the tradition of *tiffin* lunches, sports and

---

10 'Playwright Found Off For Hong Kong', *Ogden Standard-Examiner* (Utah), December 14, 1928.

11 'Dramatist Not on Ship Arriving in Hong Kong', *Indianapolis Star Sun*, December 16, 1928.

12 'Critically Ill', *Monroe News Star* (Louisiana), December 17, 1928.

the race club. Some would have described the city, at least among its higher echelons of *taipans* and the '400', as incestuous and with everybody's nose far too deeply into everybody else's business. At least half a dozen English-language daily newspapers were published in the city reporting its affairs to its foreign denizens. It was true there was a lower-echelon foreign population, composed largely of émigré White Russians who had fled the Bolshevik Revolution to the city, as well as the various soldiers and sailors stationed there to protect the foreign enclaves, but they counted for little in terms of gossip. The British may have been the dominant nationality in terms of the biggest *hongs* and the political elite – Britons invariably ran the Municipal Council that controlled the Settlement's affairs as well as held the top posts in the SMP and local armed detachment known as the Shanghai Volunteer Force – but the Americans were a growing power with their own firms, churches, schools, clubs, court and marshals, as well as the locally stationed Fourth Marine 'Leathernecks', to watch out for them.

It was also true that Shanghai was a very easy city to enter incognito. The port's customs and immigration regulations were lax to the point of non-existent (a fact that had attracted the stateless White Russians and would later bring European Jewish refugees from fascism to the city), and entry could be recorded under any name the visitor saw fit. In this respect, if O'Neill wished to enter Shanghai unnoticed and check in to a hotel unrecorded, then Shanghai was about the best big city in the world to achieve that aim. However, if you were a somebody, a name, a celebrity, then Shanghailanders and their press considered you fair game.

It's quite possible that the SMP realised earlier than the newspapers that O'Neill was in town, but they weren't about to inform the ladies and gentleman of the press corps. Someone had anonymously tipped off Shanghai's Special Branch that a dangerous American radical was in the Settlement – Shanghai Special Branch took a particular interest in 'Reds' who popped up on their turf and usually sought to move them along as quickly as possible. Clearly O'Neill's IWW membership and his Bohemian socialist friends in Greenwich Village had been noted. For as long as O'Neill was in town the SMP kept watch outside the Astor as assiduously as did the press corps.

The Shanghai runaround

Who gave the game away remained a mystery. Most assumed an employee of the Astor in return for a few dollars from a newspaperman. Who was staying at the hotel, where they went at night or who was seen leaving their room in the early hours, perhaps rather shamefacedly, was always saleable information in Shanghai. Perhaps it was a flatfoot from the SMP, bored with standing around on a freezing corner in December with the chill winds whipping off the Whangpoo River waiting for O'Neill to emerge. Or perhaps an outraged Dr Renner annoyed at being duped gave the game way, or was he in on the ruse? . . . for that was what the whole letter and supposed midnight flit out of town had been. In fact Eugene O'Neill was, according to the hotel's management, still comfortably ensconced in his room at the Astor curled up in his sickbed. He had gone nowhere.

Dr Renner denied he had been in on any subterfuge and had not known O'Neill was still in Shanghai and added:

> I don't understand O'Neill. Apparently he disliked my services.
> He had a right to dismiss me but he shows no appreciation
> for my kindness and his actions are most unethical.[13]

Henry Wasser, commanding the reception desk at the Astor against all comers, was straight-backed and tight-lipped. He confirmed O'Neill was still a guest, but refused to reveal his plans except to say he was a 'very sick man and is not seeing anyone'.

But nobody had actually seen O'Neill, not even Renner, and some refused to believe he was still in the hotel. Was O'Neill really up in his sick bed, or was this just more misdirection, while in fact he was long gone out of town and had planned this altercation with

13   'Eugene O'Neill Discovered Again in Hotel', *Wilkes-Barre Times Leader* (Pennsylvania), December 18, 1928.

Renner to throw the press off his scent once again? Randall Gould, the famously acerbic local chief correspondent for the United Press (and later to become the editor of the *Shanghai Evening Post and Mercury* and one of the city's most respected and long-serving newspapermen) believed it was. In fact he believed he'd got O'Neill – in Manila. Where Gould led, many other local reporters followed.

Thanks to a UP stringer in Manila, Gould believed he had his man. A passenger bearing an uncanny resemblance to O'Neill had arrived in the Philippines capital aboard the German steamship, the ss *Coblenz* of the Norddeutscher-Lloyd line. After Manila the ship would sail for Bremen, via various Asian ports, and then across the Atlantic to New York. Gould's Filipino stringer identified the man he thought to be O'Neill travelling under the alias of the Reverend William O'Brien. The stringer felt sure he was right, questioned the man, who (he claimed) admitted he was indeed Eugene O'Neill, was intending to sail for Genoa in Italy and then travel to the resort of Rapallo.[14] The story was picked up on the wires and ran in numerous newspapers across America.

But Gould was not a man to fall for a ruse more than once. A stringer's identification from a photograph; a man claiming to be O'Neill? Gould demanded clear evidence as to the clergyman's true identity. The good Rev. produced an American passport in the name of Eugene Gladstone O'Neill, born October 16th, 1888. Furthermore, he had letters in his handwriting and others addressed to him; he then produced his notebooks for the reporter to verify the handwriting and he even allowed the man a glance at his bankbooks. He finally gave the Manila stringer an autograph. The chase was over – Gould had indeed found his man. But his man was now gone from Shanghai, aboard a steamer bound for Europe and refusing to leave his cabin until the ship set sail westwards. At noon on December 19th, 1928 the ss *Coblenz* set sail from Manila for Europe. O'Neill made one final comment to the pressmen ashore – that because of the fuss in Shanghai he'd failed to do what he had come there for, namely to study the Chinese theatre, but

14 'O'Neill Playwright, in Manila as "Rev. O'Brien"', *Modesto News Herald* (California), December 18, 1928.

that he had now, aboard the *Coblenz*, finally begun work on a new play.[15]

Back in Shanghai Renner still denied any involvement in O'Neill's escape from the city. It had been a ruse perpetrated by the Astor House Hotel on O'Neill's behalf to let him escape unnoticed while the press believed him still firmly in his sick bed. He had been tricked too. Henry Wasser at the Astor merely commented that the hotel had served their esteemed guest as he so wished and facilitated his unmolested journey onward. And so the story of Eugene O'Neill's disappearance, reappearance and second disappearance in Shanghai died.

The newspapermen may have been pleased with themselves for tracing O'Neill to Manila and uncovering him. But none of them – not in Shanghai, nor in Manila – had got the real story of Eugene O'Neill's winter 1928 sojourn in the city. None of them ever mentioned or worked out that O'Neill had not been alone in his hotel room. They never discovered that he had regularly gone out and explored the city, its streets and nocturnal delights in the company of others. They never got the story of the woman that came to Shanghai with Eugene O'Neill and what they got up to in one of the world's wildest towns.

15   'Dramatist is O'Neill and is Aboard Ship', *Daily Chronicle* (De Kalb, Illinois), December 19, 1928.

Part Two – High times in Shanghai

Preparing to head east

The origins of O'Neill's Shanghai sojourn go back to the start of 1928, the point at which he decided that his future lay not with his wife Agnes but with Carlotta Monterey. He set his course and started to disentangle his marriage. Agnes, now aware of his relationship with Monterey and that it was more than just a fling, came to New York to sort out a settlement under the guidance of their joint attorney, Harry Weinberger. Agnes was to receive six to ten thousand dollars annually (depending on O'Neill's earnings) and the use of the Spithead property in Bermuda. Somehow Carlotta found out Agnes was in Manhattan and a frightful argument ensued with O'Neill, which led to a temporary break-up. Eventually Agnes, and their three children, left New York for Bermuda and O'Neill reconciled with Carlotta.

Meanwhile, good reviews were coming in for the Broadway production of *Marco Millions*[16] and *Strange Interlude* was in rehearsal.

Opinions on Carlotta Monterey's acting skills among New York's theatrical community were mixed, though all seem to have agreed that she was extremely beautiful. The gossip columns were starting to note O'Neill and Monterey as an item and neither wanted that sort of attention while things still weren't finally legally settled with Agnes. They began to formulate plans to sail for Europe once *Strange Interlude* had opened, which it did on January 30th, 1928 to good reviews despite some critics' concern about its marathon length. *Strange Interlude* significantly increased O'Neill's bank account – his combined royalties from the theatrical production,

16   Including from Brooks Atkinson, the highly influential *New York Times* theatre critic, who would, shortly after Pearl Harbor in 1941, switch beats dramatically and become the paper's China correspondent for the duration of World War Two.

Eugene and Carlotta

his share of the movie rights and sales of the book of the play topped $275,000 (about $4 million in 2018 money). Financially O'Neill was set. He decided to leave town.

Travelling incognito was not a novelty for O'Neill. In February 1928 he had told everyone he was heading to California and then booked passage to London under an assumed name. Carlotta was also booked on the same liner. He got out of New York without the press realising his true destination. In a springtime Europe O'Neill and Carlotta's relationship blossomed. London, Paris, Biarritz beckoned and O'Neill, through moving hotels and resorts regularly and a bit of light-hearted subterfuge, managed to avoid the interest of the English and French press. Consequently little gossip of his breakup with Agnes or the new relationship made the American newspapers. He was slightly annoyed that Agnes was asking for more money, but then his financial circumstances had changed rather dramatically since the first settlement negotiations. The news of the divorce, as already mentioned, did emerge in the newspapers in June, though Agnes did not mention Carlotta by name. That effectively ended the correspondence between O'Neill and Agnes, though it would be another year before she did finally file suit.

In July O'Neill mentioned to the Theater Guild's Theresa Helburn in New York his idea of travelling to Asia to see the India and Far East of Rudyard Kipling (an author he had loved as a boy) and that he might leave around October for Hong Kong. First he completed his next play, *Dynamo* (to be the first in a trilogy of plays on the failure of materialism). Once this was done it was a busy time making arrangements and packing, although their plans were rather of the 'play it by ear' variety with a planned voyage to Hong Kong and then . . . well, they'd see.

Eventually, on October 5, the couple boarded the majestic ss *André-Lebon* of the French Messageries Maritimes line at Marseille and began the long voyage east to China. Accompanying them was Carlotta's personal maid and secretary, Tuve Drew, known usually as Mrs Drew, a stout blonde Swede with a husband and child back in England. Mrs Drew handily happened to be both a skilled masseuse and a trained nurse.

The journey to Shanghai was of several weeks' duration. O'Neill celebrated his fortieth birthday sailing through the Red Sea, though the couple were unmolested as the bulk of the other passengers were French and had no idea who their famous travelling companion was. It should have been a pleasant journey – Eugene working on a sketch for his next play[17] and Carlotta relaxing on deck – but Carlotta felt a sense of foreboding. On October 14th she wrote in her diary, 'Something awful is going to happen – *I know it!*'[18]

The ship made a brief stop at Djibouti, a rather fly-blown French colonial possession on the Horn of Africa with little to recommend it to tourists, and then pressed on to the British colony of Ceylon and the port of Colombo. Later some press reports would claim that O'Neill got sunstroke at Colombo, though his biographer

17   O'Neill was working on *It Cannot be Mad*, a play about the rise of an automotive industry billionaire, which he never finished. According to Robert M. Dowling, *Eugene O'Neill: A Life in Four Acts*, (New Haven: Yale University Press, 2014), p. 360.

18   Stephen A. Black, *Eugene O'Neill: Beyond Mourning and Tragedy*, (New Haven: Yale University Press, 1999), p. 363.

Louis Sheaffer believes this happened at the next port of call, Singapore where he went swimming in water Carlotta thought 'sewer infested'.[19] After Singapore, Messageries Maritimes ships crossed the South China Sea to French Indo-China and put in at Saigon, a city O'Neill described as 'fascinating in a queer sinister way'.[20] The couple took a day trip to Cholon (Saigon's Chinatown) but, it seems, O'Neill's real discovery in Saigon was the city's gambling casinos on the infamous Rue Catinat. Other pleasures also tempted O'Neill in Saigon, though he showed restraint. Sending a postcard of an opium smoker to the journalist and critic Benjamin De Casseres, whose ideas on Nietzsche had influenced him (O'Neill had taken *Thus Spake Zarathustra* as shipboard reading), he wrote:

> *I've never fallen for this brand of Nirvana, but this guy looks as if he couldn't be altogether wrong! I'm staying in Saigon awhile – most interesting place so far.*[21]

As was reported in some newspapers later it seems O'Neill did catch flu in Saigon and had to submit to the ministrations of Mrs Drew. He certainly seems to have lost a pile at the gaming tables, which did not best please an increasingly exasperated Carlotta.

Eventually the *André-Lebon* docked in Hong Kong's impressive Victoria Harbour with the famous Peak rising above the colony. Hong Kong had been their intended first stop, but O'Neill was still out with the flu and Mrs Drew declared Hong Kong too damp for his health. He told friends that he was planning to continue east and eventually to stay a while in Japan. And so they remained on board and continued up the South China coast to Shanghai where they disembarked, passing by the notoriously lax customs officials, and checked into the Palace Hotel in mid-November.

19   Louis Sheaffer, *O'Neill: Son and Artist*, (London: Paul Elek, 1974).
20   Black, *Eugene O'Neill*, p. 362.
21   Crosswell Bowen, *The Curse of the Misbegotten: A Tale of the House of O'Neill*, (London, Rupert Hart-Davis, 1960), p. 188.

A tense and terse Shanghai

Things were a little tense between Eugene and Carlotta by the time they checked in to their separate suites at the Palace. As usual O'Neill registered them incognito and in different rooms to avoid the city's snoops and hacks that might be looking for a story. The American newspapers were still reporting O'Neill as AWOL and details of his marriage break-up with Agnes still occasionally surfaced in the New York gossip columns. The Palace was certainly swank digs. Right on the Bund waterfront, it was a European-style hotel, all redbrick Victorian neo-Renaissance, and had opened in 1908. In the 1920s it was the smartest hotel on the strip of grand buildings that fronted out onto the teeming Whangpoo River and looked across to the busy wharfs and (warehouses) of the Pootung shore opposite and the vista of small farms and villages beyond. The rooms were sumptuous, newly installed elevators whisked guests up to their floors, hot water was on tap, radiators beat the chill of Shanghai's cold winters and cloth-slippered staff moved quietly along the corridors with room service trays and guests' fresh laundry.[22] Going about their business they may well have heard the odd screaming match from the adjoining suites occupied by O'-Neill and Monterey.

The confinement of a long voyage, the daily repetition of each other's company and cabin claustrophobia hadn't helped their moods. O'Neill's taste for outdoor swimming had given him sunstroke either in Colombo or Singapore, and what was either a bad cold or a mild influenza in Saigon. Carlotta had warned him not to go swimming and worried about the bacteria and diseases in the water. But it was his new-found love of the roulette wheels in Saigon (and his not insubstantial losses spinning those wheels) that really sent her into a rage. She screamed at him and he screamed back. She resented his stubbornness and he declared himself tired of her incessant nagging. O'Neill was feeling confined and so, when they were out strolling along the Bund on one of their first days in Shanghai, he chanced upon an old acquaintance called Alfred Batson, he jumped at the chance of some male company and an

22   The Palace is now the Swatch Art Peace Hotel on the Bund.

opportunity to get away from Carlotta for a while. Batson recalled their meeting that day:

> I was walking past the Palace Hotel one morning at the
> corner of Nanking Road and the Bund when I saw a tall
> man in front of me. I was sure it was O'Neill, and with him
> a beautiful woman. Shanghai was like a small town as far as
> the foreign population went in those days and any foreigner
> stuck out like a sore thumb. I walked up to the man, looked
> at him, and said, 'It is!'.[23]

O'Neill had first met Alfred 'Red' Batson in Cape Cod with the Provincetown Players and then again later in Greenwich Village. The adventurous redheaded man was sure to appeal to the side of O'Neill that had gone away to sea as a young man. Born in Boston and briefly attending Harvard, Batson joined the Canadian Army and served in Europe in World War One. To achieve this he seems to have taken Canadian citizenship and so ever after is referred to as Canadian in just about every report concerning him. After the war he decided to become a 'soldier of fortune', jumped a ship in San Francisco and went briefly to Central America, joining the army of General Juan Bautista Sacasa in Nicaragua, where the general was staging a sort of counter-coup. Even so there wasn't much action to be had in Nicaragua and the US Marines ordered Batson to leave the country. He took their sternly offered advice and walked through Honduras, Guatemala and Mexico back to the United States and eventually to Greenwich Village and O'Neill's table in the Golden Swan Saloon one night. But he didn't tarry in Manhattan long. Batson joined China's fledgling Nationalist Army that was then accepting foreigners with Western military training who might make good officers and trainers. It appears he did join up, for a while anyway, but seems to have found himself in Shanghai at some point in 1928 and been offered a newspaper job. Batson promptly swapped his black Nationalist uniform and rifle for a locally tailored Saigon linen suit, notebook and pencil.[24]

23   Arthur & Barbara Gelb, *O'Neill*, (London: Jonathan Cape, 1962), p. 681.

'Red' Batson, who was still only twenty-eight years old despite his many adventures, was in Shanghai working for the *North-China Daily News*, a paper technically owned by British interests but invariably reflecting the particular mind-set of the Shanghailander – all business, and intent on boosting Shanghai's role globally, while retaining the extraterritorial privileges of the city's unique status. The *North-China* was the most established and widely read of the half dozen or so China-coast English-language papers and employed a large staff of various nationalities who all worked out of its offices and presses at No. 17 Bund. The building, known as 'The Old Lady of the Bund', was just a block along the waterfront from the Palace Hotel. O'Neill was delighted to meet Batson but begged him, 'Do me a favour, just keep me out of the paper.'[25] Batson agreed; he didn't think his editor, the staunchly British O.M. Green, a man not well versed in New York theatrical trends, would recognise the name anyway. Red offered to show O'Neill the sights while he was in town. O'Neill jumped at the chance to escape the increasingly terse atmosphere of the Palace Hotel.

Shanghai might have been one of the most wide-open cities on earth in 1928, but it was also one of the most tense. Nineteen twenty-seven had been one of the bloodiest in the treaty port's history. Ceded by the Chinese after the First Opium War in 1842, it was a village raised to a major port in the intervening years. The Americans had merged their small concession with the larger British one in 1868 to form the International Settlement, where the foreign population had its own courts, justice system, municipal council, police force, armies and the Volunteer Force to protect the Settlement's borders. The French retained their own adjacent concession and largely managed their own affairs. The city had grown phenomenally as the entrepôt for the Yangtze trade, eclipsing Hong

24 Batson told many of his stories, particularly about his time in Central America in his memoir, *Vagabond's Paradise*, (Boston: Little, Brown & Company, 1931). He certainly knew how to spin a yarn and so perhaps these memoirs should be read with a touch of caution.

25 Sheaffer, *O'Neill: Son and Artist*, p. 314.

Kong and Singapore as the major trading post in Asia. Mass construction had thrown up Western-style hotels, theatres, the inevitable racecourse, streets of smart housing alongside myriad lanes cheek-by-jowl with rookeries of smaller, cramped dwellings. The city had largely avoided any major bloodshed or wars due to its unique international status. But Shanghai, a city of modern ideas both in culture and politics, was not completely immune.

In April 1927 the city's streets had literally run with blood. Chiang Kai-shek and his ruling Kuomintang Party had vowed to unite China and drive out the scourge of the warlords. He began his campaign in the south, from Canton, and moved north, towards the Yangtze and Shanghai. In Shanghai Chiang faced another threat – strongly organised labour unions and an emergent communist force. Communist-led strikes broke out in Shanghai. On April 9th Chiang declared martial law in the city outside the foreign concessions and planned a purge of the recently formed Communist Party. Things escalated – severe beatings led to deaths, the army opened fire killing more strikers. Officially, over a thousand communists were arrested, some three hundred executed and more than five thousand went missing. Many foreign journalists, who watched the events, claimed the slaughter was far worse.

Eugene O'Neill could not but have been aware of the unrest. The British still had a garrison of 3,000 soldiers to support troops stationed in the Settlement from Italy and France as well as the American Fourth Marines and several ships of the US Asiatic Fleet, the Royal Navy's China Squadron and the French Navy moored on the Whangpoo. Batson took him to the Municipal Police's crime museum, where he was given a tour by no less than George Gilbert, the chief of the Shanghai detective squad. The museum described many macabre forms of Chinese torture and laid bare the general state of criminality in the city. O'Neill was particularly fascinated, as so many foreign sojourners were over the years, by the exhibit on the traditional 'death by a thousand cuts' method of getting a suspect to talk! Shanghai was in many respects a Western city, a highly modern metropolis, and not the magical Orient O'Neill had imbibed in his boyhood Kipling. Shanghai was not what he had expected; he was angry with Carlotta, he was not writing and in a city with numerous, as he would later say (with tongue firmly in cheek), 'wholesome virtues', he began drinking again.

On the town

Not surprisingly O'Neill's jaunts to the city's bars, nightclubs and casinos with Batson did little to improve Carlotta's temper. In her suite at the Palace with nobody for company, except her maid Tuve Drew, she felt trapped; trapped in a town full of excellent restaurants, glamorous nightclubs and smart hotel lobbies in which to see and be seen. She had snuck out briefly while O'Neill was sightseeing with Batson and gotten a tour of the city from the Palace's Swiss manager. But that had been her only escape. Her Broadway career was on hold, Agnes was still stalling on finalising the divorce and O'Neill insisted on them remaining incognito in Shanghai.

When O'Neill returned from one of his nights out on the town, steaming drunk, Carlotta was waiting for him and a fight started. He accused her of spying on him; she claimed she was worried for his health. It was true the drink wasn't going to help him get over his bout of flu quickly. Carlotta claimed O'Neill eventually exploded and slapped her hard; so hard she almost toppled over. He then, rather nastily, called her 'an old whore'. O'Neill admitted later to Red Batson that he'd taken 'a poke' at her.[26] She walked out of the room, told Tuve Drew to pack their belongings, checked out of the Palace and moved across the Soochow Creek to the Astor House Hotel and the close attentions of the manager, Henry Wasser.

The fight, and Carlotta's departure to another hotel, did little to change O'Neill's behaviour. Batson recalled meeting him for breakfast the next day at the Palace and he was already drunk. The following evening, around November 20th, the two embarked on an epic bar crawl. From the Palace they headed over to the Avenue Edward VII, the 'Avenue Eddy' to Shanghailanders, and into the

26   Sheaffer, *O'Neill: Son and Artist*, p. 315.

French Concession. Their first stop was the notorious strip of bars on Rue Chu Pao San, known as 'Blood Alley'. The narrow street was home to two dozen bars, mostly of the hole-in-the-wall variety. Some of them hadn't even got electricity and just used kerosene lamps, but they weren't afraid to give themselves some grand names – the Palais Cabaret, the 'Frisco, Mumms, the Crystal, George's Bar, Monk's Brass Rail, the New Ritz and The Manhattan. Inside were sailors, soldiers and the foreign 'driftwood' of Shanghai mingling with a League of Nations of prostitutes – Cantonese from the south, Koreans, French-speaking Annamite girls and White Russian women. Carl Crow, an American journalist who had swapped Missouri for Shanghai fifteen years before O'Neill arrived commented that you didn't have to hang around Blood Alley long before you'd get to witness a 'knock-down-and-drag-out fist fight between British and American sailors that usually ended with the tall, tough, turbaned Sikh constables of the SMP wading in with their bamboo lathis to break up the ruckus.'[27]

From Blood Alley they headed back into the Settlement and up the Bubbling Well Road to the small street known as Love Lane, another strip of entertainment joints including the Saint Anna Ballroom (very popular with the local Fourth Marine contingent), Van's Dutch Inn and Madam Margaret Kennedy's infamous mansion-sized brothel staffed mostly by American working girls.

Fairly well liquored up by this time they finally ended up at the St George's Café, a mid-market dance hall patronised by both Shanghailanders and Chinese customers. The St George's, on the major thoroughfare of the Bubbling Well Road, was well established, a barn of a place and known to everyone. The owner, Jimmy St James, was a long-term face about town who also had arrangements with the visiting liners to bring in tourists and which, in a practice not followed by Shanghai nightclubs wishing to avoid trouble, also allowed sailors and soldiers of various nations entry. The night often ended in brawls.

---

27 Paul French, *Carl Crow – A Tough Old China Hand: The Life, Times, and Adventures of an American in Shanghai*, (Hong Kong: Hong Kong University Press, 2006).

Shanghai was a fairly wild town in 1928. But it wasn't yet quite the equivalent of Manhattan; its 1930s zenith as the sin Mecca of the Far East was still a few years away. However, fun could be had quite easily and till the early hours and booze was incredibly cheap for those with American dollars. The St George's was a taxi-dance establishment – a large dance floor with rattan tables and chairs round the edges. Chinese and White Russian women sat with their backs to the wall, fanning themselves, waiting to be asked to dance. You bought a strip of tickets, you asked a girl to dance, you gave her a ticket, which she later cashed in with the management. The girls would encourage you to hand over more dance tickets, buy more booze and were often open to 'off-the-books' arrangements at the end of the night.

O'Neill was half drunk when he got to the joint; closing time was basically sun up. He ordered champagne and got to drinking yet more. O'Neill found the girls sad looking and started buying bottles of champagne for them, against Red Batson's advice – Red knew that the girls would mark O'Neill as a moneybags and the champagne was probably just cold tea. O'Neill threw a lot of cash about and became ever more drunk. Eventually they left and O'Neill collapsed on the curb outside the nightclub and opposite the large and imposing Bubbling Well Police Station. The Sikh officers changing shifts at the station saw him sprawled on the pavement and laughed at another casualty of Shanghai's ferocious nightlife. O'Neill told Batson he'd been 'a son of a bitch to Agnes'[28] but that he'd 'make Carlotta a helluva husband.'[29] After a long confession of his woes mixed with a large dose of self-recrimination O'Neill began to vomit repeatedly and turned decidedly pale. Batson got him back to the Palace Hotel in a rickshaw, up into his suite, and called the house doctor.

28   Sheaffer, *O'Neill: Son and Artist*, p. 316.
29   Arthur & Barbara Gelb, *O'Neill*, p. 683.

Country Hospital

Enter Dr Renner

The Palace's house doctor was Alexander Renner, who swiftly appeared, along with his wife Theresa. For O'Neill it was perhaps a slightly odd consultation. Renner began attending to his patient, slumped on the bed, while his wife, having ascertained that this was indeed Mr Eugene O'Neill the famous American playwright, pulled out a typewritten manuscript of a play she'd penned and began reading it out loud to the patient. As Renner tried to find a suitable vein for an injection in O'Neill's arm, his wife kept asking the playwright if he was still listening. He wasn't; he was in a bad way.

Dr Renner insisted O'Neill be moved to the Settlement's Country Hospital, out to the west of town on the Great Western Road.[30] They got O'Neill into an ambulance and drove him the couple of miles to the hospital. In 1928 the area around the Country Hospital was still largely undeveloped and quiet, except for a British army shooting range nearby, which did nothing for patients' peaceful recuperation. The facility had only opened a couple of years previously and was pretty close to state-of-the-art. The Country, run by the Municipal Council, was one of the best hospitals in Asia, with an accident and emergency ward. It had been designed by the émigré Hungarian architect Ladislav Hudec, who contributed so many modernist buildings to Shanghai's architectural treasure

30   Now the Huadong Hospital on Yan'an West Road.

trove. Renner attended O'Neill at the hospital and Red Batson visited; when O'Neill asked him to smuggle in a 'pint of liquor' he refused and got an earful for his attempt to help his friend's recovery.[31]

Carlotta meanwhile had heard of O'Neill's hospitalisation and to find out his condition she befriended the Renners. Dr Alexander Renner was invariably described in the newspapers in 1928 as Austrian, though he appears to have been born in Budapest in 1884. Certainly he had grown up in the old Austro-Hungarian Empire, before it was blown apart by the Great War. He'd studied medicine at Pázmány Péter Catholic University in Budapest. He was seen as a caring physician, a nerve specialist (then meaning a psychiatrist), but advertised himself in Shanghai later as a specialist in 'women's diseases and obstetrics' by training. After service in World War One he married Theresa and they moved to Shanghai. In the city's International Settlement he opened his own practice as a general practitioner with a surgery at a prestigious central address – 11b Nanking Road, adjacent to the Chinese-American Bank – and also acted as house doctor for the nearby Palace Hotel when required.

But it was Theresa Renner who became Carlotta's close friend and confidante. With Theresa as company Carlotta was finally able to get out and about in Shanghai and see the city, escaping the confines of her hotel room. The two women were approximately the same age; Hungarian-born Theresa was just a year or two younger than Monterey, from a minor aristocratic background and with an artistic bent. As a young woman she had studied the piano under Béla Bartók at Budapest's Royal Academy of Music. Dr Renner was a well-respected man, with a steady and decent income from his practice, but it was Theresa who guided their move into the higher echelons of Shanghailander society. She emerged as quite the hostess at the Renners' residence at 1369 Rue Lafayette in the heart of the French Concession. They had invited Albert and Elsa Einstein to a New Year's Eve dinner when the physicist visited the city in 1922 *en route* to Japan; the Bengali poet Rabindranath Tagore (who had a large following of admirers in China) stayed with them.

They hosted parties for many visiting artists – the concerto pianist Mischa Levitzki after his farewell performance at Shanghai's Lyceum Theatre in 1925; the German poet Bernhard Kellermann who was retracing the steps of Marco Polo in 1926 with his companion the Austrian artist Lene Schneider-Kainer; the Hungarian Orientalist scholar Dr Felix Valyi. The Renners, who had a keen interest in traditional Chinese painting, also hosted a number of highly esteemed Chinese artists. Among them were the painter Chao Shao-an, who specialised in beautifully rendered flower-and-bird paintings, and Fu Tienian, who specialised in nature scenes and decorated beautiful traditional fans. The Renners were, in short, a highly connected, a highly cultured and, it seems, a highly liked couple in Shanghai.

Carlotta had befriended Theresa partly to get more news of Eugene's hospital stay, but she also talked about her relationship with him. Theresa recalled, 'In almost no time we were like sisters, devoted sisters. We went shopping every day . . . and she used to pour out her complaints about O'Neill.'[32] The two certainly made an attractive couple – the brunette Carlotta Monterey and the blonde Theresa Renner, both invariably referred to as 'beauties'. Indeed it seems they soon became inseparable. The only small fly in the ointment was that Theresa, who had been raised with servants in her native Hungary, disapproved of Carlotta's treatment of Tuve Drew, who she considered hard done by and spoken to with great impoliteness by her mistress. New World money didn't match Old World manners in Theresa's view. Quite a few people noted Carlotta's snobbishness and offhand treatment of servants, hotel staff and various ship's crews. Later the crew of one liner she sailed aboard dubbed her 'Queen Mary' for her behaviour. However, others were obviously very attached to her – regardless, Tuve Drew was sticking with her loyally, while Henry Wasser at the Astor Hotel was devoted, indeed appears to have been quite smitten with her.

The Renners became the willing conduits for messages between Carlotta and O'Neill. O'Neill passed notes to her via Dr Renner

32 Sheaffer, *O'Neill: Son and Artist*, p. 317. Of course we don't really have Carlotta's view of how close they were and it was the case that Theresa dined out on the O'Neill story for many years subsequently.

and Carlotta sent back messages to O'Neill via Theresa. Eventually the Renners effected a bedside reunion and the two managed to patch things up and once again declared their undying love for each other. By the end of November they were writing and returning several notes a day back and forth delivered at each end by Chinese messengers (who they referred to as 'coolies'). Eugene had certainly got his romantic head back on – in late November he sent a message to Carlotta at the Astor on Country Hospital headed notepaper:

> *Dearest! And God bless you! This in much haste to catch your*
> *coolie back.*
> *I love you – always and forever!*
> *Forgive me! I'll be a good 'un in future – do my damndest best to!*
> *A million kisses, Blessed! Good'night*
> *Gene*[33]

Eventually Carlotta began to visit O'Neill in person and sit by his bed talking and reading to him. Red Batson arrived one day to find them deep in conversation and decided to slip away and leave them undisturbed. He never saw his old friend again, though several weeks later, after the O'Neill furore in Shanghai had died down, he received a silver cigarette case in the post engraved with the words: – *To Alfred Batson, from 133 Macdougal Street to Shanghai. Gene O'Neill, 1928.*[34]

O'Neill's health (and it seems his temperament too) was slowly improving under Dr Renner's care; the lovers were reconciled, cooing rather than shouting, but now word of O'Neill's surfacing in Shanghai after being incommunicado for months was about to burst as a major news story. If the trip to Europe, the long voyage East and the few weeks in Shanghai had in any way actually ever been as restorative, peaceful and calming as intended then they were about to become a stressful and exhausting game of cat and mouse with the world's press.

33   Eugene O'Neill to Carlotta Monterey, c.25–30 November, 1928. Letter No. 265. Eugene O'Neill, in Eds. Travis Bogard & Jackson R. Bryer, *The Selected Letters of Eugene O'Neill*, (New Haven: Yale University Press, 1988).
34   Arthur & Barbara Gelb, *O'Neill*, p. 683.

'Missing In China'

The news was out. O'Neill's gallivanting round the bars and dance halls of Shanghai, his hotel reservations and then hospitalisation couldn't remain secret for long. Especially not after Carlotta started being seen around town on the arm of Mrs Renner too. However, it was perhaps a genuine fan who revealed the playwright's presence in the city.

Missing In China

EUGENE
O'NEILL

O'Neill, noted American playwright, has disappeared in Shanghai, where he was suffering from a nervous breakdown. He left a letter for his physician in which he complained that he was unable to work unmolested in China.

Strolling with Red Batson one day the two had wandered into a bookstore that stocked a variety of American titles. O'Neill was delighted to see a copy of his play *Desire Under the Elms* on the shelves and even more delighted when the young Chinese clerk in the store admitted he was a great fan of its author. For once O'Neill let his vanity get the better of his desire for anonymity. He purchased the book, signed it and presented it as a gift to the clerk. The clerk was keen to show everyone his book, signed that very day by the actual author himself, right here in his bookstore. Batson, realising that eventually someone would get the story, decided he'd better get the scoop himself and so, on December 8th, the *North-China* ran a small piece by Batson noting O'Neill's arrival in the city to recover from a recent illness and stressing the playwright's desire for peace and quiet while resident in the Settlement. The city's press corps read the short piece, realised something was up, and the chase was on.

O'Neill's health was improving but that didn't stop the Associated Press releasing a story on the wires the day after Batson's article claiming that O'Neill was 'confined to bed' suffering bronchitis and a nervous breakdown due to the exertions of travel and overwork. The story ran widely in myriad American papers that took the AP feed.[35] From Shanghai O'Neill cabled his lawyer Harry Weinberger, who immediately put out a statement saying his client's illness was much exaggerated. But the fact was that after the initial discovery that O'Neill was in China there wasn't much newsworthy to say. Left at that the story might have disappeared altogether. It ran for a day or two as provincial papers caught up with the wires but that, it seemed, was that for the 'O'Neill is Missing' tale.

That is until O'Neill personally engineered the story of his sudden and dramatic disappearance from Shanghai, the letter announcing his departure and disgruntlement at Shanghai and Dr Renner as well as the mystery of where he'd gone. In the end it was O'Neill himself who gave the story legs and ensured the press resumed their interest and stuck with it to the bitter end, while smart Shanghailanders were annoyed at being categorised round the world as 'snoops and gossips'.

And so the circus began – Dr Renner read the letter to the press; wire service stringers crowded shipping offices and despatched other stringers to docksides in Japan, Manila and Hong Kong to keep watch for the fleeing playwright; Shanghailander sensibilities were outraged; the press corps got insulted about doing nothing more than requesting an interview; and Dr Renner and Theresa told everyone their feelings had been hurt by an ungrateful O'Neill. However, in all the ensuing coverage Carlotta Monterey's name never appeared.

Flight to Manila

After being discharged from the Country Hospital O'Neill had moved to the Astor to be with Carlotta again. He found Henry Wasser, the manager, a willing accomplice in keeping his movements secret. Once there they had hatched their escape plan, in the full belief that the press barrage that had filled the lobby for several days would continue indefinitely. O'Neill roped Alexander and

35   Including, as an example, 'Eugene O'Neill Recovering', *Brooklyn Daily Eagle*, December 10, 1928.

Theresa Renner into the escapade, and Henry Wasser too. And so it was executed.

Wasser agreed to keep the news of O'Neill's departure secret. He would simply say, if asked (and, of course, he was going to be asked), that their guest was resident in his room, recovering and not admitting visitors. The Renners agreed to appear surprised, and even hurt, at O'Neill's dispensing with Alexander's services. Meanwhile passage was booked on the German ship, the *Coblenz* under false names. And so Tuve Drew packed their cases and the three left the hotel by the rear entrance. They exited onto a small lane at the rear of the building, called Astor Terrace, and made their way along the dark alley, past Madame Madani's Massage Parlour, a fortune-teller's storefront and a few other small, and perhaps questionable, businesses that clustered there, to Astor Road that ran down the eastern side of the hotel.[36] There a taxi was waiting to take them to the Customs Jetty at the Bund. After the per-functory leaving formalities they walked down the pier onto a waiting launch that took passengers the twelve miles downriver along the Whangpoo to the waiting ocean liners at the terminals at Woosung. There they boarded the *Coblenz*, O'Neill listed on the passenger manifest as the Reverend William O'Brien, while Car-lotta was listed as 'Miss Drew', pretending to be Tuve Drew's daughter. They settled into their berths – once more with Carlotta in one stateroom and 'O'Brien' in another. The *Coblenz* upped anchor and sailed for Manila. The next morning Dr Renner, surprise on his face, read O'Neill's letter to the assembled press at the Astor Hotel. Henry Wasser then instructed them all to leave so his lobby could return to some semblance of normality.

Randall Gould's eagle-eyed stringer in Manila was Walter Robb. Robb, and his wife Dolly, had arrived in the Philippines in 1907 and were to stay there for thirty-five years. Robb would become the Philippines correspondent for the *Chicago Daily News*, and in 1928 he was supplying editorial to anyone interested including the local *American Chamber of Commerce Journal*, which he edited for many

---

36 Astor Terrace no longer exists, though a trace of it can be found on Jinshan Road down the eastern side of the Astor House Hotel building that is now blocked off half way down by later additions to the hotel.

years.[37] Part of a freelancer's life in a posting like Manila was meeting visiting liners and seeing if anyone interesting disembarked that might be worthy of a column inch or two. The hunt was on for O'Neill and, despite the Astor management's protestations that he was upstairs in his sickbed, Randall Gould wasn't buying it. Robb had been put on alert and armed with a photograph of the playwright. He spotted O'Neill immediately. O'Neill came clean, took Robb to his stateroom and showed him his documents and handwriting and Robb got cabling back to Gould in Shanghai.

What Robb didn't discover was that Carlotta was locked in the adjacent stateroom listening to the newsmen 'scurrying about' while she kept quiet. Robb thought O'Neill looked washed out and that the Far East had taken its toll on his health. In fact he feared the playwright might be about to relapse. The *Coblenz* stayed in Manila a couple of days and Robb met with O'Neill several times. Robb was loosely acquainted with the writer and editor of *The American Mercury*, H.L. Mencken, who had commissioned him to write several articles on the Philippines. Knowing Mencken would be interested in the O'Neill story he wrote to him in New York on December 20th saying that the playwright's 'vision was dull and wandering, his attention sluggish, his mind worked only by the most obvious effort of his will. He was gracious to everyone, but he was physically shot.'[38]

O'Neill was probably still not fully recovered from the combination of sunstroke, flu and alcohol. He may well have still been in the throes of depression and/or a breakdown. Carlotta, in her diary, noted his drinking and his use of potassium (which was then believed to stave off the cravings for alcohol).[39] But he may also have still been dissembling somewhat. In Manila, O'Neill's major objective was for the pressmen not to work out that Carlotta was aboard the *Coblenz*. Rumours had been whispered in Manila of a

37 Later Robb was to gather many of his insightful and observant pieces on the Philippines between the world wars in *Filipinos: Pre-War Philippines Essays*, (Manila: Araneta University Press, 1963).

38 Walter Robb, Letter to H.L. Mencken, 1928, The George Nathan Collection, 1913–1958, Division of Rare and Manuscript Collections, Cornell University Library.

39 Black, *Eugene O'Neill*, p. 365.

woman in O'Neill's party, but nobody had come up with a name. To further put them off the scent O'Neill left the ship and Carlotta to take a whirlwind tour of old Manila's Intramuros district within the ancient city walls. He knew the press would follow him. Speaking to a journalist from the *Manila Tribune,* he praised the old town and admired Filipino traditions, but gave no details of his arrangements or onward plans. On December 21st the *Coblenz* steamed out of Manila Bay, the hunt for Eugene O'Neill finally done with. O'Neill, it seems, even looked back on it all with a wry smile. Following an anxious cable from the playwright Lawrence Langner, and another from an old family friend in America who'd both been alarmed by stories of bandit kidnappings, critical ill-nesses and even the playwright's premature death in China, O'Neill cabled back to Langner: 'Feel well now. Much idiotic publicity Shanghai, Manila. My discovery, disappearance, kidnapped, ban-dits, death, etc. Merry Christmas to all.' And then to the old family friend: 'News of my death premature. Now I'm in a class with Mark Twain.'[40]

'The most ridiculous farce I've ever run into!'

After the shenanigans at Manila had been uncovered and reported, the news cycle moved on. The Shanghai press corps went back to reporting what most interested those in the city's 'hermetically sealed glass case'[41] – i.e. what was happening in Shanghai. After their brief moment in the limelight, Walter Robb and the Manila press corps went back to writing about the country's tobacco monopoly, the arrival of a new American governor-general from Washington and an early January earthquake in Luzon's Central Province.

The *Coblenz* arrived in Singapore on Christmas Eve with O'-Neill claiming he was well. But it wasn't so. He felt Carlotta was nagging again, though the midnight flit from Shanghai and her confinement on the *Coblenz* since couldn't have helped her mood

40   Arthur & Barbara Gelb, *O'Neill,* p. 686.
41   Quote from Arthur Ransome, 'The Chinese Puzzle', *Guardian,* May 2, 1927.

much. O'Neill started to hide away in the stateroom of F. Theo Rogers, whose cabin was next to Carlotta's. Given O'Neill's studious avoidance of the press, Rogers might seem a strange shipmate, being, as he was, an American entrepreneur who had been secretary to Manuel Quezon, the most prominent local politician in the country, and then general manager of the *Philippines Free Press* newspaper. Rogers wrote that O'Neill was 'gentle' and Carlotta 'domineering', but did admit that O'Neill drank too much brandy on the voyage.[42]

O'Neill's drinking led to very heated arguments between the couple once more. The combination of cabin fever and constant rowing all got too much for Carlotta. The *Coblenz* put in at Colombo on New Year's Day 1929 and Carlotta, without telling O'Neill, went ashore along the shaded landing jetty and checked in to the Grand Oriental Hotel that overlooked the harbour. She instructed Tuve Drew to stay on board and look after O'Neill. As the *Coblenz* pulled out of Colombo Carlotta sat on the terrace of her room at the GOH, as it was generally known, and watched the *Coblenz* and O'Neill disappear over the horizon. The next day she booked passage on the Dollar Line ship the *President Monroe* and left Colombo.

What followed was a barrage of wireless telegrams between the two ships. Both were in fact heading in the same direction and were not that far apart. Tuve Drew telegrammed Carlotta to report that O'Neill was distraught at her leaving and was threatening to drink himself to death. Carlotta was concerned and so started sending telegrams directly to O'Neill. He seemed to recover somewhat after she made direct contact and Mrs Drew reported his drinking slightly abated. Across the Arabian Sea and into the Red Sea both ran up substantial bills with the wireless operators. Both ships passed through the Suez Canal and put in at Port Said. As the gangplank of the *President Monroe* was lowered Carlotta saw a weeping O'Neill rush up the wooden stairway.

But it wasn't quite a Hollywood ending. The second officer on the *President Monroe*, George W. Stedman Jr., told O'Neill's biog-

42   Sheaffer, *O'Neill: Son and Artist*, p. 320.

rapher Louis Sheaffer that the reunion, in view of everyone 'was a combination of name-calling, insults, jumping up and down, screeching, hair-pulling, stamping feet, wrestling, and finally winding up in a passionate embrace smothering each other with kisses and hugs. From then on they were like a couple of lovebirds.'[43] Reunited they sailed on to Genoa where a chauffeur met them and drove them to the French Riviera where they installed themselves in the Villa Les Mimosas in Cap-d'Ail adjacent to the Principality of Monaco. Carlotta wrote to a friend, 'I have found peace!'; O'Neill, seemingly back in rude health, telegrammed the Theater Guild in New York and asked if there was an opening date fixed yet for his new play, *Dynamo*? Eugene O'Neill, America's most notorious playwright, was, it seemed, back in the game.

And perhaps Shanghai hadn't been so bad after all? At least with hindsight. Shortly after arriving at Cap-D'Ail O'Neill wrote to Horace Liveright, the founder of the Modern Library: 'Had a wonderful trip East and got a lot out of it in spite of snooping reporters and severe illness.'[44] To George Nathan, the New York drama critic, he wrote, 'The trip to the Far East was all I expected of it and more. . . . Also the publicity mix-up in Shanghai and Manila was particularly exasperating and threatening at the time although the humorous side of it strikes me now. It was really the most ridiculous farce I've ever run into!'[45] Writing to his son Eugene Jr., O'Neill said that he was considering writing a new play, set on an ocean liner travelling to the Far East and involving a mixed-race Eurasian woman and her involvement aboard with an American poet fleeing the reality of America and its cultural imperialism for the Orient.[46] O'Neill's good friend, and sometime editor, Saxe Commins was delighted, and not a little surprised given the press reports of their sojourn in Asia, to receive snapshots from Eugene and Carlotta of the pair dressed in Chinese costumes bought in

43   Sheaffer, *O'Neill: Son and Artist*, p. 322.
44   Arthur & Barbara Gelb, *O'Neill*, p. 686.
45   Letter from Eugene O'Neill to George Nathan, February 14, 1929. Contained
      in *'As Ever, Gene': The Letters of Eugene O'Neill to George Jean Nathan*,
      transcribed and edited by Nancy L. Roberts & Arthur W. Roberts,
      (Rutherford (N.J.): Fairleigh Dickinson University Press, 1987), p. 87.
46   Bowling, *Eugene O'Neill*, p. 366–367. He never wrote the play.

O'Neill by Mai-Mai Sze

Shanghai. Later he visited the couple in France and saw Carlotta open drawers stuffed with handmade lingerie also made in Shanghai. Mai-Mai Sze, the daughter of a Chinese diplomat and a New York-based artist who drew what became a famous portrait of O'Neill, became friends with the couple later and heard them tell many stories of their trip to China. She recalled that the two sounded just like any other ordinary tourists who'd ever visited Shanghai.

And afterwards?

Tuve Drew had been slightly stunned by the events of the trip. Not least that some news reports and gossip columns had intimated that she was far more than simply Carlotta's maid and secretary, but was also O'Neill's mistress. Tuve headed back to her husband and child in England to reassure them that she was still, most definitely, Mrs

Drew. Tuve Drew was often described as being 'stolid', 'serious' and 'stern'. She stuck by O'Neill and Carlotta throughout the trip, saw probably more of the couple's tempestuous fights and passionate makings up than anyone else, and seems to have calmly tolerated their constant high jinks. She was professional above all else. After the events in Shanghai O'Neill wrote to the *New York Times* art critic Louis Kalonyme that although Mrs Drew had been 'shocked to death, she presented a stolid front and lied like a major and a good scout.'[47]

Alexander and Theresa Renner remained in Shanghai. Dr Renner always maintained that he had not been in on O'Neill's midnight flit. However, they clearly were friends. While in Shanghai both O'Neill and Monterey wrote in the Renners' guest book. O'Neill penned: *To Mme Renner with deep feelings of gratitude and friendship always. Eugene O'Neill Shanghai, Dec. '28.* Carlotta wrote: *To that charming and real woman.* And, if Alexander Renner was really disappointed at O'Neill's dismissal of his services and 'unethical' behaviour it seems he soon forgave him. O'Neill and Monterey moved from Cap-d'Ail to the more secluded Château de Plessis at St Antoine du Rocher, near Tours. Alexander and Theresa Renner travelled from Shanghai to stay with them in 1929, less than a year after the supposedly hurtful events. Later the Renners left Shanghai and settled in Southern California.

Alfred 'Red' Batson became a highly prolific author, writing many, many stories for *Argosy*, an American pulp fiction magazine. In 1933 he published another book, *African Intrigue*, and then was lured to Hollywood to write screenplays.

Carlotta Monterey never did return to the Broadway stage. Instead she stayed with Eugene O'Neill for the rest of his life. The divorce

47   Arthur & Barbara Gelb, *O'Neill*, p. 685.

from Agnes Boulton eventually came through and the couple were married in Paris in July 1929. Her life was not without its challenges. She suffered from addiction to potassium bromide and repeated bouts of fighting with O'Neill led to several separations and reconciliations, though they never divorced. Carlotta died in the Valley Nursing Home in Westwood, New Jersey in November 1970.

Eugene O'Neill became prolific again after his Shanghai sojourn. Among his best-regarded plays that came after 1928 were *Mourning Becomes Electra* (1931) and the comedy *Ah, Wilderness!* (1933) – just about his only work to have a happy ending. In 1936 he received the Nobel Prize for Literature. After a decade-long break he returned with *The Iceman Cometh* in 1946. His personal life was slightly more troubled – as well as the continued arguments with Carlotta, in 1943 O'Neill disowned his daughter Oona for marrying Charlie Chaplin when she was eighteen and Chaplin fifty-four. He never saw Oona again. He was also distant from his other children.

O'Neill continued to battle alcoholism and depression as well as severe tremors in his hands that prevented him from writing. He died in Room 401 of the Sheraton Hotel in Boston, in November 1953, at the age of sixty-five. His last words were: 'I knew it. I knew it. Born in a hotel room and died in a hotel room.'[48] He left many unfinished manuscripts and play ideas. Carlotta complied with his final wishes and destroyed all these manuscripts after his funeral.

48   Dowling, *Eugene O'Neill*, p. 529.

Nearly Snubbed by Shanghai:
Douglas Fairbanks & Mary Pickford (1929)

'You have done a great deal to undermine the honour and dignity of the Chinese people.'

The king and queen of Hollywood head to China

In 1929 Douglas Fairbanks pretty much had it all. He'd been acting in silent movies since 1915 with virtually every performance hailed as a success. In 1920 he had met and married Mary Pickford – 'America's Hero' had married 'America's Sweetheart' and film fans and cinema audiences loved them both. Fairbanks earned a phenomenal salary that made the studio bosses wince; with Pickford, Charlie Chaplin and the director D.W. Griffith he had co-founded his own movie studio, United Artists, and had begun to successfully make the transfer from silent movies to the new medium of the 'talkies'. Fairbanks was a household name across America and a star across the globe wherever there were cinemas – *The Mask of Zorro, The Three Musketeers, Robin Hood, The Thief of Bagdad, The Black Pirate* and *The Gaucho* were all internationally popular and much-loved Hollywood movies.

Part of the attraction of these movies, and of Fairbanks, to movie fans abroad was attributed to the fact that they were mostly about heroes who stole from the rich and gave to the poor with plenty of swashbuckling along the way. Fairbanks had earned the nickname 'The King of Hollywood' by the time he married its reigning 'Queen of the Movies', Mary Pickford and he showered her with diamonds and precious stones befitting a monarch. Their eighteen-acre estate in Beverly Hills, dubbed 'Pickfair', was more impressive than most royal palaces. In 1929 they were the most prominent and most photographed celebrity couple in the world.

As the 1920s closed, Fairbanks was arguably at the peak of his career, but he was in his mid-forties and his health and his ability to swing from chandeliers were failing, due largely to the effects of his chain-smoking. With Pickford he made the talkie *The Taming of the Shrew*, an adaptation of the play by William Shakespeare. The studio (United Artists naturally) figured the two of them on screen together was a sure-fire money earner. It was a good movie,

Pickfair

though didn't make as much money as the studio hoped – audiences recently pitched into the Depression after the Wall Street Crash largely didn't warm to it. Still, Pickford's first talkie, *Coquette*, had done well and her star was still firmly in the ascendant. Unlike so many other silent-era actors who had dense foreign accents or particularly squeaky voices, Denver-born Fairbanks and Canadian-born Pickford could have a future in talking pictures.

Despite Fairbanks's career recession and the effects of the Depression upon the American movie industry, Douglas and Mary remained massively popular abroad – audiences in Europe and Asia still packed cinemas to see their movies. It was decided that as the poster boy and girl for the new technology of American talking pictures, Hollywood's golden couple should undertake a world tour. First stop was London, then Paris and on to Switzerland. All went swimmingly – massive audiences, clamouring fans, reams of press coverage and some good deals signed. From Europe they sailed for Egypt and then headed east from Suez to Southeast Asia and eventually to China. The tour continued to be a success – wherever they went adoring fans mobbed them. In Egypt the streets of Cairo were blocked for hours. It was hoped that the Far East would be a repeat of these triumphs.

Trouble brewing

Fairbanks hadn't planned to make *The Thief of Bagdad*. After the success of *Robin Hood* in 1922 he'd thought a pirate movie was the best follow-up. A skull-and-crossbones adventure film was actually planned out – a storyline was researched, a treatment prepared, costumes and sets were assembled on the United Artists lot in Hollywood. Then, to everyone's surprise, Fairbanks walked into the planning room full of models of Spanish galleons, pirate camps and maps with X's marking where the gold was, and declared, 'Let's do an Arabian Nights story instead.' So the researchers, screenwriters, props, sets and costume people all switched from Caribbean pirates to mythical old 'Bagdad'.

Fairbanks had stayed up late the previous few nights reading Sir Richard Francis Burton's translation of *One Thousand and One Nights* (often known in English as *The Arabian Nights*), a collection of Middle Eastern and South Asian stories and folk tales compiled in Arabic during the Islamic Golden Age (i.e. the eighth to thirteenth centuries). Filming the whole thing (sixteen volumes in total) was obviously impossible, so Fairbanks settled on *The Thief of Bagdad*, a lush fantasy of an Arabian fairy tale. And so the carpenters began to construct a facsimile of ancient Bagdad on the United Artists lot – city walls, minarets, domes, bazaars, winding stairways and a caliph's palace. Raoul Walsh was brought on board as director and hundreds of raffish-looking extras recruited out of LA's many dive bars and shebeens to portray the denizens of the old Bagdad souk.

When released in 1924 the movie was generally considered a success – certainly the *New York Times* praised its beauty and the *New York Sun* thought it 'sensitive'. It showcased Fairbanks's trademark acrobatics and athleticism. It was one of the most expensive films of the 1920s, costing over a million dollars, while the special effects of a magic rope and flying carpets were state of the art for the time.

The Thief of Bagdad won awards around the world, from Poland to Japan. Ever looking towards the next picture, Fairbanks moved on to *Don Q, Son of Zorro*.[49]

---

49   Ralph Hancock and Letitia Fairbanks, *Douglas Fairbanks: The Fourth Musketeer*, (London: Peter Davies, 1953).

Through the 1920s, Fairbanks and his beautiful new wife Mary Pickford were becoming the biggest celebrity couple in the world. By 1929 Fairbanks had been elected the first president of the Academy of Motion Picture Arts and Sciences. In May of that year he presented the second Oscars ceremony where Pickford picked up the award for Best Actress for *Coquette*. Then they agreed to the worldwide tour promoting the talkies, and Hollywood and, of course, themselves.

And now here they were, December 1st, 1929, arriving in what was then known as the Straits Settlements (now Malaysia and Singapore). In Penang they stayed in the best hotel, the Eastern and Oriental, the E&O, known by the local wags as the 'Eat and Owe', and one of the famous chain of hotels across the Far East owned by the Armenian Sarkies brothers (who also founded Raffles in Singapore and The Strand in Rangoon). They were photographed on the vast seafront lawn gazing out over the Straits of Malacca – they enjoyed *tiffin*, *stengah* whisky and sodas on the veranda, frolics by the pool. Then the newspapers brought trouble from China. . . .

Censored!

Hearing that Fairbanks and Pickford were coming to Shanghai, and that they planned to visit the local film studios, China's government censors got around to watching *The Thief of Bagdad*, even though by 1929 it was nearly six years old. They didn't like it. The problem was one particular scene. In the movie the Caliph of Bagdad's daughter, 'The Princess' (played by the silent star Julanne Johnston), has a Mongol slavegirl (who remains nameless in the film). Ahmed, the genial thief of Bagdad (Fairbanks) breaks into the princess's private apartments. The slavegirl (played by the Chinese-American actress Anna May Wong in only her fourth film appearance, and the one that would be her breakout role to stardom) sees Ahmed hiding and raises the alarm. The next day the princess witnesses a parade of three suitors vying for her hand in marriage. One is a Cham Shang, Prince of Mongols (played by the Japanese actor Sojin Kamiyama in his first Hollywood movie), of whom she is terrified. She is now in love with Ahmed who, in disguise, parades as one of her potential suitors. Cham Shang learns from the Mongol slavegirl that Ahmed is merely a common thief and unmasks him to the caliph. Ahmed is caught, tortured, about to be ripped apart by a giant ape until the love-struck princess helps him escape. Eventually, after some twists and turns, the spurned prince and his army capture Bagdad. Ahmed must use his magic to re-conquer the city and rescue the princess. In the course of this Cham Shang is thrown out of a palace window and left to dangle from a pole by his queue (or pigtail, as the press reported it at the time).

The Thief of Bagdad had previously been shown in Shanghai and other major Chinese cities to packed houses of film fans – both in international treaty ports and Chinese-controlled cities – soon after its release in 1924. It did not encounter any opposition or criticism at the time. However, by 1929 the Nationalist government was more keenly aware of slights to Chinese sensitivities, even in a fantasy where a Japanese actor played a Mongol prince in a fantastical ancient Bagdad. The government had formed a censorship committee based in the capital Nanking, which publicly took offence at the movie and criticised it strongly. The government issued a formal notice: Fairbanks and Pickford were to be ignored socially and all formal courtesies were to be withdrawn.

Fairbanks and Pickford were scheduled to arrive at Shanghai in a week's time, on December 10th.

Welcome to Shanghai?

To some extent the Nanking government's threatened boycott of the two Hollywood stars was irrelevant. They were due to spend the entirety of their stay within the foreign-controlled International Settlement of Shanghai – technically not even placing their feet upon sovereign Chinese soil. The Chinese government could not order the Shanghai Municipal Council that administered the International Settlement, or the Conseil Municipale that ran the adjacent French Concession, to do anything. It could not ban films from cinemas in the Settlement or Frenchtown. In this respect it was a hollow threat.

Mingxing Studios welcomes Pickford and Fairbanks, 1929

However, the couple were scheduled to meet with local Chinese movie stars, including Butterfly Wu (Hu Die) and the staff and management of the local Mingxing (or Bright Star) Film Studio, one of the big three film studios in Shanghai (the others being Tianyi and Lianhua). These studios were based within the foreign settlements (for various reasons that partly included avoiding censorship by Nanking), but were obviously subject to influence from the Chinese government which could ban their movies from cinemas outside the international treaty ports. It could all get very embarrassing, cause a lot of bad publicity in non-treaty port published newspapers and periodicals, and, if the Shanghai movie studios were penalised by Nanking, prove costly for the Chinese film industry. Along with Fairbanks and Pickford on their tour were representatives of the American film industry – keen to sell talk-ing-pictures technology to the Chinese studios and which those studios were keen to buy. It would be in nobody's interest – Chinese or American – to have this 'royal visit' go down in flames.

As Fairbanks and Pickford approached Shanghai, contradictory messages were heard from China – local Chinese film fans were said to be excited at the impending arrival of Hollywood's most famous couple while organisations sympathetic to, or controlled by, the Nanking government issued formal notifications of the order to boycott the visit and shun the delegation. The order stated that *The Thief of Bagdad* portrayed a Chinese in an 'unsavoury role, thereby damaging the nation's prestige.'[50] Another Chinese patriotic organisation formed a committee to boycott Fairbanks and Pickford specifically. They issued a statement that accused Fairbanks and *The Thief of Bagdad* of doing 'a great deal to undermine the honour and dignity of the Chinese people.'[51] English-language newspapers in Shanghai, Hong Kong and along the China coast, as well as in America, Britain, Singapore and Australia went on to report that 'Chinese film companies have been ordered to refrain from entertaining the visitors under a threat of a cancellation of privileges.'[52] The *Pittsburgh Post-Gazette*'s headline was 'Shanghai Intends to give Douglas Fairbanks and Mary Pickford the Cold Shoulder.'[53] Some scrambling needed to happen to avoid a calamity as Fairbanks and Pickford boarded their steamer for Shanghai and the Nationalist government called upon Shanghai's Municipal Council not to permit them to disembark upon arrival.

It was left to the local offices of United Artists to sort the mess out. We can't be entirely sure who did the sorting, who averted the PR disaster and saved the Fairbanks-Pickford Far East tour, but it's a pretty solid bet that Norman Westwood was involved in the process somewhere. Westwood was, for more than two decades, effectively the chief representative of Hollywood in China. He was one of two main American movie studio representatives in Shanghai at the time, the other being Al Krisel, of whom more later. Westwood was usually described as representing Universal Pictures in the country, but certainly at various times (and often overlapping) he also represented Warner Bros., First National Pictures and

---

50   At the time the Nationalist Chinese government claimed sovereignty over the whole of Mongolia, hence the notion of a 'Mongol Prince' being 'a Chinese'.

51   'The Film Provocative', *The Manchester Guardian*, December 7, 1929.

52   See, among others, 'Famous Film Stars Face Social Boycott in China', *Sydney Morning Herald*, December 3, 1929.

53   *Pittsburgh Post-Gazette,* December 3, 1929.

a host of smaller American studios, production companies and distributors.

Westwood was originally from England and had emigrated to Vancouver, Canada, as a young man. He first turned up in Shanghai in 1916, a movie pioneer showing Charlie Chaplin two-reelers and early silent westerns in halls, theatres and tents – wherever he could erect a screen basically. He started out showing the movies in Shanghai and then, as the number of cinemas burgeoned, started copying and distributing them, licensing cinemas to show them throughout China. He represented the film studios as well as the equipment manufacturers and so also helped American firms sell cameras, projectors, screens and other kit to Chinese production companies and cinemas. A percentage of the royalties made it back to America and studios saw a China revenue stream. For the camera and projector manufacturers Westwood's sales in China helped make up the shortfall caused by the slump in spending due to the Depression at home. Naturally they all rather liked Norman West-wood and encouraged him to expand his business. It's also safe to say Westwood loved Douglas Fairbanks's movies too. Later, in 1937 when Westwood was preparing to leave China after more than two decades and retire to his farm in British Columbia, he told the *Santa Cruz Sentinel* the secret of his success in Asia: 'if you want to pack a Chinese theatre – show an action picture, one with lots of thrills.'[54] *The Thief of Bagdad* had certainly fallen into that winning category.

Westwood would regularly travel between Shanghai and Los Angeles, on the lookout for new movies, cameras and projection equipment and distribution deals with new studios (at that time called 'American Exchange' agreements). He personally loved westerns and action movies, but also brought comedies, detective and romantic pictures to China. In the mid-1920s there were only a hundred or so purpose-built cinemas in China – Westwood's circuit was confined to Shanghai, Hong Kong, Tientsin, Peking, Harbin, Canton and Hankow. However, Westwood was keen to encourage Hollywood not to rest on its laurels and think they'd

---

54 'Movie Pioneer in China Comes Home: Enters Retirement', *Santa Cruz Sentinel,* February 23, 1937.

always dominate the market. There were a growing number of British and continental European films being screened in China as well as local product. Already in 1926 Westwood was telling American newspaper readers that, 'Shanghai is now the Hollywood of China. There are fifty Chinese production companies there, using Chinese directors, cameramen and actors. The general conception that the Chinese are way behind the times is all wrong.'[55] As well as encouraging Chinese audiences to flock to Hollywood movies, and for the studios to buy American sound technology, the Fairbanks and Pickford tour was about improving relationships between the American and the Shanghai film studios – there had been talk of Hollywood filming English-language adaptations of some Chinese classics and also Shanghai's movie studios making Chinese versions of some profitable Hollywood franchises. To be shunned by the likes of Tianyi, Mingxing and Lianhua would be very bad for business.

It seems Westwood found a solution to the problem, one that saved 'face' all round, got Fairbanks off the hook and kept the tour on track. It was simple really – Westwood blamed Raoul Walsh for creating, writing and directing the scene and giving Fairbanks no choice but to act as he was told (conveniently ignoring the fact that Fairbanks was a co-founder of United Artists and so therefore Walsh was, technically, an employee of his). Raoul Walsh didn't care – he was in Hollywood filming *Hot in Paris*, a musical with Victor McLaglen and Fifi D'Orsay and had no intentions to ever visit China.[56] Walsh took it on the chin in the Chinese press as the insulter of Chinese dignity and all was clear for Fairbanks and Pickford to dock at Shanghai without an official snub. The Chinese press excoriated Walsh, forgave Fairbanks and the boycott and social privileges were restored; the local film studio tours back on; the paparazzi-accompanied nightclub visits reconfirmed and the Chinese fans were unleashed.

And so on Monday December 9th, 1929 Douglas Fairbanks and Mary Pickford steamed into Woosung from Hong Kong on the

---

55 'Tongue Tips', *Pittsburgh Press*, September 18, 1926.
56 This is now a 'lost film' and no copy of it is believed to exist.

P&O liner ss *Rajputana*. When Fairbanks and Pickford arrived on their lighter at the Bund they were mobbed by thousands of Chinese movie fans. Norman Westwood had saved the day.

Doug and Mary do the town

All Shanghai – Chinese and Shanghailander – loved celebrity. The newspapers went into great detail concerning Pickford's clothes, hairstyles and especially her collection of jewellery. Fairbanks was declared the most handsome man that ever graced the silver screen. *Liangyou*, a leading cinema magazine, described Fairbanks as a *wuxia mingxing* (martial arts star).[57] Wherever they went for the few days they resided in the International Settlement flash bulbs popped as a throng of photographers followed them. Crowds pursued them, people waved and blew kisses from windows above the streets and shouted compliments from passing trolley cars. After all the potential disruption of *The Thief of Bagdad* fracas Fairbanks was keen to be on his best behaviour and not antagonise the government. He joshed with local newspaper photographers who asked him to pose standing on his head and regularly stopped to greet the public for their own photographs.

And, if you looked closely, you'd also see two other men – European, large build, extra bulky in their overcoats, serious looking and watching everything – two Shanghai Municipal Police detectives. The armed men, one of whom was William 'Bill' Fairbairn,[58] were assigned to the couple to watch them wherever they went. The police claimed that every robber, cat burglar and pickpocket in Shanghai – Chinese or foreign – had set their sights on nabbing Pickford's gems. It was well known, and widely reported, that Pickford had brought much of her famed jewellery

57   Eds: Paul Pickowicz, Shen Kuiyi & Zhang Yingjin, *Liangyou, Kaleidoscopic Modernity and the Shanghai Global Metropolis, 1926–1945*, (Leiden: Brill, 2013), p. 3.

58   Bill Fairbairn (aka 'The Shanghai Buster') was a noted specialist in knife fighting and unarmed combat, a subject that naturally interested screen swashbuckler Fairbanks. The two men must have discussed fighting techniques at some length as Fairbanks agreed to contribute a preface to Fairbairn's book *Scientific Self Defence*, published in 1931.

collection to Shanghai with her, including the 182-carat 'Star of Bombay', a breath-taking blue star-shaped sapphire that was set into a platinum cocktail ring. Fairbanks had bought it for Pickford in 1920 when they married. Rich pickings for any of Shanghai's legion of thieves able to get close enough. The detectives went everywhere with the celebrity couple – even when they addressed an assembly at the Shanghai American School!

Fairbanks visited the Mingxing Studios, the major business engagement of the trip. Mingxing was the best established of Shanghai's three major film studios and considering a move into sound. The studio was known for their left-leaning 'social problem' movies, though the studio was profit driven. Mingxing was based in a large European-style mansion. Fairbanks toured the studio and had a group photograph taken with the actors and staff.

The visit to Mingxing was organised by Alexander 'Al' Krisel, a friend but also rival of Norman Westwood. Krisel's company, General Film Exchange, was a distributor for United Artists in Asia – his territory covering China, Japan, the Philippines and India. At various times he also represented Twentieth Century Fox, Paramount, Walt Disney and Warner Bros., as well as Sam Goldwyn and David O. Selznick in the region. Krisel also had a toe in the European movie business and represented the French studio Gaumont in Asia. Krisel, like Westwood, also dabbled in representing camera, projector and screen manufacturers. He lived with his family in Shanghai in a sizeable three-storey villa with a large garden on Route Francis Garnier in the French Concession, not far from Madame Chiang Kai-shek's family villa.[59] Given the nature of Krisel's work the guest list for dinner was often impressive and had included Charlie Chaplin and his wife Paulette Goddard when they visited Shanghai and, of course, during their 1929 stay, Fairbanks and Pickford. Krisel's downtown office in the Settlement was pretty impressive too. General Film Exchange took the top floor (with a

59   The Krisel family was forced to leave Shanghai in 1937 following the Bloody Saturday bombs. Al Krisel's son William had been born in 1924 in Shanghai and spoke fluent Mandarin. During World War Two he returned to China to serve as 'Vinegar' Joe Stilwell's special-aide and translator and then returned to America to become a noted architect.

Majestic Ballroom

large balcony) of the Capitol Building on Soochow Road South, not far from the Bund. The Capitol was a combined theatre, cinema and office block with an imposing spire that had only been completed the year before. Here Krisel previewed new American and French movies for cinema managers and also had offices that arranged the Chinese and Japanese language subtitling.

As well as business visits like Mingxing Studios and private dinners, such as that at the Krisel's Frenchtown residence, Fairbanks and Pickford did go out on the town. At the swank Majestic Hotel, on McBain Road and just off the Bubbling Well Road in the heart of the Settlement, Shanghai's '400', the height of Shanghailander society, sat around in big French-style rattan chairs on a two-inch thick Peking carpet, among palm fronds set in bamboo boxes. They sipped cocktails in the hotel's Winter Gardens conservatory at tables layered in white linen. There was also a giant domed ballroom. Fairbanks and Pickford visited and both took a turn with the establishment's resident exhibition dancers, Joe and Nellie Farren. Mary Pickford's police bodyguards sat close by the dance floor to ensure none of her jewellery accidentally fell into Joe's jacket pocket!

A commercial success

The Shanghai newspapers and movie fan magazines loved Hollywood's golden couple; film fans chased around town to see them; Shanghai's film stars got their pictures taken with them; Shanghailander high society invited them to dinner. And plenty of equipment got sold too. The Mandarin-language *Sing-Song Girl Red Peony* premiered as China's first feature talkie in 1931. Chang Shih-chuan was the extremely canny and fast moving boss of the Mingxing Film Studios and a founding father of Chinese cinema. With the playwright Hung Shen (Hong Shen) he directed *Sing-Song Girl Red Peony*. It starred Butterfly Wu, the biggest Chinese movie star of the day, and was a 'sound-on-disc' movie, using a phonograph disc to record the sound in sync with the film. However, Chang opted to use Pathé equipment, probably sold to him by Al Krisel. Several years later the rival Tianyi studios made China's first 'sound-on-film' talkie. With this American technology the sound accompanying the picture was physically recorded onto photographic film. Talking pictures had arrived in China.

Fairbanks and Mary Pickford, with Captain and Mrs Waard on the junk 'Amoy', which crossed from Shanghai to Canada in 1922

Douglas Fairbanks and Mary Pickford visited Shanghai and China several more times over the 1930s, both together and separately. In 1931 Fairbanks was accompanied around town by his same SMP bodyguard Bill Fairbairn. Fairbanks's acting career had indeed peaked – he only made four more movies after his 1929 trip to Shanghai, though these included the classic *The Private Life of Don Juan* in 1934. He visited Shanghai again in 1931 to record footage for his documentary *Around the World with Douglas Fairbanks,* which also took him to Tokyo, Yokohama, Angkor Wat, Siem Reap, Rangoon and across India. In 1933 Fairbanks and Pickford separated after he began an affair with a former lingerie model and West End theatre dancer Sylvia, Lady Ashley. Fairbanks and Pickford formally divorced in 1936 and he married Sylvia, freshly divorced from Lord Ashley. Mary Pickford retired from acting in the early 1930s but remained closely involved with United Artists until 1955–56 when both she and Charlie Chaplin sold their shares in the studio. She netted three million dollars for her stake. Fairbanks died of a heart attack in 1939 at just fifty-six years of age; Mary Pickford died in 1979 at eighty-seven.

After the divorce from Fairbanks, Mary Pickford continued to live at Pickfair and receive visitors there. The highlight of any visit to Pickfair was the large collection of Chinese and other Asian objets d'art collected by Fairbanks and Pickford on their trips to the East.

Shanghai Gestures:
Louis L'Amour (1933)

'No one belongs in Shanghai.
Everyone is either just going or coming.'

The Wild East that came before the Wild West

Louis L'Amour was America's most prolific writer of westerns. He also wrote historical novels, some science fiction and several collections of short stories. Perhaps only Zane Grey is better remembered in the western genre. L'Amour claimed to be just 'a storyteller, a guy with a seat by the campfire' yet aficionados of the genre praise his historical accuracy and eye for detail. L'Amour sold a couple of million copies of his eighty-nine novels; thirty have been filmed. However, while his westerns mostly remain in print and are still much loved by fans of the genre, L'Amour is less well remembered for having sojourned in Shanghai during what he called his 'knockabout' or 'wandering' years and having written excellent short stories that feature the city. These are mostly snapshots of the city in the 1930s, including shortly after the Japanese attack on the Chinese areas of Shanghai in the summer of 1937. For those looking to recapture the essence of the authentic Shanghailander experience at that time these works, especially his short story 'Shanghai, Not Without Gestures' (1939), are classics waiting to be rediscovered.

Born in North Dakota in 1908, Louis Dearborn LaMoore was an avid reader as a young man, particularly admiring the *Boy's Own* adventure stories of the prolific and very patriotic British writer G.A. Henty. He remained addicted to books despite his family falling on hard times in the 1920s. Louis was forced to leave home at just fifteen and started to work through a list of jobs during those self-declared 'knockabout years' that would give him a long CV in the style of Jack London – dabbling at professional boxing (a skill taught by his father and older brothers), working as a longshoreman, cattleman, lumberjack, elephant handler, fruit picker and gold prospector. He went to sea on an East India schooner and travelled to the Far East. His voyages and travels took him across all the western states of the USA and then onwards to England, Japan, China, Borneo, the Dutch East Indies, Arabia, Egypt, and

Panama. It is possible L'Amour also travelled inland when visiting India. In a story that appears to be as much memoir as fiction ('A Friend of the General') he suggests that he visited Chabrang in India and perhaps travelled as far as Tibet, though these journeys may have been more through his prolific reading than in reality. L'Amour certainly did write a story set in Tibet ('May There Be a Road') that suggests a wide reading on Tibetan and Central Asian history and some anthropological knowledge of western China's tribes and customs.

Young Louis L'Amour

After the 'wandering years' Louis settled with his family once again in Choctaw, Oklahoma in the late 1930s, changed his surname from LaMoore to L'Amour and began writing short stories and pieces of reportage. These soon began regularly appearing in America's burgeoning legion of pulp magazines that provided a good living to more than one prolific provider of short stories during the Depression. Much of L'Amour's early writing was based on his previous travels – the various adventures of the mercenary sea captain, Jim Mayo, being obviously based on his own seafaring years. War intervened and L'Amour joined up, serving in World War Two as a tank commander in Europe. Still an avid and wide-ranging reader, it was only after his service that he settled on writing as a full-time career and published his first full-length western novel in 1950. He went on to write eighty-eight further novels (the majority being westerns), fourteen short-story collections, and two full-length works of non-fiction. He personally wrote the movie adaptations of several of his novels. At the time of his death in 1988 at eighty he was hailed as 'one of the world's most popular writers ever.'[60]

When it comes to Shanghai, L'Amour's 'Shanghai, Not Without Gestures' – published in *Rob Wagner's Script* magazine in May 1939 – is excellent. *Script* was the creation of Rob Wagner, an artist, screenwriter and movie director, who became intrigued by the fledgling motion-picture business and moved to California to take a closer look at it. His wife suggested he could make more money writing about the movies than jobbing as an artist around the studios. Taking her advice, he founded *Script* in 1929 and, through his wide network of contacts in Hollywood, persuaded any number of luminaries of the early industry to contribute – Edgar Rice Burroughs, Walt Disney, William Saroyan, Ogden Nash and Dalton Trumbo, among others. He also coaxed stars better known for their screen work to write articles, including Will Rogers, Edward G. Robinson and Charlie Chaplin. Wagner was a self-declared socialist and championed the work of like-minded leftists, such as Upton Sinclair and Max Eastman, in his magazine.

Most *Script* articles focussed on the movie business, the rise of a celebrity culture around the silver screen, and the emergent visual and literary arts in general. L'Amour's 'Shanghai, Not Without Gestures' is a short story that has no immediate connection to the cinema, though the title obviously refers to the controversial 1926 Broadway play by John Colton that would later become a Josef von Sternberg movie in 1941, *The Shanghai Gesture*. Like that movie it is a noir-ish piece concentrating on the anonymity of the city, its 'otherness' and the displaced and adrift characters – the 'beach-combers', as they were often called in Shanghai – who inhabited the International Settlement and French Concession. It focuses on the community of foreigners living in the city, the 'Shanghai-landers', with an American encountering a White Russian émigré. Several years later, in 1941, L'Amour published another short story set in Shanghai – 'The Man Who Stole Shakespeare' – again in

60   James Barron, 'Louis L'Amour, Writer, Is Dead; Famed Chronicler of West Was 80', *New York Times*, June 13, 1988.

Script.[61] This story too focussed on the foreign 'driftwood' of the International Settlement, their loneliness, desperation and isolation within the teeming modern city.

L'Amour in Shanghai

Just how much time L'Amour spent in Shanghai, as well as exactly when, quite where and just what he was doing are shrouded in some mystery. Partly this mystery is due to nobody ever asking L'Amour about his Shanghai sojourn, and partly it's down to his own later myth making. After the war, when he had become a household name and on just about every bookshelf in America, stories did the rounds about his time in Shanghai. In interviews he recalled supplementing his merchant seaman's pay with boxing bouts in various Asian ports – 'My biggest purse was $1,800 in Singapore – I won by a knockout in seven rounds'. In the same interview he claimed to have fought a 250lb Russian in Shanghai and felled him with a stomach punch that put the man down for the count.[62] Other stories floated in the ether – that L'Amour had helped recover US$50,000 in sunken treasure off the coast of the Portuguese enclave of Macau; that he had ridden with Mongol bandits; that he had witnessed a beheading in the deep interior of western China; and that he had fought with the Nationalist Chinese army led by Chiang Kai-shek. Though all of these are possible – and all certainly have happened to other people and could have happened to L'Amour too – the evidence for these claims is scant to non-existent.

What we do know is that L'Amour took a job on a merchant ship sailing from San Pedro, California to the port of Singapore. L'Amour was initially attracted to the Far East after having read *The Arabian Nights* as a boy. He had also developed a fascination with Marco Polo, reading Irish novelist Donn Byrne's *Messr. Marco Polo* (1921), a retelling of the Polo legend that was a bestseller when it was published. L'Amour followed Byrne's rather anecdotal life of

---

61   Louis L'Amour, 'The Man Who Stole Shakespeare', *Rob Wagner's Script,* Vol. 25 No. 590, March 8, 1941.

62   Both anecdotes are from Donald Dale Jackson, 'World's Fastest Literary Gun: Louis L'Amour', *Smithsonian Magazine,* 1987.

Polo by reading the two-volume edition of *The Travels of Marco Polo* (1877) with notes by the old Asia Hands Henry Yule and Henri Cordier – a far more scholarly tome. From there he lapped up Yule's *Cathay and the Way Thither: Being a Collection of Medieval Notices of China* (1866).[63] A fascination with China had begun. On the way to Singapore L'Amour's merchant ship docked in Japan. He went ashore in Kobe where, in solid sailors-ashore tradition, bar fights ensued. L'Amour, already a keen amateur boxer, developed an interest in martial arts, Japanese swordsmanship and the ideas of Bushido and what it meant to be a samurai.

L'Amour signed on to a ship again. This one headed for the Dutch East Indies and he arrived there, still barely eighteen years of age. Later, when L'Amour set himself to writing short stories (on the hop 'in ship's fo'c'sles, bunkhouses, hotel rooms – wherever I could sit down with a pen'[64]) he fell back on his store of memories of the Dutch East Indies, recalling Gorontalo and Amurang in Sulawesi, Belawan in Sumatra and Balikpapan in Borneo. In Belawan, the busy port of Medan in Sumatra, L'Amour found a small bookstore. Falling into conversation with the shop's proprietor he first heard about the *Sejarah Melayu* (*Malay Annals*). He was fascinated but only many years later did L'Amour finally locate a copy. Though he eventually focussed on westerns he never lost his fondness for Indonesian-set stories – L'Amour's first movie script, written in the early 1950s, was the Anthony Quinn vehicle for Universal Pictures, *East of Sumatra* (1953).

He seems to have been in Singapore in British Malaya around 1926 or 1927. Of the year we can't be certain, but L'Amour did write that on May 14th of whichever year it was he was there reading a copy of Kipling's *Departmental Ditties* (1892), which he had purchased from Muhammed Dulfakir's bookstore. Such a bookstore did indeed exist, owned by a Mr Muhammed Dulfakir[65] at No. 46

---

63   Wonderfully we are able to trace L'Amour's life through his reading as his autobiographical *Education of a Wandering Man* (New York: Bantam, 1989) is essentially a list of what he was reading and when throughout his life. Somewhat of a gift to any biographer!

64   L'Amour, *Education of a Wandering Man*.

65   Though spelt Mohammed in the directories of the time.

High Street,[66] close to Fort Canning Park. Dulfakir both sold and published books[67] as well as stocking a wide range of English periodicals and newspapers. Dulfakir's was part bookstore, part stationers and part newsagents; a must-visit location for anyone sojourning in the port and craving English-language reading materials. It was a treasure trove for any enquiring minds in Singapore and many Chinese and others living there read English perfectly well. British Intelligence in the port worried that Mr Dulfakir was stocking copies of Lenin's *Will the Bolsheviks Maintain Power?* and that copies were being snapped up by radical young Chinese. When not in Dulfakir's bookstore L'Amour hung around the Maypole, a sailor's bar (which may or may not have actually existed) that he described as 'non-descript.'[68]

From Singapore he found another ship bound for Shanghai and took up on-board with a shipmate known as 'Russian' Joe Smith. Russian Joe (who was not Russian and whose moniker L'Amour never determined the origin of) swapped books with him in their bunks as they crossed the South China Sea (sailing through two typhoons). One that had a particular appeal for him was, perhaps unsurprisingly, Joseph Conrad's 1899 novel *Lord Jim*, a tale of a merchant ship sailing from the Malay peninsula in bad weather with a hold full of Muslim pilgrims going on the Hajj. L'Amour would return to *Lord Jim* and to Conrad, both for pleasure and inspiration, again and again.

Russian Joe's own stories were as good as anything in Conrad. He claimed to have jumped ship at Taku Bar, just outside the treaty port of Tientsin and from there somehow washed up down in Shanghai. He'd picked up a woman in a Shanghai bar and gone back with her to her lodgings. She was, according to L'Amour's retelling of Russian Joe's shipboard tale, educated but fallen to drink after being deserted by her husband who'd disappeared in western

---

66 I believe Dulfakir's changed premises several times over the years – though always on High Street.

67 Especially publishing vocabularies and dictionaries covering the major dialects and languages spoken in Singapore – English, Malay, Hokkien, Hindustani and 'Nipponese' (i.e. Japanese).

68 I can find no other reference to the Maypole bar in Singapore except for L'Amour.

China. The woman died of chronic alcoholism soon after Russian Joe met her. The dead woman's relatives ordered him to vacate her lodgings. As he'd been paying her rent by panhandling in the Settlement (where the sight of a white beggar was so distressing to Shanghailanders that the takings were good enough for bed, board, meals and to get drunk every night) he gathered up her belongings, including thirty books, as recompense and moved on. He passed the books on to L'Amour. Among them was the copy of *Lord Jim*.

Quite where L'Amour stayed in Shanghai is hard to pinpoint, as is the number of times he visited the port and the duration of those stays. His major visit seems to have been in 1933 and 1934. His initial contacts in the city was a list of recommended spots provided by 'Oriental Slim', a boxer L'Amour had known in San Pedro before shipping out East. Slim was apparently familiar with Shanghai, Hong Kong, Tientsin and Saigon having, so he claimed, fought as a mercenary in a bunch of Asian armies – official and warlord – shacked up with a myriad of local girls, and spent a lot of time drunk in various bars along the China coast. L'Amour mentions both reasonably upmarket addresses where he may have resided as well as typical sailor joints, such as those in Hongkew and along the city's notorious Rue Chu Pao San, the 'Blood Alley' bar strip,

'Blood Alley' (Rue Chu Pao San), Shanghai

in the French Concession. He also hung out in a sailor's joint called the Olympic and made friends with a Scottish ex-British Army Officer called Haig who had supposedly converted to Buddhism, though L'Amour was convinced he was really with British Intelligence. The two briefly shared an apartment on the Avenue Edward VII, known by Shanghailanders as 'Avenue Eddy', that formed the border between the International Settlement and the French Concession.

Thanks to Haig's friendship and introductions L'Amour seems to have become part of a literary salon based around a Eurasian brother and sister. The sister spent her days painting in the Chinese style and her brother wrote 'very elegant poetry'.[69] L'Amour began to enjoy a world of parties with artists and intellectuals that formed the bulk of the salon. Most of the other guests came from Shanghai's Eurasian community. He continued his habitual reading and lapped up China-set works – he reports reading *Lord Jim* again in Shanghai, as well as more Conrad, the China novels of Ann Bridge[70] and plenty of Somerset Maugham, James Hilton's *Lost Horizon* (1933) where plane crash survivors discover Shangri-La, Alice Tisdale Hobart's bestseller *Oil for the Lamps of China* (1933) and her earlier China-set novel, *By the City of the Long Sand* (1926).

L'Amour wrote: 'Long ago I considered writing an entire book of short stories about Shanghai, but war and revolution changed the situation, leaving it still an important city and one of the great ports of the world but lacking in some of the variety and colour it formerly possessed.'[71] In the end he only wrote four stories set in Shanghai: 'Shanghai, Not Without Gestures', 'The Man Who Stole Shakespeare', 'A Friend of the General' and 'The Admiral'.

Each of these stories reveals a different aspect of Shanghai between the wars, the places L'Amour saw and the people he met while sojourning in the city.

69 L'Amour, *Education of Wandering Man*.
70 L'Amour would have been reading Bridge's China-set novels shortly after their first publication – *Peking Picnic* (1932) and *The Ginger Griffin* (1934).
71 Louis L'Amour's introduction to his short story 'The Admiral' contained in the collection *Yondering* (New York: Bantam, 1980), which also includes his other three Shanghai stories.

Sampans on the Whangpoo

In his first Shanghai story, 'The Admiral', first published in 1938 in *Story*,[72] one of the most prestigious literary periodicals of its day, L'Amour writes in the first person – as a merchant seaman on a jobbing tramp steamer arriving at the great port of Shanghai for the first time. The opening is a familiar and oft-recorded scene in sailor's memoirs of the first half of the twentieth century – arrival in Shanghai aboard a ship on the Whangpoo River, mooring at the Wayside Piers in Hongkew, observing the clusters of *sampans* with their inhabitant families bobbing around the larger ships. One *sampan* in particular returns to L'Amour's ship every day begging for 'bamboo' (any kind of firewood) or 'soapo' (soap), which the *sampan* dwellers assumed the foreign sailors have in large quantities and was eminently sellable or tradable for them. The *sampan* contains a family – a mother and grandmother, a boy and two girl children, and no father. The boy, L'Amour estimates him at five years old, is particularly friendly and the crew dub him the 'Admiral'.

The sailors take to the Admiral and pass out gifts of chocolate and a red silk handkerchief he takes to wearing around his head. L'Amour and his shipmates are a mixed bunch of hard characters – one, Tony, is rumoured to have killed a cop in Baltimore, another an angry and belligerent drunk, another a black cook from Georgia – but they all genuinely care for their adopted *sampan*. Then there

Sampans on the Whangpoo River

72   Louis L'Amour, 'The Admiral', *Story*, Vol. XII No. 68, March 1938.

is an accident when the young Admiral falls from the *sampan* into the river when a large Dollar Line steam ship passing too close rocks the *sampan*. As the young boy is sucked towards the giant propellers of the far larger ship Tony dives in to try and save him. The sailor manages to save the Admiral and return him to his family *sampan*. That night L'Amour's tramp steamer weighs anchor in Shanghai with a cargo bound for Hong Kong.

Later L'Amour's tramp steamer makes the run back to Shanghai with a fresh cargo. The crewmen carve wooden ships for the Admiral, they talk about the small toys and trinkets they'll buy the little lad as gifts when they see him again. They eventually arrive back at the Whangpoo River and moor up once again at the Wayside Piers. But their floating family are nowhere to be seen until they spot their half-sunk *sampan,* probably smashed by the propellers of another large ship, a terrible hazard for the *sampans* of the Whangpoo. The tough collective of sailors aboard the tramp steamer stand on the deck and see the Admiral's 'little red silk handkerchief flag, fluttering gallantly from the wreckage.'

'No one belongs to Shanghai'

'Shanghai, Not Without Gestures'[73] captures the mood and feel of Shanghai in the aftermath of Japan's invasion of China in August 1937, Bloody Saturday. It begins at an auction of household goods, presumably those of a foreigner who is evacuating the city as so many did at the time. L'Amour (for it seems he is writing once again as himself essentially and so we'll assume this story is at least semi-autobiographical and that this occurred during one of his final Shanghai sojourns before settling more permanently in the United States) attends the auction and meets a woman there. The auction is on Kiangse Road, a few blocks back from the Bund, in the heart of the International Settlement. L'Amour establishes his Shanghai credentials when he states: 'There was always an auction some-where, it seemed. Today it might be on Range Road, or somewhere

---

73   Louis L'Amour, 'Shanghai, Not Without Gestures', *Rob Wagner's Script,* Vol. 21 No. 581, May 13, 1939.

along the Route Frelupt, tomorrow it would be in Kelmscott Gardens. Household effects, usually, for people were always coming and going.'[74] All these streets did exist in various parts of the city and were heavily populated by foreigners.

L'Amour conveys the transience of Shanghailander life, the vagaries of the post-1937 'Solitary Island' (or *Gudao* to the Chinese) period of the Shanghai Settlement. Japan had surrounded the International Settlement and adjacent French Concession, but was not to move in and occupy those foreign-controlled portions of the city until immediately after Pearl Harbor in December 1941 – Shanghai was effectively cut off from the rest of China. The story establishes the boundaries of the 'Solitary Island' and reveals an intimate knowledge of Shanghai's geography. Range Road ran parallel to the very northern boundary of the Settlement in the Hongkew district above the Soochow Creek – by late 1937 it was a frontline between the Settlement and Chinese Chapei, close to the heavily bombed North Railway Station.[75] Route Frelupt was to the south, in the French Concession, while Kelmscott Gardens, also in Frenchtown, was close to the border with the Settlement. Range Road and Route Frelupt were major roads, as was Kiangse Road, close to the Settlement's major administrative buildings of the Municipal Council and the SMP. Kelmscott Gardens was just inside the French Concession; it was a small lane off the Avenue Roi Albert and close to Avenue Joffre, the main thoroughfare of the French Concession and close to what became known as 'Little Russia' for its profusion of White Russian–run shops, stores and cafés. If L'Amour had managed to get a list of road names from some source without ever actually knowing them it is highly unlikely it would have included the small and little-recorded Kelmscott Gardens.

Outside the auction it is raining, suitably reflecting the rather depressed atmosphere at the sale. These are, as L'Amour notes, 'dark days' for Shanghai. The woman who attracts L'Amour's attention is not there to buy but merely to escape the downpour outside. Meanwhile inside 'Soochow curtains, chests of drawers, brass-

---

74   This and all subsequent quotes in this section from Louis L'Amour,
     'Shanghai, Not Without Gestures'
75   Now the Shanghai Railway Museum on Tianmu Road East.

topped tea tables' – the odds and ends of people's lives are up for auction. Within two paragraphs we are in the Shanghai of post-August 1937, geographically, descriptively and emotionally. A city surrounded by an enemy army, a city threatened, a city whose foreign population is being hollowed out by evacuation and war jitters, but also a city that is trying to carry on as before, to find a new normalcy.

L'Amour's woman escaping the rain is typical of the 'China Coaster'. The American author Harry Hervey, who had spent time in China and Indo-China, wrote the detailed treatment that became Josef von Sternberg's 1932 movie *Shanghai Express*. In that film Marlene Dietrich famously played Madeleine (aka Shanghai Lily), described as a 'coaster'. Hervey explained in his treatment – 'a coaster is a woman who, although not technically a person of easy virtue, makes her living off men up and down the China coast.'[76] They are so common in Shanghai stories, because they were so common in Shanghai.

L'Amour assumes she lives in a room with little more to her name than 'some worn slippers, a few neat, rather worn frocks, a Japanese silk kimono. Probably there would be a picture on the old-fashioned dresser, of a man, of course. He would be an army officer, grave and attractive.' L'Amour engages her in conversation and she confesses that, 'Yes, I am often lonely.' They go for coffee. Her dress is shabby, her accent intrigues him, but he cannot place it, though it reminds him of a pre-war Shanghai when the narrator was younger, 'before the shells of Nippon blasted Chapei into smoking ruins and destroyed the fine tempo of life.' L'Amour is newly (re)arrived in Shanghai; the woman a long-time resident but, as she says, 'No one belongs in Shanghai. Everyone is either just going or coming.' She declares that ultimately she belongs in Shanghai because she belongs nowhere, intimating her stateless refugee status as a White Russian. In fact, she is China-born, in Nanking. It is

---

76 Harry Hervey, *Shanghai Express: A Treatment*, Hoover Institution, Stanford. Hervey's treatment is longer than usual at thirty three pages and contains much explanatory information on Shanghai, 'coasters', warlords etc. It was however Jules Furthman who eventually wrote the script for the movie, changing some details and names from Hervey's original treatment.

her father who is the émigré from Russia ... and, in a common stereotype, he is a drunkard who has fallen from Madeira, 'vodka then, and finally samshu and Hanskin.'[77] Her father eventually succumbed to the drink and left her an orphan, alone in Shanghai.

The Shanghai of 'Shanghai, Not Without Gestures' is a modern city, a noir city, as so often portrayed both by modernist writers of a more literary output such as André Malraux, Yokomitsu Riichi or Vicki Baum in their novels *La Condition Humaine* (1933), *Shanghai* (1931) and *Hotel Shanghai* (1937)[78] respectively, as well as the pulp fiction writers who covered the city including John Richard Finch and L. Ron Hubbard, and Chinese modernist writers such as Mu Shiying, Eileen Chang/Zhang Ailing, and Zhang Henshui. Streetlights glowing through the fog, heavy rain, a taxi skidding around a corner in a cloud of spray, coffee drinking – these are its staple features. L'Amour is a merchant seaman of some education and literary interests opting to stay ashore awhile and is living in slightly better Western-style accommodation with a Chinese servant, shelves of books and Chinese woodcuts adorning the walls. In his apartment the White Russian woman showers – another modern convenience of Westernised Shanghai – and informs him she is a secretary.

As the woman talks the narrator riffs on Shanghai and China: 'Outside was China. Outside was Shanghai. Three million people: English, French, Dutch, American, Sikh, German, Russian, Portuguese, Spanish, Dane, Norwegian, Japanese, Hebrew, Greek, Armenian, Malay, and, always and forever, the Chinese. Outside was the Whangpoo, a dark river flowing out of China, out of old China into new China, and down to the sea. Outside were rivers of men flowing back and forth along the dark streets, men buying and selling, men fighting and gambling, men loving and dying. Three million men and women of all colours and kinds, opening

77 'Samshu', usually spelled *samshoo*, is a spirit distilled from millet or rice (and more common in southern China than in Shanghai); 'Hanskin' may be *hanshin*, a Japanese grain spirit. Both were cheap and often home-brewed.

78 Malraux's *La Condition Humaine* is best known in English as *Man's Fate* (or sometimes *Man's Estate*) while Baum's *Hotel Shanghai* (in German) first appeared in English as *Nanking Road* and later as *Shanghai '37*.

countless doors, eating the food of many countries, speaking a hundred languages, praying to many gods.'

It transpires that the Russian woman is homeless. Her rent unpaid, she has been evicted from her lodgings. L'Amour lets her stay, offers her his own bed and opts himself for the daybed in the other room, but says, 'If you change your mind . . . well. . . .' The story ends and we leave these two 'Shanghai types' to their future.

A thief on the Avenue Eddy

L'Amour's 1941 short story, 'The Man Who Stole Shakespeare',[79] reprises many of the same Shanghai themes as 'Shanghai, Not Without Gestures'. The story appears to be set around the same time with the narrator (again it appears to be L'Amour himself) renting a room in a lodging house on a narrow street just off the Avenue Edward VII. The Avenue Eddy, as Shanghailanders knew the street, had been where L'Amour and his friend, and suspected British intelligence officer, Haig had briefly shared an apartment. The rent is low and the communal front door opens out onto the street beside a moneychanger's stall. L'Amour enjoys people-watching from his window. Again the representation of the city is of a modern, cosmopolitan, multinational metropolis. L'Amour takes long walks at night, drifting *flâneur*-like through Shanghai's neon-lit streets. Rain, fog and coffee are omnipresent once again.

Wandering the night-time city, he is caught in a rain shower and steps into a Western bookstore in the French Concession where he encounters a man called Sterne whom he observes shoplifting. L'Amour (let's assume this is again effectively autobiography) does nothing as he does not consider the theft of a book by a poor man to be a crime. The thief is a Shanghailander of indeterminate nationality, small, academic looking, but clearly down on his uppers, with frayed clothing and a worn overcoat. To L'Amour books are as much a human necessity as food or water. He has observed the man browsing Burton's *Anatomy of Melancholy* (1621),

79 'The Man Who Stole Shakespeare', *Rob Wagner's Script*, Vol. 25 No. 590. March 8, 1941. All quotes in this section from that edition of the story.

Huysmans' *Against the Grain* (1884) and Richard Hakluyt's *Divers Voyages* (1582) before deciding to steal a slim volume of Shakespeare. Curious, L'Amour is anxious to know which of the Bard's plays the man has selected. The thief hides the book within his worn overcoat and runs away towards the busy Thibet Road that leads off the Avenue Eddy heading from the French Concession back into the International Settlement. L'Amour pursues him and observes him turning into a small lane, a *lilong*, and entering a crowded *shikumen* tenement building. L'Amour follows him and gains entry into the thief's basement room. The much smaller man is scared at this broad-shouldered stranger barging in to his lodgings – 'Possibly he had visions of being found in the cold light of dawn with a slit throat, for such things were a common occurrence in Shanghai.'

The basement is dimly lit and lined with shelves of books. The stolen book is *Henry IV Part One* and the shelves contain classics from Tolstoy, Dostoyevsky, Carlyle, Byron, Verlaine, Baudelaire,[80] Voltaire and others. These are the man's evening company, his companions, his only consolation in his dislocated, displaced life on the China coast in Shanghai. His name is Meacham and, though L'Amour never fully determines his past, it appears he worked once for one of the old foreign trading companies, or *hongs*, of Shanghai and had spent many years in the interior of China.

The two men talk about literature. L'Amour confesses a love of books as companions on long, lonely voyages; for Meacham books are a link to a life lived before his current state of impoverishment in Shanghai. Meacham claims to have trouble with his eyesight and so L'Amour agrees to read to him – he will gain access to books he has not ever had a chance to read; Meacham will be able to rest his strained eyes. The choice is wide – Gissings' *Private Papers of Henry Ryecroft* (1903), Laurence Sterne's *Sentimental Journey* (1768), Locke's *An Essay Concerning Human Understanding* (1689). . . . They begin with Thomas Hardy's *The Return of the Native* (1878). Then, rather oddly, Meacham hands L'Amour a copy of *Elsie's Girlhood* (1872) by Martha Finley, a book of advice for a young girl about to become

---

80   Obviously a natural for the shelves of any Shanghai *flâneur*!

a woman. L'Amour assumes Meacham is kidding, handing him such a child's book.

L'Amour believes Meacham has a secret but he cannot divine it. For a while L'Amour has to go upriver to do a job for a man he calls Dou Yu-seng, who it appears owns the entire building L'Amour is living in and has 'affiliations with war lords and at least one secret society.' He infers Dou is a criminal. 'Dou Yu-seng' is a variant spelling of Du Yuesheng, the Shanghai crime lord and boss of the city's dominant Green Gang. While on this job and away from Shanghai L'Amour muses on Meacham's secret and then realises the truth: 'He never guessed that I knew, and probably for years he had hidden his secret, ashamed to let anyone know that he, who was nearly seventy and who so loved knowledge, had never learned to read.'

Milton's last deal

Louis L'Amour's final short story related to Shanghai was 'A Friend of the General'.[81] It concerns a fictional mercenary in 1920s Shanghai who later becomes a general, and a Shanghai-based gunrunner to China's Northern Warlords called Milton. It seems that the general and Milton are wholly fictional, yet swirling around them in L'Amour's story are a number of very definitely real old Shanghai characters.

L'Amour claims to have met the general in the newly liberated Paris after World War Two. L'Amour was in Paris in 1946 with the US Army, which again gives this story the veneer of perhaps being at least partially autobiographical. L'Amour is dining with a colourful cast including a countess, her sister, an American naval attaché, a stateless White Russian émigré of 'indeterminate age', a 'fragile blonde actress' who had been in the French Resistance, a homesick American major and a monocled Baron. The general is absent, reputedly gone to Tibet it seems via Baghdad and Chabrang in India. The general is a man about whom legends accrue – his

81 'A Friend of the General' was first published in L'Amour's short-story collection *Yonderings* in 1980, and all quotes below are from that edition.

involvement in Latin American revolutions, Near and Middle East tribal uprisings, North African campaigns with the French Foreign Legion, and eventually China. However, L'Amour is in luck – that evening the general has returned to Paris. Despite the legends that swirl around him his appearance is not that impressive: 'He was not tall, and he was – corpulent. He was neatly dressed in a tailored grey suit with several ribbons indicative of decorations.'

L'Amour realises that he knows the general, that he was one of a number of mercenaries in the pay of various Chinese warlords who used to gather for drinks in Shanghai before the war when L'Amour had been in the city. He dines with the general and they discuss Chabrang (a small village in Ladakh on the road out of Chinese Sinkiang[82]) and also to having been in China during the Warlord era. They discover they shared a mutual acquaintance, a man named Milton. This Milton was in his early forties at the time L'Amour knew him, a golfer, an enthusiastic Shanghai Race Club member, owner of a champion Mongolian pony, and with an apartment on the smart Bubbling Well Road close by the track. He was also an arms dealer who greatly profited from selling guns and ammunition to the Northern Warlords in the 1920s. However, his wealth had been dissipated on beautiful blondes and gambling. He needed one last, large deal to escape his gambling debts and flee to Paris with his favourite blonde mistress. So Milton shipped guns into Shanghai disguised in piano boxes – Shanghai Customs (eminently bribable) assumed Mr Milton to be the Settlement's premier dealer in grand pianos and looked the other way. Milton repacked his cases with straw and pieces of rusty old lead pipe, placing a few guns on top to give the impression of a full consignment of arms as ordered. He was considered reputable by the warlords as he had never cheated them before and so they did not expect any problems with his consignments. He loaded the piano boxes onto a junk for delivery and collected his down payment of $3,000. He planned to sail from Shanghai that night, to Suez then Europe.

---

82 Turkestan, or, as it is better known today, Xinjiang. L'Amour did claim to have travelled to Chabrang, though this may not be factual.

But there was a problem. His mistress, wanting to attend a swank party that night, had traded in the tickets and exchanged them for the following day's sailing. Milton panicked at first before recovering his calm, believing that the slow moving innocuous junk would take at least a week to reach the Northern Warlords. Milton believed all would work out well – his mistress would be the toast of the party, they would take the ship the following day and his debts would be a thing of the past. The warlords, upon discovering his fraud, would be angry but they would eventually forget him and get back to their main occupation of fighting each other.

The next morning L'Amour is awoken by a friend banging on his door insisting he accompany him to the Bubbling Well Road. There, outside Milton's house, was one of the rusty pipes he'd placed in the crates instead of the guns – atop it was Milton's severed head.

Adventurers one and all

'A Friend of the General' also suggests once again the long-running rumour that L'Amour served in the Nationalist army of Chiang Kai-shek. This doesn't appear to be true[83] but his description of Shanghai's arms dealers and mercenaries seem to indicate more than a passing acquaintance with this sub-set of Shanghailander society.

The story is set in Shanghai during China's Warlord Period. Though the tale is told in hindsight, L'Amour notes the heightened tensions in the International Settlement after the Shanghai Massacre of 1927. We can sense that L'Amour knew some of the other places where his mercenary acquaintances hang out. He notes the Carlton Café on Ningpo Road near the Bund, where he claims to have first met the general before the war. The Carlton Café was a real, and extremely well-known, venue run by the famous 'Octoroon' and former inmate of Folsom Prison, Louis Ladow.[84]

---

83 There is no evidence I can find for this rumour though foreigners did indeed serve as advisers to Chiang's army – see the case of 'Red' Batson in the chapter on Eugene O'Neill.

84 For more on Louis Ladow and the Old Carlton Café see the chapters on Florence Broadhurst and Terese Rudolph who both danced there at slightly different times.

The Carlton Café did indeed, as described in L'Amour's short story, occasionally have boxing bouts as part of its floorshow. L'Amour himself may well have boxed there to make some extra money, often enough to learn that the objective was to win, but not by such a degree as to scare off future opponents or disgust the crowd with a little too much blood and gore.

THE OLD CARLTON

DINE and DANCE

Imported California Vegetables, Fruits and Meats
—— OUR KITCHEN ——
is under Foreign supervision

A Snappy Dance Orchestra
and
Cabaret Show

In conjunction with
LADOW'S TAVERN
Cabaret de Luxe
Famous throughout the Orient
4-5-6 Ningpo Road, Shanghai

At the start of the story L'Amour gathers a cast of characters in the 'Astor Bar'. This is presumably in the Astor House Hotel.[85] The Astor House, its grillroom, bar and twelve-table billiard room was popular with Shanghai's foreign press corps and temporary sojourners. At the time of L'Amour's story the Astor's bar was famously manned by three well-known bartenders: Happell, Hill and Bobbett, who mixed mean cocktails. Sojourners including the likes of Emily Hahn and Edgar Snow were regulars while André Malraux uses the hotel extensively in *La Condition Humaine*. The Astor Bar usually had some sort of musical entertainment; most memorably noted in several memoirs were Irene's (scantily clad) 'Seven Little Sensations' and the house band for many years was 'Serge Ermoll and His Orchestra'.

L'Amour notes the soldiers-for-hire but places us in the 1930s by noting that it was the fliers who were in most demand by the warlords. L'Amour lists several notable real China sojourners with links to warlord and mercenary forces – 'One Armed' Sutton, General Rafael de Nogales, Joseph Trebitsch-Lincoln, as well as harking back to note Frederick Townsend Ward from the days of the Ever Victorious Army and the Taiping Rebellion (1850–64).

85 Again there is more information on the Astor in the chapters on Eugene O'Neill and C.C. Julian. The Astor House became the Pujiang Hotel at No. 15 Huangpu Road. It closed as a hotel in 2017 and is scheduled to reopen as a museum.

L'Amour could obviously not have encountered the Salem-born Townsend Ward who died in 1862, though would have known the story of his leading a mercenary army against the Taiping Rebels to defend Shanghai and his dying at the Battle of Cixi, near Ningbo. However, he certainly could have met, and could hardly have missed if he'd encountered him, Francis 'One Armed' Sutton.

Sutton had lost his arm at Gallipoli in World War One and then become a mercenary and adventurer in South America, Siberia and Korea before arriving in China and becoming a major-general in the warlord army of Chang Tso-lin (Zhang Zuolin), the so-called Tiger of Mukden. Sutton's major occupation was arms dealing and gun running and he did have the China concession for Stokes Mortar, a popular and easily operated and manoeuvred weapon that warlords bought by the score. Sutton was certainly in China at the time and died in Hong Kong while interned by the Japanese in 1944.

De Nogales was a slightly different character – certainly a mercenary, he was Venezuelan-born but served with the Ottoman Empire's army in the Great War and was awarded the Iron Cross by Germany's Kaiser Wilhelm II. After the war he moved to Nicaragua to fight with the forces of Augusto Cesar Sandino. However, despite rumours that he had come to China, it seems that in reality he probably never did. He died in Panama in 1936. Nevertheless, rumours and legends, presumably heard by L'Amour in Shanghai, grew up around his supposed China exploits.

Ignatius Trebitsch-Lincoln however did come to China and his life is one of the most mysterious of any Shanghai sojourner. A small-time thief originally from Hungary, he had fled to London in 1904 and managed a few years later to gain British citizenship, adding the 'Lincoln' to his name. He was elected as a member of parliament in England for a few years but gave it up as, in those days, MPs weren't paid. He moved across Europe working as a confidence trickster. During the Great War he offered to spy for most of the major combatant powers, working for the Germans and eventually fleeing to England. The Americans handed him back to the British who put him in prison on the Isle of Wight for three years and then deported him back to the ruins of the post-war former Austro-Hungarian Empire. In Berlin he hung around the fringe of Weimar politics but ended up being deported again before turning up in China. He spent much of the 1920s working for various warlords in China before claiming to have had a deep spiritual awakening and becoming a Buddhist abbot in Shanghai. Come the Japanese attack on Shanghai in 1937 he appears to have turned his allegiances to serving Tokyo and the Nazis. He certainly never lacked ambition – he appointed himself the new Dalai Lama upon the death of the Thirteenth Dalai Lama in 1933 and received Japanese support for his claim, but was rejected by the Tibetans. He eventually died in Shanghai while working for the Japanese occupiers in 1943.[86]

Did L'Amour know any of these mercenaries – Sutton, De Nogales or Trebitsch-Lincoln? Did he ever really work for Du Yuesheng or serve in Chiang Kai-shek's army? He might have known all these people and done all these things. He might just have sat in bars in Shanghai and heard anecdotes he later wove into his own short stories with himself as the narrator. Either way, his stories have left us several evocative accounts of inter-war Shanghai that depict the modernity and alienation of the cosmopolitan city.

Back to the West

Though the Wild West was to be L'Amour's major literary stomping ground for the bulk of his post-war writing career, it seems he did plan to return to China. Towards the end of his life, in 1984, L'Amour embarked on a planned trilogy of novels set, not in the old West, but in twelfth-century Europe and the Middle East. The first of this medieval trio was *The Walking Drum* (1984) which follows a Frenchman's journeys and adventures across the Near and

---

86   Townsend Ward, Sutton, De Nogales and Trebitsch-Lincoln are all worthy of further study. I would recommend Caleb Carr's *Devil Soldier: The Story of Frederick Townsend Ward*, (New York: Random House, 1992); Charles Drage's *General of Fortune: The Story of One Arm Sutton* (London: White Lion Publishing, 1973); Rafael De Nogales's autobiography *Memoirs of a Soldier of Fortune*, (New York: Garden City Publishing, 1932) and; Bernard Wasserstein, *The Secret Lives of Trebitsch Lincoln*, (New Haven, CT, Yale University Press, 1988).

Middle East. In an afterword to the novel L'Amour told readers that he intended to continue his Frenchman's adventures and create a series of novels, the next to be called *A Woman Worth Having*, which would take his hero across India and then one more book to complete the trilogy. It was never titled but L'Amour said in an interview that its story would move to China. Due to his declining health, he was unable to complete either novel and died four years later in 1988.

A Warm Welcome for Charlie Chan: Warner Oland (1936)

'Shanghai is an unhealthy place for you. If you are wise, you will not leave this ship.' [87]

87   Anonymous note delivered to Charlie Chan aboard ship as he arrives at Shanghai, *Charlie Chan in Shanghai* (Twentieth Century Fox Studios, 1935)

Hollywood has more problems in China

In 1929 Douglas Fairbanks Sr and Mary Pickford had finally
received a warm welcome from Shanghai's movie community and
social elite after what, for a nail-bitingly long time, had looked like
being a major PR disaster for Hollywood's golden couple. During
the inter-war years Hollywood's producers, directors and stars were
regularly to encounter problems in China with both the censors
and aggrieved audiences. Thanks to its problematic representations
of Chinese people, culture and history, relations between America's
movie capital and the Nationalist government were fraught, a
situation registered by a series of recurring spats.

China's own movie capital was Shanghai – home for the country's
major film studios and to most of its glamorous stars. By 1927 the
country had a total of 181 film-production companies, of which
over 150 were based in Shanghai, mostly within the International
Settlement and Frenchtown. Shanghai was also home to most of
the country's purpose-built cinemas, which screened movies from
Hollywood and Europe as well as those made locally. The Nanking
government was naturally interested in what people were watching
as were Special Branch in the Settlement – the Branch's 's3' division
dealt with film censorship. Though the censors had little influence
in the foreign-controlled treaty ports, Nanking controlled which
films were approved and which were to be censored or banned in
most of China. And they were pro-active.

One of the major issues for the Nanking government was that
Hollywood movies often denigrated Chinese people or culture and
featured white actors playing Chinese roles in yellowface. The
Nanking censors could, and did officially take objection, but it was
also the case that movie fans sometimes reacted to negative portrayals of themselves too. Silent-era comedy star Harold Lloyd's first
talkie *Welcome Danger* in 1930 was partly set in San Francisco's
Chinatown and featured some negative portrayals of Chinese

people. The film received repeated choruses of loud booing in Shanghai cinemas.[88] This audience outrage, which the SMP reported almost turned violent in a couple of instances, led to a change in policy in the Settlement. At the urging of cinema managers fearing a costly boycott by Chinese patrons, the SMP agreed to liaise with the Nanking censors and potentially follow their lead on banning films. *Welcome Danger* was withdrawn after a short run in the Settlement and an apology issued to Chinese patrons by cinema managers.

Following this the government censors, the SMP, S3 and cinema managers monitored foreign films for negative portrayals of Chinese. Fu Manchu, queue pulling, Chinese-American actresses in skimpy costumes – all could potentially cause offence. One major exception to this though was the Swedish-born American actor Warner Oland, a white European who over his long career played many Chinese characters in yellowface but was best known both in Hollywood and in China for his numerous Charlie Chan detective films.

Charlie Chan

Charlie Chan was the creation of Earl Derr Biggers, a Harvard graduate originally from Ohio who had been a journalist for the *Cleveland Plain Dealer* newspaper. Biggers had found some success with novels and plays before he created Charlie Chan, a character he based upon a real life-Hawaiian detective, Chang Apana (Chang being his family name) of the Honolulu Police Department.[89] Charlie Chan wasn't a straight representation of the real Chang – the rather corpulent detective of the novels physically resembles Biggers himself more closely in his build than the rather slight Chang Apana – who also never spouted cod Chinese aphorisms at every opportunity either. But the Charlie Chan books were

88 'Shanghai Protests American Pictures: Lloyd's 'Welcome Danger' is Reason', *Honolulu Star-Bulletin,* April 26, 1930.

89 For much more on Biggers, Chan and Chang Apana see Yunte Huang, *Charlie Chan: The Untold Story of the Honorable Detective and his Rendezvous with American History,* (New York: W.W. Norton, 2010).

bestsellers and made Earl Derr Biggers a household name and one of the most-borrowed authors from American public libraries. Biggers wrote just six Charlie Chan novels, while the movie franchise was to continue up to the 1980s, creating over fifty more stories about the detective. Biggers did very well financially out of the franchise and moved to California, dying there at just thirty-eight of a massive stroke in 1933. Chang Apana died just months later in Hawaii at sixty-two. Fox acquired the screen rights to the character from Biggers' widow Eleanor in 1934.

For his part, Warner Oland was born Johan Verner Olund to a family of Lutheran shopkeepers in a small Swedish village in 1879.[90] His family emigrated to Massachusetts when Oland was thirteen. He decided upon a career on the stage and trained at Curry's Dramatic School in Boston. After graduation he moved to New York City and began his career reciting Shakespeare sonnets Off-Broadway. In 1906 the flamboyant Russian actress Alla Nazimova spotted him and hired Olund to tour with her theatre company performing Ibsen plays around the country. He made good money with Nazimova and became quite wealthy combining the vogue in America for modern Scandinavian drama with an ever-continuing demand for Shakespeare. Olund became a great advocate of Scandinavian drama in America. With his wife Edith, a portrait painter from Boston and something of a socialite, he translated many of Henrik Ibsen and August Strindberg's plays into English.

Johan Verner Olund moved out to California around 1910, changed his name to Warner Oland and started appearing in silent movies. He made the transition, often tricky for actors with foreign accents (though Oland had eradicated all traces of his original Swedish vowels), from silents to talkies, appearing in the phenomenally popular early talking picture *The Jazz Singer* with Al Jolson in 1927 as Cantor Rabinowitz, an orthodox Jew.

90   To the best of my knowledge no dedicated biography of Oland has so far been published.

Oland in 'Charlie Chan's Secret' (1936)

Oland, who was bulky, fitting Biggers's characterisation of his detective as 'very fat', began playing Charlie Chan in 1931 with the Fox Studios' movie *Charlie Chan Carries On*. Oland's style was perfectly suited to the laid-back, mild-mannered Canton-born, Hawaiian-Chinese detective. The Charlie Chan franchise quickly became a massive money earner for Fox who saw an emerging series of Charlie Chan movies located in different countries.[91] Indeed, Oland as Chan was the only consistently profitable movie star for the Fox Studio in the early 1930s (and arguably for any major Hollywood studio in the aftermath of the Wall Street Crash), until Shirley Temple came along with her reliably money-making films. Between 1931 and 1937 Oland appeared in sixteen Charlie Chan films. Each movie was budgeted at around US$275,000, and took under

91   A plan that was followed with Charlie going to London, Paris, Egypt and Shanghai before a break in his world tour for a few movies and then off to Monte Carlo, Honolulu, Rio de Janeiro and Panama, as well as American locations including New York, Los Angeles, New Orleans and Reno.

thirty days to shoot. On average, Fox made three Chan pictures a year.

Warner Oland probably got the role of Charlie Chan because he had already appeared in several films as an Asian. In 1917 he'd played a Japanese spy in *Patria*; Wu Fang in a 1919 crime caper *The Lightning Raider*; Li Hsun in *Mandarin's Gold* the same year; Charley Yong in *East is West* (1922), described as an 'Oriental Thriller'; Fu Shing in *The Fighting Adventurer* (1924); a Chinese bandit chief in *Tell it to the Marines* (1926), and then three outings as Sax Rohmer's Yellow Peril villain Dr Fu Manchu before he was cast as Charlie Chan.

After playing Chan the Chinese roles just kept on coming. Oland was Fu Manchu again in the 1931 movie *Daughter of the Dragon* with Anna May Wong and the Japanese actor Sessue Hayakawa. Then, in 1932, Oland played the mixed-race Henry Chang in Josef von Sternberg's *Shanghai Express* with Marlene Dietrich and, once again, Anna May Wong. He also appeared in the 1934 adaptation of Somerset Maugham's novel *The Painted Veil* with Greta Garbo – Oland played General Yu. Then, in 1935, Oland played Ambassador Lun Sing in the Loretta Young and Charles Boyer movie *Shanghai*. In fact between 1931 and 1937 it seems Oland rarely played a white man!

His regular co-star in the Charlie Chan movies, Canton-born Chinese-American actor Keye Luke, recalled that Oland didn't need make-up when he played Chan; he would simply curl down his moustache Manchu-style and shave up his eyebrows while sometimes sticking on a small goatee beard. Many genuine Chinese mistook him for one of their own countrymen. Oland claimed (whether true or not is unclear) that his Russian grandmother was of part-Mongolian descent while his good friend and the movie journalist Rob Wagner also suggested that he might actually have some Asian blood.[92] Yunte Huang, a Chinese-American academic

92   It is not entirely clear whether Oland himself or the Hollywood press
     machine came up with the Mongolian ancestry story. The slightly later
     Hollywood actor Yuliy Borisovich Briner, or Yul Brynner, also sometimes
     claimed to be part Mongolian and born on Sakhalin, an island then divided
     between Russia and Japan. It does seem Brynner was of Swiss-German,

who has thought extensively about the cultural significance of Charlie Chan, wrote that Oland became so steeped in the role that he would sometimes stay in character and talk in Chan's pithy aphorisms off-screen. However, this may simply have been Oland performing for journalists who visited the Fox Studio's commissary to see the actor eating a lunch of 'Mandarin Chicken'. Huang suggests too that Oland's fondness for the bottle perhaps slowed his speech on screen, and accounted for the perennial grin. Although Oland had a problem with alcohol for many years, this may be overreaching a bit to explain his off-screen persona. Huang also notes that Oland, 'studied the Chinese language and read up on Chinese art and philosophy', though once again this is perhaps more the product of the Fox Studio's press office than reality.[93]

Oland's Charlie Chan movies were all approved by the Nanking censors. Warner Oland became a massive star in China, Hong Kong and throughout Southeast Asia where large ethnic-Chinese populations lived. All nine Chan movies starring Oland that had been made by the time of his trip to Shanghai had been screened in the city.[94] Chinese intellectuals (invariably at the time of a leftist political orientation), and the Nationalist film censorship board, not only approved but liked the movies. The novelist Lu Xun reputedly never missed seeing whichever new Chan movie was playing at the Shanghai cinemas.

Why was Charlie Chan, and particularly Warner Oland's portrayal, so popular in China? While Oland had fallen foul of the censors when *Shanghai Express* was put on the banned list in 1932

Russian, and partial Buryat (a Mongol sub-group admittedly) ancestry and born in Vladivostok.

93   Yunte Huang, *Charlie Chan: The Untold Story of the Honorable Detective and his Rendezvous with American History*, (New York: W.W. Norton, 2010). Oland would occasionally tell the press he was studying 'Chinese', although he only ever speaks a few Chinese words in the Charlie Chan films. If he had been studying Chinese, then he doesn't seem to have achieved any significant proficiency.

94   By March 1936 *Charlie Chan Carries On*, *The Black Camel*, *Charlie Chan's Chance*, *Charlie Chan's Greatest Case*, *Charlie Chan's Courage*, *Charlie Chan in London*, *Charlie Chan in Paris*, *Charlie Chan in Egypt* and, most importantly perhaps, *Charlie Chan in Shanghai* had been screened in the Shanghai International Settlement.

(along with the Frank Capra–directed movie *The Bitter Tea of General Yen*, also released that same year), Charlie Chan was embraced as a positive role model rather than a demeaning yellow-face portrayal of a Chinese. Certainly the Charlie Chan character – solving mysteries, law abiding and enforcing, clean living (a family man who only drinks sarsaparilla) – was more approved of than the devilish Dr Fu Manchu or the white-slaving, opium-smuggling Chinese characters more usually associated with Hollywood. It was also the case that Biggers's novels had been quite anti-Japanese and although this wasn't always a factor played up in the movies it may have won him some support among the higher echelons of the Nationalist government in the 1930s, often (with the exception of Chiang Kai-shek) American-educated, highly proficient in English and well read.[95]

And so it came to pass that it was arranged for Warner Oland to visit China. There was of course the possibility of a PR hitch. Douglas Fairbanks and Mary Pickford, both loved by Chinese fans had famously fallen foul of the Nanking censors in the late 1920s while, for all the adoration of Oland's portrayal of Charlie Chan, his roles as Fu Manchu and in *Shanghai Express* a few years before had not gone down well with officialdom. And then there was the much more recent fuss around Oland's friend and occasional co-star Anna May Wong.

Everyone's off to Shanghai

In January 1936 Chinese-American actress Anna May Wong celebrated her thirty-first birthday with a journey to China to discover her roots and meet her relatives in her ancestral village near Canton. She planned to start her trip in Shanghai – always a useful destination for any China trip combining a fair dose of publicity

95   Several early silent film versions of Biggers's Charlie Chan novels featured Hollywood-based Japanese actors – the character actors George Kuwa and Kamiyama Sojin, and the early 1920s matinee idol Sessue Hayakawa. These films were not mentioned as part of the Chan franchise the Chinese Nationalist government approved of. Sadly, Kuwa and Sojin's performances as Chan are 'lost' films now.

and the paparazzi pack with a chance to tour China. Wong certainly wanted to get away from Hollywood in 1936. She had tried so hard to be cast in the movie of Pearl Buck's China-set bestseller *The Good Earth*, but she'd been cruelly overlooked, bizarrely considered 'too Asian' by MGM Producer Irving Thalberg who chose the German actress Luise Rainer for the part Wong so badly wanted. Anna May Wong's China trip was sponsored by the Hearst newspaper empire and she took along the celebrated Chinese cameraman H.S. 'Newsreel' Wong. The artist, set designer, and film director Harry Lachman and his wife, the Chinese-American vaudeville entertainer Jue Quon Tai, threw a going-away party for the actress at their sumptuous Beverly Hills home just before she set sail for Shanghai. The papers reported that 'all Hollywood' attended the party. Warner Oland certainly did.

Los Angeles-born Anna May Wong had made her screen debut in 1919 as an extra in *The Red Lantern* starring Warner Oland's old boss Alla Nazimova as a Eurasian woman who falls for a missionary, gets involved with the Boxers and inevitably dies. In 1927, Oland and Wong had worked together for the first time in the Warner Brothers film *Old San Francisco,* written by Daryl F. Zanuck. The movie was considered a big picture for the studio that year. Although it's essentially a silent movie it does use the human voice as part of the score at several key moments, indicating that 'talkies' were just around the corner. Wong was cast as 'Lotus: A Flower of the Orient'. Warner Oland played her husband, the rather white and European-sounding Chris Buckwell. Such was the ridiculousness of the cinema at the time that Oland and Wong could not be seen to kiss on screen. In what is otherwise a fairly standard story of land grabbing in California in the Spanish colonial era, Buckwell, who maintains defiantly at one point that he will 'keep the Mongol inside Chinatown', turns out to be Chinese by birth, imprisons his dwarf Chinese brother in a cage and, in private, wears Chinese robes and worships a statue of the Buddha. Lotus dies in the end – as indeed did most characters Wong played in American films.

A few years later in 1931 Oland and Wong worked together again in *Daughter of the Dragon* playing Fu Manchu and Long Moy, his daughter. Oland had made his first Charlie Chan movie earlier in the year. It had been an instant success with audiences and he was now best known for that role. Oland liked Anna May Wong and the feeling seems to have been mutual. She was not long back from Europe where she had made a string of successful films in England and Germany including *Piccadilly* (written by Arnold Bennett and directed by E.A. Dupont). On the first day of filming *Daughter of the Dragon* on the Paramount lot Oland (who didn't pay too much attention to scripts before shooting started) asked her what roles they were playing this time. When she told him, he responded: 'Husband and wife?; father and daughter? This is getting pretty incestuous.'[96] Pay scales in Hollywood then were as bad as ever – Oland was paid US$12,000; Wong just US$6,000.

A year later Oland and Wong worked together once more on Josef von Sternberg's *Shanghai Express.* This was film fare of a higher quality (though disliked by the censors in Nanking as noted above). Jules Furthman developed *Shanghai Express* as a script from a detailed treatment by Harry Hervey, who had travelled extensively in China and Indo-China.[97] The Oland-Wong screen relationship took another twist when Oland, as Chang, an incognito Chinese warlord, rapes Wong's courtesan Hui Fei. She later stabs Chang to death. The train continues to its destination, Shanghai. Hui Fei walks out of the station alone. Unusually for an Anna May Wong film, she did get to stay alive![98]

96   Quoted in Misa Oyama, *The Asian Look of Melodrama: Moral and Racial Legibility in the Films of Sessue Hayakawa, Anna May Wong, Winnifred Eaton, and James Wong Howe,* (University of California, Berkeley, 2007), p. 102.

97   Harry Hervey recounts some of his experiences of China in his travelogue *Where Strange Gods Call* (New York: The Century Company, 1924) and finally has a well-deserved biography in Harlan Greene's *The Damned Don't Cry – They Just Disappear: The Life and Works of Harry Hervey,* (Columbia, SC, University of South Carolina Press, 2017). Jules Furthman had, to the best of my knowledge, no direct experience of China but obviously enjoyed writing about it – as well as *Shanghai Express* he scripted the Clark Gable–Jean Harlow Malay pirates adventure *China Seas* (1935), *The Shanghai Gesture* for von Sternberg (1941) and the reworking of *Shanghai Express* for the communist era, *Peking Express* (1951).

Anna May Wong and Oland in 'Shanghai Express' (1932)

And so Anna May Wong was delighted to see Warner Oland at her going-away party. The two talked and Oland said he was also hoping to get to Shanghai later in the year and would love to meet up with her, which she thought a wonderful idea. However, their visits wouldn't overlap. As Oland explained, 'I am still Charlie Channing. This time in the Circus.'[99] Oland was committed to film *Charlie Chan at the Circus* for Fox. Such was the speed of filming that the movie was already in cinemas across the United States by April, by which time Oland himself was in China.

---

98 For more on Anna May Wong see Graham Russell Hodges, *Anna May Wong: From Laundryman's Daughter to Hollywood Legend*, (New York: Palgrave Macmillan, 2004).

99 Yunte Huang, *Charlie Chan*, p. 254.

Charlie Chan in Shanghai

Over in China things had not gone well for Anna May Wong. She was criticised by Chinese nationalists for stopping off in Japan *en route* and visiting Tokyo and Kyoto on the way to Shanghai. However, she was assured that despite some grumblings in the Chinese press about her praising Japan (in reality she did little more than politely describe the temples of Kyoto as 'really lovely') a warm reception would still await her in Shanghai from film fans. But the Chinese media had its claws out, accusing her of having played too many demeaning roles – particularly her role as the Mongol slave in 1924's *The Thief of Bagdad* with Douglas Fairbanks Sr, which was considered degrading by many Chinese moviegoers, and was the movie that had caused so many problems back in 1929 when Fairbanks and Pickford visited. There had also been complaints about the 1927 silent Charlie Chan movie *The Chinese Parrot*, which had starred the Japanese actor Sojin Kamiyama. Wong had played a scantily clad nautch girl, belly danced, and once again was accused of degrading Chinese women. The Nanking government was in the middle of a campaign, the New Life Movement, which attacked the 'modern woman' and urged young women to be more demure. Anna May Wong's skimpy movie costumes were pointed to as examples of what they didn't want to see.

Still crowds flocked to see her ship arrive in February and she was fêted around Shanghai wherever she went by legions of loyal Chinese movie fans. She also had some influential friends in Shanghai, including the Chinese opera star Mei Lan Fang, the writer Lin Yutang, and the actress Butterfly Wu. China's star international diplomat Wellington Koo, and his fashionable Chinese-Indonesian wife Oei Hui-lan, who were about to leave for Paris where Koo was to be Chinese ambassador, gave a celebrity-studded lunch for the actress.[100] But overall it was a troubled trip – the Chinese press never stopped criticising her.

100 Wellington Koo (Gu Weijun) had been educated at St John's University in Shanghai and Columbia. He was perhaps most famous as a diplomat for leading the Chinese delegation at the 1919 Paris Peace Treaty and refusing to sign the final agreement at Versailles as part of China's protest over Japan's occupation of Tsingtao and Shandong province. From 1922, Koo served as

By contrast Oland arrived in Shanghai aboard the Canadian Pacific Steamship's RMS *Asian Empress* at the end of March to a rapturous welcome from fans and officials alike who referred to him as 'the honourable Mr Chan'. It was Oland's first, and only, visit to China. He was fifty-six and billed as an 'Ambassador of Good Will' from America to China. Where Chinese-American Anna May Wong had met a mixed reception and a fair amount of hostility for demeaning Chinese women on film, Warner Oland, a white European man who adopted a cod Chinese accent in film after film was mobbed. Every Chinese newspaper, magazine and film fan publication interviewed Oland, with the actor occasionally slipping into his Charlie Chan persona spouting the usual aphorisms and telling local journalists, 'Visiting the land of my ancestors makes me so happy.'[101]

Later, when his return ship docked in San Francisco, Oland recalled that there had been a sumptuous banquet provided for him by one or another organisation in Shanghai every night of his stay. There is a short newsreel of his visit – it's late March and Shanghai

Newsreel – Oland in Shanghai

China's foreign minister and then finance minister. He was the acting premier in 1924 and again in 1926 during a period of chaos in Peking under the warlord Zhang Zuolin in 1926–27. I have written in more detail about Koo, his career and role in the Versailles Treaty, as well as his relationship with his third wife Oei Hui-lan in *Betrayal in Paris: How the Treaty of Versailles Led to China's Long Revolution*, (Beijing: Penguin North Asia, 2014).

101 This was a line he, as Chan, delivers to journalists covering the great detective's arrival at the Bund in *Charlie Chan in Shanghai* (1935).

is still chilly before spring finally arrives. Oland is walking through what appears to be the old town wearing a heavy overcoat, surrounded by Chinese fans and curious onlookers, accompanied by his wife Edith. He examines birdcages and has his trademark Charlie Chan moustache that everyone recognised. The Mayor of Shanghai, Wu Te-chen, presented him with a moustache comb at a huge banquet he organised in the actor's honour. Walking through Shanghai's streets Oland seems happy, the fans and locals seem adoring and interested. Oland claimed they called him 'Chan Charley', or 'Honourable Chan', wherever he went.

By the time he arrived Shanghai cinemagoers had had a chance to see the film Oland had made the previous year and which perhaps interested them more than any other in the franchise so far, *Charlie Chan in Shanghai*. In that film, the twelfth in the franchise, one of the best and also one of the funniest, Oland actually sings a supposed Chinese folk song to some children aboard a ship bound for Shanghai.[102] Rumours appeared in the Shanghai newspapers and Chinese film fan magazines that Oland was fluent in Chinese and, as Oland himself recalled in an interview in Hollywood, after the trip back home: 'Everywhere I went, people addressed me in Chinese. I was always introduced as "the Honourable Mr Chan".'[103]

For lovers of old Shanghai, *Charlie Chan in Shanghai* is an interesting curiosity. It was an original screenplay and not an adaptation of one of the Earl Derr Biggers's novels. Directed by James Tinling, who made several of the Charlie Chan and Mr Moto movies for Fox, and starring Chan movie regular Keye Luke as Number One Son along with Irene Hervey as the damsel in distress captured by an opium-smuggling ring, there are some shots of genuine Shanghai inserted into the movie. You can see the majestic sweep of the Bund with all its landmarks – the Customs House, the Cathay Hotel and other major buildings, as well as an up-close image of the Bund landing stage where ship's passengers were

102 A concoction called 'The Song of Princess Ming Lo Fu', in English, which includes an inside joke reference to 'the mighty emperor Fu Manchu'.

103 'Warner Oland Enthused about Reception He Got in China as "Ambassador of Good Will"', *Dayton Herald*, June 30, 1936.

Oland and Keye Luke on set

offloaded from lighters, all surrounded by *sampans*. There's a pretty good mock up of a Shanghai River Police boat complete with Shanghai Municipal River Policemen aboard. Additionally there's also a recreation of the Shanghai Municipal Police switchboard with Shanghai-born actor James B. Leong answering the phones in a (not altogether accurate) SMP uniform.[104]

And then there's the Versailles Club, where Charlie goes to follow a clue. Though a Hollywood invention it's a rather good facsimile of a Shanghai waterfront bar as in the disreputable Hongkew bar district around Wayside Road. It's called the 'Versailles' because that's 'where all nations meet', referring to the post-Great War Paris peace treaty signed in Versailles. Although (to the best of my knowledge) no actual Versailles Club existed in Shanghai it feels authentic. There are sailors drinking beer, White Russian cabaret dancers, and Shanghailanders correctly ordering whisky sodas (the '*Stengah*' – the house drink of old Shanghailander society). The

104 I have no idea what the Shanghai Municipal Police switchboard room looked like in real life, but it's an interesting recreation.

cabaret dancer is dressed in a revealing number and does a sort of shimmy-cum-belly-dance routine, which was a favoured dance style of the period in Shanghai. The actress playing the cabaret dancer is Joan Woodbury, who appeared in several Charlie Chan movies.

Warner Oland left Shanghai after ten days and arrived in the British Crown Colony of Hong Kong on the *Empress of Asia* on April 9th. Again he was feted upon arrival – Charlie Chan films were also extremely popular with audiences in Hong Kong. Anna May Wong also happened to be in town, about to go over the border back into Guangdong province to visit her ancestral village of Chang On, near Taishan. Before leaving the colony she arranged a special celebratory Cantonese dim-sum lunch for Oland and his wife. Then Oland boarded another liner and sailed back to America stopping briefly in Hawaii, home of the original inspiration for Charlie Chan, Detective Chang Apana.

Know Him? It's Hollywood's Charlie Chan

Oland and his wife Edith in Hawaii, February 1936

Chinese Charlie

Shortly after Oland's 1936 visit, Charlie Chan mania increased a couple of notches back in China. Xiaoqing Chen, a graduate student of the University of California, Irvine translated the original six Earl Derr Biggers Charlie Chan novels into Chinese. This was a big deal – previously only English-language readers in China had had access to the original novels. Additionally, Chen was a prolific and gifted translator – as well as Biggers, Chen translated Gorky! He also wrote his own detective stories featuring the character Huo Seng, a sort of Chinese Sherlock Holmes who solved crimes by use of rational deduction.

Additionally there were Chinese versions of the Charlie Chan movies, made initially in Shanghai during the 1930s and then in Hong Kong after the Japanese invasion of the Shanghai Settlement forced the studios to relocate. The Chinese series started with *The Disappearing Corpse* in 1937. Others swiftly followed: *The Pearl Tunic* (1938), *The Radio Station Murders* (1939), *Charlie Chan Smashes an Evil Plot* (1941) and *Charlie Chan Matches Wits with the Prince of Darkness* (1948, in Hong Kong). In most of the Chinese versions, directed by Xu Xinfu, the actor Xu Xinyuan (no relation) played Chan. The police detective is now a private eye (or 'consulting detective' of the Sherlock Holmes variety) who has a smart daughter, Man-na, assisting him rather than a son. The series, which was a bit low budget, was known in China as *Chen Charli Hui Guo* (*Charlie Chan Comes Home*). Unfortunately most of these films have been lost, though it has been suggested that Xu Xinyuan's portrayal of Chan Charli borrowed elements of Oland's characterisation – his walk, talk and dress.[105] The phenomenon of a Chinese actor imitating a white Swedish-American actor playing a fictional Canton-born, Honolulu-raised Chinese detective is intriguing. Indeed the Chinese films were popular and came to the attention of the American press who commented on this conundrum.

105 See Yunte Huang, *Charlie Chan*, p. 258.

The end of Charlie

Talking to the American newspapers upon his return from China, Warner Oland said that his trip to Shanghai, brief as it was, had provided him with many ideas for developing his character. These included (once again) learning Chinese and working on his calligraphy. But the Fox Studios schedule remained as concentrated as ever – by mid-May Oland was on set with Keye Luke again, filming *Charlie Chan at the Racetrack* shuttling between the Fox Studios lot and the Santa Anita race track. As ever he had little idea of the story and maintained that he only read the script the night before so that he never knew the twists and turns at the end and they came as much of a surprise to himself as they did to the audience.

But the rapid production schedule had taken a toll on Oland's health. Nurses were assigned to him on set, ostensibly to stop him drinking during filming. They were not overly successful. It was reported Oland was exhausted and needed rest. For the last eight Charlie Chan movies Oland was signed by Fox exclusively to play the part and do no other films. He had always been a heavy drinker, but the punishing filming schedule and, perhaps, the dissatisfaction of being a classically trained actor continually playing one, rather simplistic, part over and over again in what were, essentially, just very popular B-movies, accentuated his problems with alcohol.

In 1937 Oland was stopped by police in Los Angeles wandering around his neighbourhood in nothing but his underwear, walking his miniature schnauzer dog and seemingly unaware of his surroundings. He had a full breakdown shortly afterwards and was diagnosed with alcoholic dementia. At the end of her tether, Edith, Oland's wife of thirty years, began divorce proceedings.

In January 1938 filming began on *Charlie Chan at Ringside*, the sixteenth Charlie Chan movie. After a few days shooting Oland walked off the set with alcohol-induced delusions and suffering from pneumonia. Negotiations between Daryl F. Zanuck, Oland and the Screen Actors Guild led to a new contract for three more Charlie Chan movies in 1938 and 1939 paying Oland us$30,000 each. But filming never seriously restarted. Zanuck suggested a break for Oland to recover his health. Oland decided to return to his mother's home village for a visit. In Sweden he also tried to reconcile with his estranged wife. However, he contracted bronchial pneumonia again and died there on August 6th, 1938 – just fifty-seven years old. He was buried in Southborough, Massachusetts where he and Edith had lived for many years alternating between there, a large house in Santa Barbara (both filled with *chinoiserie* objects and collections of Chinese curios) and, for a time, a 7,000-acre ranch on the island of Palmeto de la Virgen, off Mazatlan, Mexico. A long career playing a Chinese villain, Fu Manchu, and a hero, Charlie Chan had been, if not always the greatest of dramatic challenges, at least highly lucrative for Oland.

Fox wasted no time, taking the existing film footage from *Charlie Chan at Ringside* and hastily reworking it for their other Asian franchise, the Mr Moto films with Peter Lorre. *Mr Moto's Gamble* is an oddity in the series with its Charlie Chan-like script and Keye Luke making a 'guest appearance'. *Mr Moto's Gamble* was a massive success at the box office.

Oland's passing was mourned by movie fans in China. Fox tried to keep the Charlie Chan series going, such was its profitability for the studio. Sidney Toler played the role for a further eleven movies, but never managed to achieve the fan support that Oland had while the scripts were generally considered lower quality than previously. Total war had broken out in China and so Hollywood lost that revenue stream. In 1942 Fox sold the rights to the Charlie Chan franchise to Monogram Pictures, a low-budget studio, which made six more Charlie Chan movies with the actor Roland Winters. They're generally considered dismal. When Charlie Chan is remembered now, or appears occasionally on cable channels (or more usually nowadays is watched on YouTube), it is the Warner Oland movies that are remembered.

Two Poets Meet in Frenchtown:
Langston Hughes & Irene West (1933)

'Shanghai is a town in another world. Here there are sky-scrapers, neon lights, night clubs, jazz bands, air-cooled movies, and warships in the harbour.' [106]

A balmy night in Frenchtown

On a hot and humid July night in 1933 two American poets could be observed engaged in deep conversation. They were sat on rattan chairs across a plain deal table on the terrace of the Canidrome Gardens Ballroom in Shanghai's Frenchtown. They sipped cocktails and enjoyed the late-evening warmth as the worst of the day's hothouse-like humidity finally abated. The Canidrome Gardens at that time was Frenchtown's swankiest scene. It attracted a cast of Shanghai luminaries. Frenchtown's upper echelons including Soong Mei-ling, Madame Chiang Kai-shek herself, were regularly spotted seated at its white-linen-covered dinner tables and dancing to the resident jazz band.

Shanghai Canidrome

106   Langston Hughes, 'From Moscow to Shanghai', *China Forum*, July 14, 1933.

The poets – Irene West and Langston Hughes – were both well known at the time, though history has chosen to record only the latter substantially. West was a white woman and Hughes a black man. Their acquaintance, cordial and based on their mutual interests in African-American music, poetry and travel, would have been impossible, if not dangerous, in most parts of the United States. However, Shanghai did not impose any formal colour bars and them drinking together bothered nobody that night.[107]

Hughes had travelled from the United States via a prolonged stay in the Soviet Union, eventually to reach Shanghai. Irene West had moved gradually out from the West Coast of America as an entertainer, sojourning in Hawaii before coming to the foreign concessions of Shanghai. In the city she had established herself as a manager and agent for a number of African-American cabaret acts, the type of which were in high demand in the Settlement and Frenchtown in the 1930s. When Irene met Langston she was managing the combustible and troublesome Mackey Twins.[108] Langston, she thought, might be an answer to her prayers when it came to those two!

Langston's long road to China

Langston Hughes was most associated with the Harlem Renaissance movement of the previous decade. His poetry had been widely published and read in the United States. Possessing a strong wanderlust he had voyaged as a merchant seaman, spent time in Paris, and then, once he had achieved some fame as a poet, toured

---

107 However, this should not be taken to indicate that all venues welcomed black patronage – most of the city's private members' clubs did impose their own colour bars as did most of the major hotels. Bars and nightclubs varied their policies, often guided by the demands of the US Army in Shanghai that feared fighting between white soldiers and African-Americans free from the racial segregation laws of their own country.

108 Hughes briefly mentions his Frenchtown meeting with West in his *I Wonder as I Wander: An Autobiographical Journey*, (New York: Rhinehart & Co., 1956). While many researchers have looked at Hughes's relationship with China and Asia and his impressions of the city, to my knowledge nobody has ever looked more deeply at his meeting with Irene West.

the southern states of America making money from readings with side trips down to the Caribbean, Cuba and Haiti. Knowing that, as a black writer, he would never be hired in Hollywood, an offer to work on a motion picture featuring a largely black cast and to be shot in the Soviet Union intrigued him.[109] Hughes spent most of his stay in the Soviet Union in Moscow where he met many of the city's cultural elite and pro-Soviet sojourners. There he had met the poet Xiao San (or Emi Sao), who was living in Moscow. Xiao San was a few years older than Hughes, who was in his early thirties, and had been a university student in Hunan province with the young Mao Zedong. Like many of his intellectual contemporaries he had travelled to France on a work-study programme and, in 1922, had joined the newly formed Communist Party of China. By the time Hughes arrived in the Soviet capital Xiao San, fluent in Russian, English, French and German, had spent many years in Moscow working largely as a translator. The two spent a number of evenings talking about socialism, poetry and China. Xiao San was a highly cultured man, with excellent connections in Moscow. Shortly afterwards Xiao San was to meet and marry the beautiful German-Jewish photographer Eva Sandberg.[110]

Also in Moscow, Hughes met and had a brief romance with the modern dancer, Sylvia or Si-Lan Chen. The daughter of the Trinidad-born Eugene Chen, a lawyer and exiled minister of foreign relations to Sun Yat Sen, Sylvia was exploring Central Asian dance.

Ultimately the movie project collapsed, unable to circumvent the Stalinist bureaucracy, but Hughes stayed on in Moscow with occasional trips eastwards to Soviet Central Asia. Lodging for several nights at a cotton commune in Turkmenistan he found himself sharing a room with a young European journalist with

---

109 Hughes's time in the Soviet Union and East Asia are recounted in *I Wonder as I Wander*. His earlier life is recounted in his first memoir, *The Big Sea*, (New York: Alfred A. Knopf, 1940).

110 Xiao San returned to China in 1939 with Eva Sandberg and they lived with Mao in Yan'an. Eva was the only white woman to live full time at Yan'an during the war. They were both arrested in 1961 at the start of the Sino-Soviet split and remained in prison until 1974, to be finally rehabilitated by Hu Yaobang in 1979. Xiao San died in Beijing in 1983. Eva Sandberg died in Beijing in 2001.

pretensions to be a novelist, named Arthur Koestler. In Central Asia he listened to the music, watched the dancers, ate the food, stayed in numerous drab Soviet tourist hotels, got sick, got bored, and eventually returned to Moscow knowing that it was time to move on.

At that point Hughes had a choice of how to get home to America. A decision that was, in distance terms, pretty much six of one and half a dozen of the other. He could either return via Moscow and wend his way through Europe and eventually catch a boat to New York from Hamburg, Cherbourg or Southampton, or, alternatively, he could continue across the USSR to the Far East and then sail to America's West Coast via China and Japan. While in Russia Hughes had managed to earn a pretty decent sum of money from scriptwriting on the aborted film project . . . but it was all in Soviet roubles. He discovered that he could buy a ticket from Moscow to Shanghai, via Peking, with his roubles, while the journey to New York would have to be mostly paid for in American dollars. Changing roubles into dollars was problematic and meant paying a ridiculously high commission to the Soviet state, so Hughes decided a journey home via the Far East a useful way to spend his Soviet earnings. The trip would exhaust his supply of roubles and leave him a meagre hundred dollars to live on in Japan and China – but Langston Hughes had been down to his last few dollars before when travelling and something had always shown up; a reading, a book-translation deal, freelance reporting work. He wasn't overly worried about arriving in China with an empty wallet.

In 1933 exit visas from the USSR were a lot more difficult to obtain than entry visas. Hughes was forced to wait around in Moscow for the slow turning wheels of bureaucracy to spit out a mass of paperwork allowing him to head east. While hanging around he met Agnes Smedley, the left-wing American firebrand recently arrived in Russia with other members of the Chen family from Chiang Kai-shek's anti-communist purge in China. Smedley also told him stories of the recent Japanese occupation of Manchuria and their bombing of the Shanghai district of Chapei.[111] For some

---

111   Smedley was referring to the so-called January 28th Incident in China, or (in Japan) the 'Shanghai Incident'. Smedley's China time is covered in more detail in the chapter 'Red Sojourners at the Zeitgeist Bookstore'.

reason the Soviet authorities didn't much like foreigners leaving the USSR via Siberia and the Russian Far East, and now it seemed his planned route would be through a minefield of the ever rumbling Sino-Japanese conflict too. It took Hughes fully three months of queuing and filling endless forms in triplicate across multiple soulless Moscow government offices to secure the permits and a berth on the Trans-Siberian Railway. All the time (as the Soviets now required permit fees to paid in hard currency) his last hundred dollars was dwindling.

Then more problems – in control now of a large swathe of north-east China the Japanese cut the China Eastern Railway Line at the Siberian border – a through ticket to Peking and then on to Shanghai was now an impossibility.[112] It would have to be the long train ride to Vladivostok and then a boat to a Japanese port. More time was wasted securing permits to transit through the heavily guarded and secretive military port of Vladivostok, home to the Soviet Pacific Fleet. Hughes amassed a large leather document case stuffed full of permits, tickets and paperwork. Finally, with every-thing chopped, stamped, signed and with the all-important receipts for payment of fees attached, he could board the Trans-Siberian train that pulled out of Moscow towards Irkutsk and then ALL CHANGE for Mongolia to the south and Lake Baikal to the north; Khabarovsk and the Amur River. And then finally Vladivostok, 'a dismal, damp, depressing and dirty frontier outpost.'[113] Beyond Vladivostok Hughes knew nobody had any use for Soviet roubles so he gave all his remaining Russian money to the chambermaid at his hotel and boarded the boat for Japan.

Onwards to Seishin[114] in Japanese-occupied northern Korea for a brief stop and then to Japan. Hughes spent his time on board in conversation with an Australian shopkeeper and his sister, the only other passengers who spoke English apart from the ship's Japanese

112   As detailed in Hughes's letter to the philanthropist and patron of the arts Noël Sullivan sent from aboard the Trans-Siberian Express, June 12, 1933, contained in Eds. Arnold Rampersad, David Roessel & Christa Fratantoro, *Selected Letters of Langston Hughes*, (New York: Alfred A. Knopf, 2015), p. 147.

113   *I Wonder as I Wander*, p. 234.

114   Now Chongjin in the DPRK.

captain who could manage a few words. Then across the Sea of Japan to Tsuruga on the west coast of Honshu and several nights in a traditional *ryokan* inn with a big wooden bathtub in the back garden. Nowadays a fairly obscure city in Japan's Fukui Prefecture, Tsuruga had been decreed an open port for trade with the United States and Europe in 1899 and was reasonably well equipped to receive Western visitors when Hughes docked. In Tsuruga Hughes had his first of many encounter with the Japanese police who took an interest in any travellers who had been in the Soviet Union.

From Tsuruga Hughes travelled overland by train to Kyoto, where he visited a *geisha* house (accompanying the Australian shopkeeper and the ship's captain, who maintained it was his favourite in the city) and a bordello. Hughes thought the place more akin to a genteel meeting of the YWCA back home than a seedy brothel. Hughes wrote that 'to cap the evening, [the captain] insisted on treating each of us to a girl at his expense.'[115] Then it was on to Nara by train, by way of Fujiyama, to see performances by the Tsukijiza Theatre Company, who performed Soviet plays as well as Eugene O'Neill. Eventually he reached Tokyo for a stay in Frank Lloyd Wright's impressive Imperial Hotel, designed in the so-called Maya Revival Style and low level to avoid destruction in an earthquake (and indeed it did survive the Great Tokyo Earthquake of 1923). Hughes was lucky with the exchange rates of the time – his small stash of American dollars was going much further than he had expected.

He stayed in Tokyo awhile, appreciated the local jazz bands with Japanese musicians, met with various Japanese writers, actors and journalists, and learnt that ships bound for China were cheap. He caught a boat for Shanghai.

---

115   *I Wonder as I Wander*, p. 240. Hughes did not elaborate on whether or not he took the Japanese captain up on his offer of a girl. The question of Hughes's sexual orientation is a much-discussed one by his biographers who, in turn, describe him as homosexual, asexual and bisexual. His Shanghai sojourn sheds no particular light on this question.

'Hot as blazes'

Langston Hughes reached Shanghai in July 1933. He was to stay for two weeks.

Hughes arrived at the height of a typical Shanghai summer, it was 'hot as blazes',[116] and he knew nobody in the city. His first days were typical of amazed visitors – opium dens, the Da Shijie 'Great World' amusement palace, the profusion of prostitutes of all ages and races on the streets, beggars with horrendous deformities, tall turbaned Sikh police officers, crowds of rickshaws jostling for fares, the great wealth and the dire mass poverty of Shanghai.

Hughes settled into a Chinese-run hotel near the International Post Office, just north of Soochow Creek in the Hongkew district. His lodging choices in Shanghai were somewhat limited, due more to lack of funds rather than overt racism. Still, despite there being no official colour bar in Shanghai, things could get ugly. The 'Chinese' YMCA on the junction of the North Szechuan and Swatow Roads accepted 'coloureds', but the American-run YMCA, which Hughes refers to as the 'White's YMCA', on Thibet Road in French-town didn't – Hughes was to remain bitter about the Jim Crow regulations at the YMCA for many years afterwards. He noted: 'Coloured people were not welcomed at the Cathay [Hotel]' and that 'none of the leading hotels in the International Settlement accepted Asiatic or Negro guests.'[117] The International Settlement's American Club on Foochow Road also maintained a colour bar (and a general gender bar except on George Washington's birthday when American women were admitted), though did admit Chinese who were graduates of American universities.

Langston Hughes was a 'name' in Shanghai. So much so that Madame Sun Yat-sen, Soong Ching-ling, invited him to dinner at her Frenchtown house for a traditional Chinese banquet. Hughes found her irresistible, as did just about everyone who met any of the famous Soong Sisters in the 1930s.[118] Hughes follows the long line of visiting American and European journalists and connected

116   Ibid., p. 246.
117   *I Wonder as I Wander*, p. 250.
118   Madame Sun Yat-sen was the widow of Sun Yat-sen and also the sister-in-law of Chiang Kai-shek.

Teddy Weatherford

sojourners who went rather weak kneed and reported back on one Soong sister or another – they all had impeccable English, perfect manners, were beautiful and great conversationalists. Madame Sun was closely acquainted with the Chen family and keen to hear of Hughes's meetings in Moscow with the various offspring of her husband's former minister of foreign relations. Hughes also dined with a number of prominent Shanghai writers and journalists including Lu Hsin (better known as Lu Xun nowadays), who was under a cloud at the time for his anti-Kuomintang views. Hughes described him as 'elderly', though Lu was only in his early fifties at the time.[119]

Hughes quickly discovered the African-American jazz and entertainment community in Shanghai. He got to know its doyen – the pianist Teddy Weatherford, who was playing early evenings at the Canidrome Gardens and then other nightclubs across town. Langston and Teddy got on swell – Teddy invited the wandering poet to his legendary after-show dinners: home-style fried chicken, hot bis-

---

119   Hughes met Lu Xun when the writer was in the early stages of tuberculosis, a
       condition which would become chronic a couple of years later combined
       with bronchitic asthma. He died in Shanghai in October 1936 at just fifty-five
       years of age.

cuits and gravy washed down with freshly mixed highballs back at Teddy's sumptuous apartment. Teddy was chauffeured from gig to gig, playing sometimes five different venues in a single evening.[120] One night he brought Hughes along with him into Frenchtown to the Canidrome to hear the band.

The routine at the Canidrome was that Teddy came in early for the first few numbers, lighter jazz for the dinner crowd. Teddy would finish up with a long version of George Gershwin's *Rhapsody in Blue* before handing over to the resident jazz band and then leave for his next gig of the evening. Before departing the Canidrome that night, he introduced Hughes to a white woman sitting out in the gardens having a smoke – Irene West. He sat down with her and they talked. Irene West was fifty-one in 1933; Langston Hughes thirty-one. He was fascinated to hear of her experiences of the colour bar in American entertainment, her commitment to African-American culture, and how she had arrived in Shanghai.

Irene West – drifting to Shanghai

Irene West was originally from Dallas. She had long been a champion of African-American culture since her days working vaudeville circuits in her teens. She'd moved from performing to booking acts and ended up specialising in bringing African-American performers out to Hawaii and then on to Shanghai and other Far Eastern venues. She was a writer too – a poet who contributed work largely to African-American magazines. Most of her literary output concerned what Americans then termed the 'race problem', about which she was passionate.

As a younger woman West had appeared in vaudeville in a number of guises including 'America's Cleverest Lady Dancer' and in 'Barnes and West', a double act with comedian George Barnes, who wore clown face. Barnes and West had toured America before the Great War and through the early 1920s on both the vaudeville circuits and at 'chautauquas' – the large tents thrown up in rural

---

120 Weatherford is a fascinating character for whom sadly space doesn't allow more discussion. However, I would recommend Brendan L. Koerner's concise but excellent e-biography *Piano Demon,* (The Atavist, 2011).

VAUDEVILLE

SPECIAL ENGAGEMENT

Barnes & West

PREEMINENT, VERSATILE VAUDEVILLE STARS

Opening at Wailuku Hippodrome, Thursday, May 11

Kahului Theater .... Friday, May 12
Haiku Theater .... Saturday, May 13
Puunene Theater .... Monday, May 15
M. A. Theater, Paia .... Tuesday, May 16

MR. GEORGE E. BARNES

MISS IRENE WEST

areas that combined vaudeville acts with speakers on topics of the day, preachers and lecturers on various subjects, all on one big, all-day bill. But she struck booking gold as Irene West and the Royal Hawaiians.[121]

West formed the group around 1912 when Hawaiian music (or at least a commercially acceptable version of it) first became something of a fad in the United States. It seems Irene ran two theatrical personas simultaneously – appearing on stage as one half of Barnes and West and then running the Royal Hawaiians as their manager. This wasn't uncommon in the hectic multi-tasking world of American vaudeville and allowed acts to double up the bookings, the income, and keep things fresh for the audiences. When she appeared in Hawaii with Barnes it was claimed they had appeared not only all over the US but also in Canada, and across Europe in London, Paris, Berlin and Madrid. It's not entirely clear, but it seems they may actually have gone on tour to South Africa, Australia, New Zealand and the Far East. They acquired the marketing moniker of 'The Dancing Globe Trotters'.

Irene managed the troupe of Hawaiians, several of whom also took the stage name 'West'. They recorded records for RCA Victor, which helped them secure yet more bookings. In 1914 they travelled to England as a headline act on the British music-hall circuit (and reputedly the first Hawaiian-themed act to appear in Britain as the craze crossed the Atlantic). As the First World War broke out the Royal Hawaiians were playing a long engagement at London's prestigious Earl's Court.

121   Alternatively known as Irene West and her Royal Hawaiian Sextette.

With war in Europe, Irene West and the Royal Hawaiians decided to head out East, via Suez, performing in the British colonies in Asia – Cairo, Alexandria, Aden, Bombay, Colombo, Rangoon, Port Swettenham,[122] Kuala Lumpur, Georgetown in Penang and then Singapore – following the steamship routes. Their repertoire included *Hawaiian Hula, Sunkist Hawaii, Wang Wang Blues* and the *Kawaihua Waltz*, alongside more mainland American fare such as *Someday Sweetheart, The Rosary* and the *St Louis Blues*. Asia loved the Hawaiian sound as much as America or Europe had and Irene West expanded their circuit to more and more locations – Saigon, Batavia (Jakarta), Yokohama. Suitably perhaps given their name The Royal Hawaiians performed in Singapore for England's Prince George, the Duke of Kent, in 1926.

Eventually West arrived in the International Settlement of Shanghai. The Royal Hawaiians played a residence at Louis Ladow's popular Carlton Café on Ningpo Road.[123] She liked Shanghai and she saw that the city had a far larger entertainment economy and nightlife than any other Far East port. She recognised that it wasn't just another colony with its acts rotated out from England, but an international city that yearned for the most modern, the latest, the new. Jazz and African-American culture were essential to that Shanghai 'new' in the late 1920s. As Irene's own performing career was coming to an end she decided the best place to base herself in Asia was Shanghai. The city was going through a jazz boom; Chinese and Shanghailander crowds appreciated African-American acts, not just Teddy Weatherford. Shanghai audiences had adored the trumpeter and singer Valaida Snow, the drummer and band leader Jack Carter, pianist William 'Bill' Hegamin, singers Midge Williams and Nora Holt, and were, soon after Hughes's sojourn in town, to flock to venues to hear Buck Clayton and His Harlem Gentlemen, Earl Whaley and His Red Hot Syncopaters and many

---

122   Now Port Klang in Malaysia.
123   For more on Louis Ladow and his Carlton Café see the chapter 'Bobby Broadhurst Teaches Shanghai to Dance'. It's not clear if Irene West herself performed at Louis Ladow's Carlton Café but, if she did, then she joins both Florence Broadhurst and Lyda Roberti as women in this collection who trod those particular boards around the same time.

others. West knew many of the acts and the managers from her vaudeville years; she knew how to handle bookings, transportation, miserly theatre managers, short-changing nightclubs entrepreneurs and dissolute showmen.

So Irene West began to specialise in bringing acts from the United States to Shanghai, most of them African-American entertainers.

The 'uncontrollable colts' of Shanghai

Sitting in the Canidrome Ballroom earlier that July evening Langston Hughes had watched with interest one of the acts that came on between Teddy Weatherford's sets – the Mackey Twins, a frenetic African-American dance act who been appearing nightly since April. Irene West had arranged the booking and was managing the Mackey Twins in Shanghai, but it was proving a decidedly stressful task. Earl Leaf, an American journalist who quit his job on the *Nevada State Journal* to move to the China coast to work on the *Shanghai Evening Post & Mercury* raved about them,[124] while

DANCING and CABARET ALL THIS WEEK 8:30 P. M. to Midnight COVER CHARGE $1.10 Including Tax YOUNG ROOF presents IRENE WEST'S Imported COLORED REVUE including those DANCING MARVELS The Mackey Twins — MARIAN BEASLEY "Snake Hips" Dancer

Teddy Weatherford thought the Twins really knew their business and could make some serious money in Shanghai . . . if they concentrated on the work.

It seems that the Mackey boys were not actually twins or even brothers. They'd both been born in the South and then hoboed to California separately before teaming up in Los Angeles and forming their act. They quickly

124 'Loose Leaf: From the Journal', *Nevada State Journal*, May 27, 1933. Though Leaf had moved to China he made a handy bit of extra cash writing an occasional journal of his Asian adventures, 'Loose Leaf', for his old employers at the *Nevada State Journal*.

became headliners at the Culver City Cotton Club and were spotted there by Louis Armstrong's band. They were elevated to supporting Satchmo's act. After Armstrong decided to take a break from his punishing schedule for a while the 'Twins' floated around – they won a Charleston contest in San Francisco; then got a spot at a nightclub in Reno. The boys were still only in their early teens. At the time Irene West was back in the States looking to put together an all-black revue show to play Honolulu and then tour the Far East. She saw the Twins perform in Reno, was impressed with their act, and signed them up on the spot. Honolulu was fine and they got great reviews. Then they got to Shanghai where the boys decided they liked the town and stayed on after the revue show finished and the other acts went back to America. West stayed on in Shanghai to manage the Mackey Twins, as best she could. By the time she met Langston Hughes it was widely believed by anyone who'd met Irene West or spotted the boys out on the town that she was seriously regretting that decision.

The Mackey Twins had been running wild in Shanghai. West called them 'uncontrollable colts'. Teddy Weatherford sympathised with Irene but he said he had to admire the boy's 'stud'-like activities. Hughes recalled that, 'Between the White Russian women and the Japanese girls the boys almost never got back to their hotel at night.'[125] By this point tearing her hair out, Irene spent every evening either banging on their hotel room door trying to wake them up for the start of their set or else scouring the town trying to find them before the nightclub managers got thoroughly sick and tired of their antics and repeated lateness and fired them. They were a major headache for Irene and she desperately needed help corralling them.

West told Hughes, 'These boys, I don't know what I'm gonna do with 'em. Them – and Shanghai together – is about to drive me nuts! I could take them to the top, the very top – if they would just behave themselves. Mr Hughes, I wish you would talk to them.'[126] She pleaded with Hughes to have a word with the Twins – 'They

125   *I Wonder as I Wander*, p. 252.
126   Ibid., 252.

give me heart failure. Now, suppose you come to our hotel tomorrow, and deliver them boys a good talking to, as one of their race.'
Irene West believed they could be playing the *Folies Bergère* in Paris or the London Palladium. So Langston Hughes caught their act again – 'two lanky, humorous-looking chocolate-brown youths with mischievous eyes, white teeth flashing in a wide smile every time they finished a complicated step. They could whirl their long legs around in the air and come down in perfect rhythm, their jazz tapping making merry percussion across the stage as they seemed to float like birds.'[127] He liked them off stage too, their infectious personalities, their constant kidding around, their obvious love of the louche, largely racially unrestricted life of China, though he worried that they had become obsessed with their amorous adventures in Shanghai. He wasn't too sure what he could say to calm them down. He had promised West he would so he did try; they ignored him, and eventually there was nothing Irene West could do to help them. The Twins got fired and packed off back to America. They never did play the *Folies Bergère* or the London Palladium.

The twain shall meet

The recalcitrant Mackey Twins weren't the only thing that brought Langston Hughes and Irene West together. Both were poets and West obviously admired Hughes as the great African-American poet of his generation while he was more than aware of her campaigning work and writing on America's out-dated and nasty racial segregation laws.

In mid-July 1933 Langston Hughes moved on – Teddy Weatherford waved him off from the jetty. Shanghai was fine – but too expensive for a jobbing poet. He departed Shanghai on the Japanese ship *Taiyo Maru*, bound for San Francisco via Kobe and Yokohama. In both cities Japanese security officials questioned him about his dinner in Shanghai with Madame Sun Yat-sen, who they considered a dangerous radical. Hughes's stopover in Tokyo was for

127   Ibid., p. 253.

several days, so he decided to visit the city again but was repeatedly stopped and interviewed by police who searched his luggage and asked him about his dealing with various artists and writers, who he'd met in Shanghai, Moscow.... Hughes was under police surveillance the entire time he was in Japan.

Irene West returned to America before World War Two broke out in the Pacific. Through the war years she wrote prolifically, producing numerous poems that sought to raise awareness and respect for the African-American fighting men in the army, navy and air force. Of the African-American soldiers fighting in the US Army, West wrote in her poem *The 'Double V' Crusaders*:

> All the races will pass, I'm proud to say,
> Thru the 'Arc De Triumph,' they're building today.
> The long suffering South, will burst in bloom
> As they march, march, march o'er defeat and doom.[128]

The 'Double V' campaign promoted 'Victory' for democracy abroad, and also within the United States for African Americans during the war. Two years later West wrote a paean to the African-American soldiers flying bombing raids with the United States Air Force. She ends the poem *Black Bombardiers* with this 'salutation':

> If Blacks must die beside the Whites –
> By the God that made us, that's Equal Rights!
> Omnipotence, Who see and hears
> Will wipe away out future tears ... Amen.[129]

Much of her wartime poetry was gathered together in a collection entitled *The Twain Shall Meet: A Volume of Race Poems by an All-White Author*, published by Irene West herself in 1944. The book was dedicated, 'to every American Negro in the United States'. It was generally praised in the African-American press and, it seems, generally ignored by the white press. After the war West lived

128   From Irene West's 'The "Double V" Crusaders', *Pittsburgh Courier*, April 18, 1942.
129   From Irene West's 'Black Bombardiers', *Pittsburgh Courier*, January 22, 1944.

mostly in Los Angeles, close to Macarthur Park. Irene West died in 1966.

Roar, China!

It's fair to say that while Langston Hughes enjoyed the jazz, the fried chicken at Teddy Weatherford's, the nightclubs and the Canidrome Gardens, he was largely critical of the Shanghai he encountered in 1933. In July that year he wrote an article entitled 'From Moscow to Shanghai' for the *China Forum*, a Shanghai-based publication started by New York socialist Harold Isaacs, which contrasted Moscow and Shanghai with Shanghai coming out of it very badly and Moscow portrayed as a workers' paradise.[130] The *China Forum* was a monthly periodical that, after Isaacs's printers refused to touch it, he and his wife Viola produced themselves on a hand press in their kitchen. The *Forum* was politically charged, railing against extraterritoriality and the Kuomintang, regularly alleging that foreign imperialism, in the form of the Shanghai Municipal Police, Special Branch and British Intelligence, was intent on smashing communism in China (a not wholly untrue assertion). It was also critical of Shanghai's exploitation of factory workers.

Roar, China! is Hughes's major poetic work concerning China. Written in 1938 when he was back in the United States and after the Japanese attacks on Shanghai and across the country, it is suffused with recollections of Hughes's sojourn in Shanghai. The work was conceived in the immediate aftermath of Bloody Saturday (August 14th, 1937) as Hughes read of the dreadful and deadly bombings in Shanghai that presaged the all-out Japanese onslaught of the Yangtze River Delta that culminated just weeks later in the horrific Rape of Nanking. *Roar, China!* was not published until some months later in the *New Masses*, a Marxist weekly magazine closely associated with the Communist Party of the United State of America, on February 22nd, 1938.

---

130 Langston Hughes, 'From Moscow to Shanghai', *China Forum*, July 14, 1933.

The poem is both a call to arms and a fierce polemic that conveys Hughes's anti-imperialist and anti-colonialist stance as well as his disgust at the Japanese attacks on China, and it makes specific references to Shanghai. He notes 'concessions', 'zones of influence' and 'international settlements' created by 'gunboats' referring of course to the creation of Shanghai as a treaty port in 1842. He also mentions his major Shanghai *bête noire*, the 'Jim Crow YMCA's'. He notes the Japanese bombing of the Chinese portions of Shanghai in the summer of 1937 and 'the yellow men' (meaning the Japanese) who dropped bombs on Chapei. Hughes goes on to mention child labour in foreign-owned factories, the gates of the foreign concessions that restricted movement for Chinese refugees and the piousness of foreign missionaries in China.

However much Langston Hughes enjoyed his Frenchtown conversations, cocktails and dinners with Irene West, Teddy Weatherford and Madame Sun Yat-sen, he refused to forget that there was another side to Shanghai that never got even close to sitting in the gardens of the Canidrome Ballroom sipping champagne and discussing poetry.

Roar, China!
Langston Hughes

Roar, China!
Roar, old lion of the East!
Snort fire, yellow dragon of the Orient,
Tired at last of being bothered.
Since when did you ever steal anything
From anybody,
Sleepy wise old beast
Known as the porcelain-maker,
Known as the poem-maker,
Known as maker of firecrackers?
A long time since you cared
About taking other people's lands
Away from them.
THEY must've thought you didn't care

About your own land either –
So THEY came with gunboats,
Set up Concessions,
Zones of influence,
International Settlements,
Missionary houses,
Banks,
And Jim Crow YMCA's.
THEY beat you with malacca canes
And dared you to raise your head –
Except to cut it off.
Even the yellow men came
To take what the white men
Hadn't already taken.
The yellow men dropped bombs on Chapei.
The yellow men called you the same names
The white men did:

> *Dog! Dog! Dog!*
> *Coolie dog!*
> *Red! . . . Lousy red!*
> *Red coolie dog!*

And in the end you had no place
To make your porcelain,
Write your poems,
Or shoot your firecrackers on holidays.
In the end you had no peace
Or calm left at all.
PRESIDENT, KING, MIKADO
Thought you really were a dog.
THEY kicked you daily
Via radiophone, via cablegram,
Via gunboats in her harbour,
Via malacca canes.
THEY thought you were a tame lion.
A sleepy, easy, tame old lion!

> Ha! Ha!
> Haaa-aa-a! . . . Ha!

Laugh, little coolie boy on the docks of Shanghai, laugh!
    You're no tame lion.
Laugh, red generals in the hills of Sian-kiang, laugh!
    You're no tame lion.
Laugh, child slaves in the factories of the foreigners!
    You're no tame lion.
Laugh – and roar, China! Time to spit fire!
Open your mouth, old dragon of the East.
To swallow up the gunboats in the Yangtse!
Swallow up the foreign planes in your sky!
Eat bullets, old maker of firecrackers –
And spit out freedom in the face of your enemies!
Break the chains of the East,
    Little coolie boy!
Break the chains of the East,
    Red generals!
    Break the chains of the East,
    Child slaves in the factories!
Smash the iron gates of the Concessions!
Smash the pious doors of the missionary houses!
Smash the revolving doors of the Jim Crow YMCA's.
Crush the enemies of land and bread and freedom!
    Stand up and roar, China!
    You know what you want!
    The only way to get it is
    To take it!
    Roar, China!

From Shanghai to Hollywood:
Lyda Roberti (1927)

*'I've seen so much of the stage and been in
the business so long I am tired, I guess.'*[131]

---

131 Lyda Roberti speaking to an interviewer in Hollywood shortly before her
death.

A clown's daughter

Hollywood has always cast its net wide in the search for screen talent. Likewise actors and actresses have been drawn to the movie capital from across the globe, China included. One such was Lyda Roberti – a clown's daughter who became an émigré in China before making it to Hollywood from Shanghai and becoming a genuine movie star.

Lyda was born in Warsaw, Poland (then part of the Russian Empire), in 1906. Her grandfather and father were both famous German circus clowns. Her grandfather had performed under their original family name of Pecjak and so, to distinguish himself, her father took the stage name 'Roberti the Clown', which later became Lyda's stage name too. Lyda's mother was a trick pony rider. The Pecjak/Robertis were a circus family and always travelling – Lyda's older brother, Robert, was born in Poland in 1905 and her younger sister Manya (Mary) was born in 1908 in Kiev. Lyda, from the age of three, was a circus performer, specialising in the trapeze as well as dance, travelling with her family and the circus around Eastern Europe. Her sister also performed in the circus ring and her brother was an accomplished musician. Come 1917 and the Russian Revolution the family fled the Bolsheviks and eventually settled in Shanghai – yet another White Russian (or technically Polish) émigré family in the city. Circus performers who had come to China tried to reform the circus in Shanghai, but it soon went bankrupt. The Chinese did not see anything special in European circus compared to their own tradition of acrobatics and popular entertainments and there just weren't enough Shanghailanders to sell tickets to. New forms of employment were required.

Lyda got a job dancing at the Old Carlton Café on Ningpo Road, near the famous Bund. Almost every foreign dancer in Shanghai seems to have danced at the Old Carlton Café in the 1920s (see the chapter 'Bobby Broadhurst Teaches Shanghai to Dance' –

Australian-born Florence and Polish-born Lyda must have been in the chorus line at the Carlton Café at approximately the same time). Through her gig at the Old Carlton, Lyda made enough money to book passage on a ship to America in 1927. There were several reasons Lyda may have chosen to leave for the United States just then. It was a tough year in Shanghai with the strikes, riots and then horrific bloodletting of the April 12th Shanghai Massacre (indeed Lyda's fellow Carlton Café dancer Florence 'Bobby' Broadhurst also left Shanghai that year in the wake of the bloodshed). Or perhaps she felt her future lay in the movies? It has also been said that she wanted to escape her abusive father who had become an alcoholic. There's no primary evidence for this, but it must have been tough for Roberti the Clown, living as a stateless émigré in a strange country and without his circus career or fame any more.

From Shanghai to America

In America with her good looks, ever-present smile, hokey Polish accent and dancing skills, Lyda quickly became a star of the vaudeville circuit. She regularly appeared as support for, and then alongside, comedy and Ziegfeld Follies star Eddie Cantor. Cantor, who was a dozen years older than Lyda, had already made the jump from vaudeville to the movies, along with his old Coney Island sidekick Jimmy Durante. Lyda with her big personality, blond wavy locks, strong look (resembling a younger Mae West) and circus clown's gift for comic timing, was a perfect foil to Cantor's trademark eye-rolling song-and-dance shtick.

Technically it was Lou Holtz who 'spotted' Lyda and put her in his 1931 Broadway show *You Said It*. Holtz and Cantor were all part of a circle of mainly Jewish, New York-based comedians who'd been born in the 1890s. Like Cantor (and Al Jolson too), Holtz started out in vaudeville and regularly performed in blackface. He moved on to create his own revues and Broadway shows that catered to local audiences and positively enjoyed hiring actors and actresses with strong Hebrew or East European accents. Lyda was Holtz's comedy actress in *You Said It*, a show produced, directed and starring Holtz. It ran for 192 performances from January 1931 to

July that same year at Chanin's 46th Street Theater – a success by
the fast turn-around standard of the times. The show featured the
usual cast of Holtz's Jewish caricatures – Holtz played Pinkie Pincus
who had to deal with Fuzzy Shawowsky and others. It was all set
on a university campus and Lyda played Fanny, Pinkie's love
interest. She had a duet with Holtz – *It's Different With Me*. It was
a success; Lyda was praised in the reviews though Holtz rather
played up her Polish origins by claiming that she spoke terrible
English when he cast her. She had arrived on Broadway and found
her stage persona – the beautiful blonde comedy actress and singer,
a 'man-eater' with a strong East European accent. She portrayed,
usually, voracious man-chasers, but she played everything for laughs
and slapstick. It was vaudeville style entertainment come to Broadway and now moving on to Hollywood.

Between 1932 and 1935 Lyda was extremely busy. She first appeared in Paramount's 1932 *Dancers in the Dark*, a romantic comedy
set in a gangster-filled nightclub – Lyda wasn't the lead (that was
the more conventionally all-American Miriam Hopkins) but she
was high up on the billing playing Fanny Zabowolski and having
some scenes with George Raft, the exhibition dancer turned movie
actor with gangster connections. The same year she appeared with
W.C. Fields in *Million Dollar Legs*. Joseph L. Mankiewicz wrote
the somewhat surreal script, which played on the fact that the
Olympics were held in Los Angeles that year. Fields had a penchant
for putting great vaudeville acts in his movies – the cross-eyed
'Happy Hooligan' Ben Turpin also appears in this film. Again Lyda
wasn't the female lead (it was Susan Fleming this time) but her
character of Mata Machree – 'The Woman No Man Can Resist' –
was a fun play on the First World War spy Mata Hari as Lyda
attempts to seduce each member of the Olympic team from the
fictional country of Klopstokia. The movie was pre-Hays Code so
Lyda's seduction techniques are fairly robust. She also got her own
song in the movie, though a rather forgettable one – *When I Get
Hot in Klopstokia*.

The press started to take note of Lyda's movie performances and
they invariably harked back to her Shanghai past. 'Lyda Roberti,
who draws a Paramount contract, waited on tables in China when

her show stranded there.' A bit of a twisting of the truth perhaps, though a little waitressing at the Old Carlton Café is not unimaginable and, of course, all good publicity. In 1933 Lyda was picked to co-star with her old vaudeville friend Eddie Cantor in his star vehicle for Samuel Goldwyn, *The Kid from Spain*. It's a typically Cantor-esque mish-mash of a movie with Eddie appearing in blackface for some not altogether obvious reason and, of course, fighting some bulls. Lyda co-starred as Cantor's love interest Rosalie. They do get two duets together, *Look What You've Done* and *What a Perfect Combination*. There was also a performance from the 'Goldwyn Girls' dance troupe who included the then completely unknown trio of Betty Grable, Paulette Goddard and Jane Wyman. Cantor was reportedly eternally grateful to Lyda, claiming she was the only woman who ever made him look sexy in a film. Her circus training meant Lyda could match any physical shtick Cantor threw her way, while she could grab attention repeatedly using her shapely leg (from behind a dressing curtain where she was obviously meant to be naked) to point a goggling Cantor towards her clothes.

Lyda appeared in a number of other movies, but never as the star. She was always the comedy support – to Paulette Goddard, Claudette Colbert and Alice Faye among others. Her parts got smaller rather than bigger, and so Lyda decided to go back to the stage rather than struggle on with the screen. She could still play up her accent and sexiness on the stage, meanwhile the Hays Code was about to be enforced on movies, removing much of the saucy naughtiness that had worked so well for her. So she appeared in a George and Ira Gershwin musical comedy *Pardon My English* as Gita Gorbel. It's a strange story but it's hard to blame Lyda for figuring that a Gershwin show is a good way to get back on Broadway! *Pardon My English* is set in a 1933 Dresden speakeasy (in a Germany where the police have banned beer and wine for some unspecified reason obviously meant to make the audience think of America's prohibition laws). Lyda sang the title song of the same name which showcased her speciality of mixed-up English of various bits and pieces of Polish, German, and near-Hungarian to comic effect. Sadly though, like Lyda's polyglottal English, the show didn't make much sense or hold together very well – there's a lot of confusing plot related to various people suffering memory loss for no good reason. Audiences weren't interested – Prohibition was on its way out and not such a racy topic in 1933. It ran for only thirty-three performances in January and February 1933 at Broadway's Majestic Theatre, got universally terrible reviews, and then disappeared into oblivion.[132] Ira Gershwin described the show as, 'a headache from start to finish'.[133]

But Lyda had much more success later in 1933 with the Jerome Kern musical comedy *Roberta.* The plot is the usual 1930s comedic musical confusion, but it does include the song *Smoke Gets in Your Eyes,* which was a smash and has obviously proved enduring with audiences. Lyda had several songs as the comic character of Madame Nunez, though none of hers were so good. The show ran at the New Amsterdam Theater for nearly 300 performances from November 1933 to July 1934. Lyda got rave reviews. In 1935 RKO Studios made a movie version of *Roberta*, but Ginger Rogers got Lyda's role and even made a reportedly half-decent attempt at mimicking Lyda's accent.

Finding love in hospital corridor

Maybe RKO considered Lyda for the movie role in *Roberta* but couldn't reach her. She was otherwise engaged when they were casting the film. Lyda had been in hospital for an appendectomy and, while stuck in her room recovering, met a fellow patient. He was the radio star Hugh 'Bud' Ernst, who was recovering from a car crash. They started wheeling themselves around the hallways of the hospital together in their wheelchairs and then walking in the gardens together as they recuperated. But Lyda had to return to Hollywood to appear in a couple of revue movies (*George White's 1935 Scandals* and *The Big Broadcast of 1936*). Still, the couple kept in touch.

132 *Pardon My English* has been revived rarely. Perhaps most oddly it was revived in Germany in 2009 as a curiosity, but it still made no sense.

133 Quoted in Philip Furia, *Ira Gershwin: The Art of the Lyricist*, (New York, Oxford University Press USA, 1996), p. 95.

Bud Ernst

Six foot, four inch Ernst was a former movie cameraman turned star radio announcer in an age where every home had, and regularly listened to, the wireless. He was also a close friend of Errol Flynn (who had himself spent some time in Shanghai as a younger man) and a keen pilot with his own plane. He flew Flynn and his French-born fiancée Lili Damita to their wedding in Yuma, Arizona, where he was Flynn's best man. He wanted Lyda to come with them but the studio wouldn't give her time off. So afterwards Ernst flew his plane to Los Angeles on June 25th, 1935. He collected Lyda when she finished her scheduled scenes that day and they flew to Yuma, were married, and then flew back to LA where Ernst dropped his new wife back on the set for her next call. Ernst recalled that he was so tired by the time they got back to California he nearly crashed the plane on landing. It was a bumpy arrival. Lyda though slept through it all and didn't realise how close they'd been to coming down in a heavily wooded forest next to the runway! Lyda was twenty-nine, though, as the press reported, maybe she was a bit older as her birth certificate had been 'lost' in the upheavals somewhere between Russian-Poland and Shanghai.

Stage and screen roles weren't Lyda's major problem. Rather it was her health, and it was deteriorating. The appendectomy, various other ailments, and a diagnosed 'weak heart' left her tired and constantly in and out of doctor's surgeries and hospitals. The couple seemed happy enough – photographed on board ship together in July 1935 arriving in New York. Lyda wore dark glasses and refused

Eagle Staff Photo
Lyda Roberti with those mysterious black goggles as she arrived on the Santa Elena with her new husband, Bud Ernst, today.

to take them off for the paparazzi quayside at the Brooklyn Piers. They had been to Panama on a belated honeymoon – she claimed the sun hurt her eyes; Bud told reporters she had a stye. Other passengers suggested a fight on-board, but Lyda denied that in her usual comic way: 'We've had several spats, but are perfectly happy.' She later gave an interview to the press from Ernst's penthouse apartment:

> I am happy for many reasons, but one of the principal ones is that my marriage will end my loneliness. It is such a change to come home to my apartment and find someone here, someone with whom I can talk over everything, and laugh a little at things that have occurred during the day. . . . There is nothing like a family to anchor one and give a feeling of 'belonging' in the world that surrounds. In my case, that is particularly true. My mother and father are far off in the Orient. . . . But how can a movie actress be lonely in Hollywood? I have been asked many times. That is simple. It takes a long time to make good friends and without good friends, one is lonesome.[134]

Still, it seems the relationship did fall apart, though never quite to a final divorce. In 1936 Lyda was living mostly in a fashionably

134 'Lyda Roberti Arrives Behind Dark Glasses', *Brooklyn Daily Eagle*, July 30, 1935.

white-walled uptown New York apartment with her dogs Herman, a cocker spaniel, and Adolph, a Dalmatian. She had a personal maid called Sonia who spoke only Polish, and a European-trained cook called Coulter who had previously worked for Lili Damita. There was talk of a divorce from Bud some time in the future, but her attorney gave no specific reasons for an annulment. Lyda would appear in the press occasionally – usually speculation about her failed marriage, or perhaps her return to Hollywood or Broadway. It was said her chauffeur was her brother Robert, who had moved from Shanghai to America. The show-business gossip columns said she was a keen tennis player, but it seems unlikely. Her heart was increasingly bothering her. Her health deteriorated to the point where she had to withdraw from a Paramount movie, *Wives Never Know* with Adolphe Menjou.

Her film roles became irregular and not great quality – a low budget 'show-must-go-on' type movie *Nobody's Baby*, and then *Pick a Star*, both made by the Hal Roach Studio, which was, by the latter half of the 1930s, a fair way past its glory days. Lyda got both jobs as a replacement for Thelma Todd, who'd made her name in movies alongside the Marx brothers and Buster Keaton, but had been found dead of carbon monoxide poisoning in her car near the home of her lover, Roland West. The inquest decided she had been locked out of her home waiting for West to return, turned on the heater in her car to wait and then succumbed to the fumes. Not everyone was buying this scenario and there were other theories including murder. The LAPD Homicide Squad investigated but the death was eventually ruled 'accidental'. It was a bittersweet return to Hollywood for Lyda after a dry spell in the movies since her marriage. Hal Roach hired her largely because Lyda did look somewhat like Todd and they were the same age. The parts were 'vampy' and made use of her accent, but had little substance and no good tunes. These films marked the end of Lyda's film career.

In 1938 Lyda suffered a series of minor heart attacks and was repeatedly hospitalised. Bud Ernst came to visit and it seems they were somewhat reconciled. He began to take charge of her care. Together they moved from New York to Hollywood in the hope that the better weather would be conducive to Lyda's recovery. On

March 12th, 1938 Ernst urgently rang Dr Myron Babcock, Lyda's
LA physician. Lyda had had a massive heart attack, brought on, it
was said, by her bending to tie her shoelaces. It was reported that
Bud Ernst was by her bedside when she died.[135] Lyda Roberti was
just thirty-two years old.

Lyda Roberti Ernst was buried in the Forest Lawn Memorial
Park in Glendale. It was a large funeral and many of her former
colleagues in vaudeville, Broadway and the movies attended. Her

Death Cuts Short Her Screen Career

body lay in rest at a Hollywood mortuary, her casket
covered in a thousand or
more gardenias (Lyda's
favourite flower). Four
hundred people attended the
wake including Eddie Can-
tor, Al Jolson, Errol Flynn,
Ginger Rogers, Joe E. Brown,
Hal Roach, Stan Laurel, Lili
Damita and Bud Ernst (they
had never finalised their
divorce).[136]

Her headstone was in-
scribed with a line from Song
of Solomon 2:17: 'Until the
day break and the shadows

---

135   'Lyda Roberti, Film Star, Dies After Heart Attack', *Philadelphia Inquirer*,
      March 13, 1938.
136   Bud Ernst was to marry several more times – once to Mary Pickford's
      daughter Gwynne. His final wife was Betty Furness, whom he married twice.
      In 1950 Ernst was despondent at having failed to make the transition from
      radio to television and was largely dependent on his wife's income. He called
      a newspaper reporter on the afternoon of April 10, 1950, and told him that if
      he went to his room at New York City's Westbury Hotel on East 69th Street
      he would get a good story. The newspaper called Furness at her Park Avenue
      home and she went to the Westbury. While Furness waited in the lobby, a
      bellboy entered Ernst's room to find that the thirty-nine-year-old had placed
      a twenty-gauge shotgun between his knees, closed his mouth over the barrel,
      and pulled the trigger. In a note addressed to Furness, Ernst claimed that he
      was 'tired of everything.'

flee away.' It is unknown if any of Lyda's family attended – her parents were still reportedly living in Shanghai, but both her brother Robert and sister Manya were apparently living in the United States.

Lyda Roberti had come a long way – from Warsaw to Shanghai and then on to Broadway and Hollywood. Perhaps she never got the best songs the Gershwins or Jerome Kern ever wrote for Broadway; maybe the movie scripts weren't always as good as they could have been. But she was admired by many of her peers and audiences. She was just thirty-two but had been performing for twenty-nine years. She was a star, even if she was not destined to become a long-lived one.

Lyda Roberti Ernst (nee Pecjak) – May 20, 1906–March 12, 1938.

The Beast Comes to Shanghai:
Aleister Crowley (1906)

'I dismissed Shanghai as a morbid dream.'

Shanghai 'magick'

The English occultist, author, artist and mountaineer Aleister Crowley, aka The Beast 666, was born in 1875. By the time he set foot in the Shanghai International Settlement in April 1906 he was already very well travelled. As a recent Cambridge graduate, in 1897, he had visited St Petersburg, most probably at the behest of British Intelligence though he was perhaps deemed a little too odd and unstable for a long-term career as an intelligence officer. Crowley had a passion for mountain climbing and had become an accomplished mountaineer, already having undertaken a daring expedition to Mexico. He had studied both Hinduism and Buddhism in India and Ceylon (Sri Lanka), and travelled through the United States, Japan and Hong Kong. He had contracted malaria on his travels and spent some time recuperating in Rangoon and Calcutta. In 1902, having recovered his health, he had joined an expedition to climb K2 (also known as Mount Godwin-Austen or Chhogori), the second-highest mountain in the world. At that time K2 had never been conquered. The party got two thirds of the way up before turning back with renewed bouts of malaria, influenza and snow blindness.

At the close of 1902 Crowley, not yet thirty, was back in Europe. Sojourning in Paris he encountered the painter, and the man who was to be his future brother-in-law, Gerald Kelly. He also met the author William Somerset Maugham, who would write a novel *The Magician* (1908) based on his encounter with Crowley.

Crowley's fascination with matters esoteric was established from a young age. He had joined the Hermetic Order of the Golden Dawn in 1898 (whose membership included such notables as W.B. Yeats and Bram Stoker – Crowley feuded interminably with both) and he was trained in ceremonial magic and the ritual use of narcotics by the Golden Dawn's leader, Samuel Liddell MacGregor Mathers.

Maugham's protagonist in *The Magician* Oliver Haddo is 'a big stout fellow, showily dressed in a check suit',[137] prone to lies and exaggeration, vainglorious and full of bombast. Haddo is mocked for his occultist pretensions but he proceeds to cast a magic spell over another man's fiancée and she becomes sexually obsessed with Haddo and elopes with him. The couple disappear to Haddo's gothic estate in the remote English countryside where he uses her in occult rituals, and finally kills her. The former fiancé kills Haddo and burns the estate and the misshapen monsters Haddo had created to the ground.

Crowley was outraged by his portrayal in the novel.[138] He responded to Maugham's characterisation of him by penning a critique of the book for *Vanity Fair* magazine under the pen-name Oliver Haddo, in which he accused Maugham of plagiarism.[139] If Crowley considered Maugham a plagiarist then the dislike was returned with Maugham considering Crowley's attempts at poetry 'verbose'.[140]

Crowley married Gerald Kelly's sister Rose Edith in 1903, ostensibly to save her from an unwanted 'arranged marriage' planned by her father. Rose had previously been married to a much older man thanks to her family's plans but he had died, leaving her a young widow. Now they were planning to marry her off once again. Though Crowley's proposal may appear to contemporary eyes as a rather gallant act, the Kelly family, including Gerald, were appalled at the turn of events; both by Rose's insubordination of her family's wishes and her choice of suitor.

And that's where the trouble really started.

Aleister and Rose (for whom Crowley does seems to have felt genuine affection, at least initially) honeymooned in Cairo in 1904

---

137 William Somerset Maugham, *The Magician*, (London: William Heinemann, 1908), p. 11.

138 In her biography of Maugham, *The Secret Lives of Somerset Maugham*, (London: John Murray, 2010), Selina Hastings claims that while Crowley publicly acted outraged he was at the same time secretly 'perversely flattered'.

139 'Oliver Haddo' (Aleister Crowley), 'How to Write a Novel! (After W. S. Maugham)', *Vanity Fair*, December 30, 1908.

140 William Somerset Maugham, *A Fragment of Autobiography*, reprinted as the preface to *The Magician*, (London: Vintage, 2000).

where Crowley claimed to have been contacted by a supernatural entity called Aiwass. Aiwass then dictated to Crowley (via disembodied voice) *The Book of the Law*, or *Liber AL vel Legis*. This was to become the foundation text of Crowley's self-invented religion, Thelema. Thelemites, as believers were called, were urged to follow their own path in life, their 'True Will'. Ritual 'Magick' (its spelling differentiating it from simple and illusory stage 'magic') is invoked by calling upon ancient Egyptian deities (with whom, presumably, Crowley had become acquainted on his honeymoon in Cairo). The founding maxim of the faith was: 'Do what thou wilt shall be the whole of the Law'. In July 1905 Rose gave birth to their first daughter whose full name was Nuit Ma Ahathoor Hectate Sappho Jezebel Lilith, though known to everyone who met her simply as Lilith (a shortening of her name for which we can assume she was eternally grateful!).

It was then that Crowley decided he would form a party to attempt the ascent of Kanchenjunga (K3) of Nepal in the Himalayas, the third highest mountain on earth. Soon after the start of the climb Crowley's fellow mountaineers, considering him reckless, wanted to abandon the attempt and turn back. Several Nepalese porters and one European climber were subsequently killed on the mountain. Crowley was generally blamed by the others in the party for the accident, having supposedly ignored their cries for help and remained in his tent drinking tea. Crowley rejected the accusations. He rejoined Rose and Lilith in Calcutta where they were waiting for him. His intention was to recuperate after the expedition but soon they all had to flee the Bengali city after Crowley was accused of killing a local man he claimed had attempted to rob him. The family went briefly to Rangoon, but this was not entirely safe for Crowley as Burma was part of the British Raj and any arrest warrant issued in Calcutta could be served in Rangoon.

The Crowleys swiftly moved on to southern and then to western China in what may have been another intelligence operation investigating the opium trade on the borders of the French Indo-Chinese Empire and the British sphere of influence in China. The family moved from town to town through Yunnan province – stopping at Yungchang, Dali and Yunnan-fu before moving into

French Indo-China and the city of Hanoi. The whole trip took around four months. Crowley smoked copious amounts of opium throughout (ostensibly to relieve the pain from having fallen off his horse forty feet down a small ravine in Yunnan – giving thanks to Aiwass for preserving his life for the adventures to come) and he worked hard on practising his ritual magick techniques. He wrote his poem 'The Opium Smoker' during this time. Crowley's poetry is perhaps an acquired taste:

> Hardly a glimmer to chasten the gloom.
> Hardly a murmur of Time at his loom.
> Nothing of sense by the poppy-perfume.
>
> Boy, as you love me, I charge you to fold
> Pipe over pipe into gardens of gold
> Such as a god may be glad to behold.
>
> Seated on high in the aeons of doom,
> Sucked as a seed into the infinite womb,
> Sealed is my soul in the sheath of its tomb.
>
> Boy, as you love me, I charge you to mould
> Pipe after pipe, till the heavens are rolled
> Back and are lost as a tale that is told![141]

Crowley had started to become distant from Rose who, under the strain of her erratic and chaotic life with him, had begun to drink heavily and was gradually succumbing to alcoholism. Eventually, in March 1906, he booked passage for Rose and Lilith on a steamer back to India. Rose had to call at Calcutta alone to collect their belongings as Crowley was still a wanted man in the city. Rose and Lilith then returned to Rangoon while the 'Beast 666', as Crowley would occasionally refer to himself, remained in French

---

141 Aleister Crowley, *The Opium Smoker (In Eight Fugues)*, 1906. This being the second fugue.

Indo-China (probably the port of Haiphong) and then suddenly announced that he was proceeding alone to Shanghai.

A date with Fidelis

The purpose of his trip to Shanghai (and of getting rid of his wife and daughter) was to meet up with Elaine Simpson. Simpson (the same age as Crowley) had been a member, a *soror* or sorority sister, of the Hermetic Order of the Golden Dawn back in London. She had then become fascinated with Crowley's *The Book of the Law* and Thelema. Simpson was born in Kussowlie, West Bengal, in 1875 to William and Alice Simpson. Her father was a reverend in the Indian Anglican Ecclesiastical Establishment. The Simpson family had returned to England, living near the Edgware Road in London. Both Elaine and her mother, Alice (who had also been born in India), had unsurprisingly joined the Royal Asiatic Society and, perhaps more surprisingly, had signed up with the Hermetic Order of the Golden Dawn in 1895. In 1899 Elaine was 'initiated' fully into the order and acquired the name *Semper Fidelis* ('Always Faithful'). Alice, who had briefly had a career on the stage as a light opera singer, was by this time a widow and the mother and daughter lived together. Crowley liked Elaine, but detested her mother whom he thought, 'a sixth rate singer, a first rate snob, with dewlaps and a paunch; a matchmaker, mischief-maker, maudlin and mud-dle-headed'.[142] Along with Crowley both Elaine and her mother were expelled from the Order of the Golden Dawn over one of Crowley's interminable rows with other members.

Despite their various global wanderings Crowley and Simpson/*Semper Fidelis* had remained in touch since his visitation by Aiwass and creation of the Thelema religion. Crowley had written that even during sexual dreams of himself with other women, thoughts of *Semper Fidelis* ran 'like a golden cord throughout.'[143]

142   From the diary of Leah Hirsig, a Swiss-American associated with Crowley, September 26, 1924, The Yorke Collection at the Warburg Institute, London.

143   Richard Kaczynski, *Perdurabo: The Life of Aleister Crowley*, (New York: North Atlantic Books, 2002), p. 93.

They visited each other every Saturday evening on the astral plane, ringing an astral bell and transporting the consciousness 'within an egg of white light' from their corporeal bodies to a non-physical realm (i.e. the astral plane).[144] Crowley claimed that Simpson's astral body was somewhat larger than her real frame at over six feet tall, and that she was partially transparent.[145] Both seem really to have believed that they could communicate this way and Crowley saw it as a high point of his week.[146]

However, astral planes aside, Elaine had married a Hong Kong–based businessman called Paul Ignatz 'Harry' Witkowski in May 1900 at St Saviour's Church on Paddington's Warwick Avenue in London. Witkowski (whose ancestry was German despite his Polish-sounding name) was eleven years older than Elaine and Jewish, though probably had converted to Christianity by the time of their marriage. Witkowski worked for the Hong Kong-and-Shanghai-based trading firm Arnhold Karberg, founded by German Jews in Canton around 1866 and engaged in various aspects of the China trade. By the 1880s the firm was operating across China in all the major treaty ports and as far north as Manchuria. Arnhold Karberg was an important *hong* and a prestigious employer. Shortly after their marriage in London, and when the couple had settled in Hong Kong, Witkowski took a seat on the board of directors of the Hongkong and Shanghai Banking Corporation representing his employers' interests.

Moving to Hong Kong, Elaine had given up attending occult meetings and, in 1901, gave birth to a daughter, Georgiana. However, she continued to have the occasional flirtation on the astral plane with Crowley of a Saturday evening from her Hong Kong bedroom. Crowley visualised her in 'a green and white room ... dressed in a soft, white wool gown with velvet lapels. "Ave Soror," ("Hail Sister") he greeted her in Latin.'[147] But officially Simpson no longer practised magick nor observed the occult rituals of either

144 Ibid., p. 92.
145 John Symonds, *The Great Beast: The Life and Magick of Aleister Crowley*, (St Albans, Herts: Mayflower Books, 1973), p. 118.
146 *Perdurabo*, p. 93.
147 Ibid., p. 92

the Hermetic Order of the Golden Dawn or Thelema. It is unclear if her husband even had any notion of her occultist past. Now, to Crowley's disgust, she wore her occult adept's regalia and robes to Hong Kong society fancy-dress parties, regularly taking first prize!

In 1902 Paul Witkowski got a promotion and Arnhold Karberg transferred him from Hong Kong up to Shanghai to look after the firm's interests there. The couple established a new home in the International Settlement. In 1904 Elaine gave birth to a second child, her son Richard Paul.

And so, in late April 1906, Aleister Crowley arrived in Shanghai for a rendezvous with Elaine, whom he invariably referred to simply as *Fidelis,* in order to combine their magickal powers and, so Crowley hoped, to finally consummate their relationship in the corporeal rather than just on the astral plane. The records of that meeting are fragmentary and contradictory and so we can only deduce from them what we can.

Consummating in the Settlement

We have few primary sources on Crowley's twelve-day Shanghai sojourn or of his impressions of Shanghai, China or the Chinese. But he had previously visited San Francisco's Chinatown and noted:

> I realised instantly their spiritual superiority to the Anglo-Saxon, and my own deep seated affinity to their point of view. The Chinaman is not obsessed by the delusion that the profits and pleasures of life are really valuable. He gets all the more out of them because he knows their worthlessness, and is consequently immune from the disappointment which inevitably embitters those who seek to lay up treasure on earth. A man must really be a very dull brute if, attaining all his ambitions, he finds satisfaction. The Eastern, from Lao Tzu and the Buddha to Zoroaster and Ecclesiastes, feels in his very bones the futility of earthly existence. It is the first postulate of his philosophy.[148]

148 Aleister Crowley, *The Confessions of Aleister Crowley*, (London: Jonathan Cape, 1969), p. 223.

Crowley was to be disappointed in his Shanghai rendezvous. *Semper Fidelis* was now Mrs Elaine Witkowski, a Far East merchant's wife, mother of two small children, and no longer his loyal acolyte and keen occultist. She complained that she felt unwell, had headaches and couldn't concentrate on the magickal incantations required – let alone any more carnal rituals Crowley had in mind. Crowley was bemused – despite their letters and conjoinings on the astral plane, *Semper Fidelis* showed him little encouragement, compassion or inspiration. She seemed to find their magick rituals embarrassing and silly; her 'magick room', supposedly set aside as a dedicated space for their magickal practice, had turned out simply to be a small drawing room. However, Crowley maintained that he recognised Simpson's green and white magick room immediately from their Saturday night astral plane visitations, right down to a cloisonné vase on a shelf.[149]

While they seem to have tried to enact some magick rituals and attempted to perform various invocations with Simpson acting as the medium, Crowley was, at the time, in a Buddhist phase and had become doubtful of Aiwass and his Egyptian influences as being one hundred per cent genuine. However, Simpson told him that she believed in the genuineness of Aiwass and that Crowley should stop hesitating and commit totally to Aiwass and the 'truth of Thelema'.[150]

If her husband was around in Shanghai during Crowley's sojourn then it does not seem the two men met or that Paul Witkowski was even aware of The Beast's presence in Shanghai. Crowley later claimed that Aiwass was also disappointed in *Semper Fidelis's* response to her 'master's' arrival. He claimed that Aiwass instructed him to leave Shanghai and return to Egypt. Aiwass apparently commanded Crowley:

> Do not take Fidelis. I do not like the relations between you
> two; break them off! Yet I would wish you to love physically,
> to make perfect the circle of your union. Fidelis will not do

149 Aleister Crowley, *The Magical Record of the Beast 666: The Diaries of Aleister Crowley, 1914–1920*, (London: Duckworth, 1972).
150 Symonds, *The Great Beast*, p. 118–119.

so, therefore she is useless. If she did, she would become
useful.[151]

However, we should remember that Simpson was Crowley's
medium to Aiwass and so, presumably, passed these instructions
along during their last invocation. The major rift between Crowley
and *Semper Fidelis* was, predictably perhaps, that she would not
sleep with him. Elaine Witkowski was insistent on remaining
faithful to her husband and Aiwass, speaking through her, seemed
to be of the same opinion. Crowley, it seems, later decided that
receiving commands from Aiwass to forget Simpson was preferable
to admitting that he had travelled to Shanghai to sleep with her
only to find her resistant to the idea.

Crowley, once again picking and choosing what received instructions he chose to follow, ignored Aiwass's supposed instructions on
returning to Egypt. On April 21st annoyed, frustrated and realising
Semper Fidelis was not going to play along with the 'consummation
rituals', Crowley took the next steamer leaving Shanghai. He
boarded the *Empress of India* bound for Nagasaki and Kobe in Japan
and then on to Canada on the Northern Pacific route. He had
originally planned to board a ship bound for San Francisco via
Honolulu, but by the time he decided to leave Shanghai all the
berths had been booked. It seems *Semper Fidelis's* feigned illnesses
perhaps saved Crowley from arriving in California just as it was
about to undergo the massive and devastating earthquake in that
city on April 18th. In his diary Crowley recalled that he spent most
of the voyage sick in his cabin.

After Shanghai

From Vancouver, Crowley travelled by train to New York, stopping
there for ten days, and spent another couple of days visiting Niagara
Falls. He then took a steamer to Liverpool arriving on June 2nd. In
England Crowley planned to raise funds for a second attempt on
Kanchenjunga. Upon arrival in London he learned that his

---

151   Crowley, *The Confessions,* p. 223.

daughter Lilith, not yet even three years old, had died of typhoid in Rangoon. Crowley blamed Rose and her alcoholism for not taking proper care of the girl, never mentioning his own long absence chasing *Semper Fidelis* and then journeying halfway round the world in the opposite direction from his family in Burma! However, it does seem that Crowley was quite distraught at the little girl's death, suffered various medical ailments that required surgery and, perhaps, had a mental breakdown before he finally reunited with Rose in Plymouth that June.

Later Crowley wrote a poem dedicated to 'Elaine W K——'

Ad Fidelem Infidelem

Ah, my sweet sister! Was it idle toil,
　　When in the flowerless Eden of Shanghai
　　We made immortal mischief, you and I,
'Casting our flame-flowers on the dull brown soil?'
Did we not light a lamp withouten oil
　　Nursed by unfruitful kisses, stealthily
　　Strewn in the caldron where our Destiny
Bides brooding – Mother, bid its brew to boil!

Ah, Sweetheart, we were barren as Sahara,
　　But on Sahara burns our subtle star.
　　Soon an oasis, now too lone and far,
Shall bloom with all the blossoms of Bokhara:
　　See! o'er the brim the mystic fountain flows!
　　Cull from the caldron the ensanguine Rose![152]

Apart from this poem Crowley's only comment on his brief sojourn in Shanghai was simply, 'I dismissed the Shanghai experience as a morbid dream.'[153] Crowley's trip to Shanghai was never reported in the newspapers, nor does he seem to have met anyone else in the city except Elaine Simpson, who herself never spoke

152　Published in Aleister Crowley, *The Winged Beetle*, privately printed, 1910.
153　Crowley, *The Confessions*, p. 224.

publicly of the meetings. Crowley and Elaine did maintain occasional contact by letter until 1928. Paul Witkowski died in 1907, aged just forty-two, while on furlough from Shanghai in Germany. In 1909, widowed and back in Europe, Elaine married a senior official with the German postal service in Hamburg, the thirty-nine-year-old Karl Julius Emil Wölker. Some reports say she became quite the society hostess in Hamburg, remaining in Germany through the Great War, until her death.

Rose gave birth to Crowley's second daughter, Lola Zaza, in February 1907 in London. She must have been conceived just prior to Crowley leaving Rose to travel to Shanghai. Crowley formally divorced Rose in 1909 with Lola Zaza entrusted to her care. Soon after the divorce Rose was admitted to an institution with alcoholic dementia and died there in 1932 aged fifty-eight. Lola Zaza Crowley died in 1990.

Crowley never returned to China though also he never completely lost his interest in the country and culture. He posed Buddha-like as 'Fo-Hi, the Chinese God of Joy and Laughter' and also published an article on Asian poetry for the August 1915 issue of *Vanity Fair* under the name of His Excellency Kwaw Li Ya (obviously a transliteration of Crowley). Crowley claimed Kwaw

Crowley as 'Fo-Hi', God of Joy

Portrait by Arnold Genthe
His Excellency, Kwaw Li Ya

Li Ya was a 'professor of poetry at the University of Pekin'. *Vanity Fair* even included an 'Editor's Note' (probably supplied by Crowley himself to the magazine):

> Editor's Note – Kwaw Li Ya is the most famous of the small group of Chinese poets known as the Yung Chang school. Of the Shen Si – or landed gentry class – he has devoted his great wealth to travelling and to studying the literatures of other nations. A fanatical adherent of the fallen Emperor, his latter years have been spent in exile from his native valleys. He is now passing a few months in New York. In religion he is a strict Taoist, and is the author of the politico-mystical romance entitled 'Thien Tao' or 'The Way of Heaven.' He is perhaps best known because of his five volumes of aphorisms.[154]

Crowley died in a nursing home in Hastings, East Sussex in 1947, a committed occultist to the end. He remains Britain's best-remembered occultist and continues to fascinate new generations of those interested in the occult and the esoteric.

154   Aleister Crowley as 'Professor Kwaw Li Ya', 'The Hokku – A New Verse Form', *Vanity Fair*, August 1, 1915, Vol. 4, No. 6, p. 46.

Interpreting the 'Shanghai Mind':
Arthur Ransome (1927)

*'The Shanghailander holds that loyalty begins at home and
that their primary allegiance is to Shanghai.'*

Shanghai is special

People have long talked about Shanghai being somehow different from the rest of China – Beijing scholars in the 1920s coined the term '*haipai*' to criticise Shanghai's self-obsessive modernity. Shanghai was a 'bubble', 'a bastard child', somehow not fully China. True, Shanghai's history was distinctly different to other Chinese cities. While it was not a crown colony, a dominion, a commonwealth, a raj or a federated state, Shanghai was a product of British imperialism – a 'treaty port'. From 1842 until 1941 Shanghai was one of initially five settlements forced from China after the First Opium War (1839–1842) and based on extraterritoriality (foreigners being exempted from the jurisdiction of local law). The Japanese invasion of Shanghai's foreign concessions after Pearl Harbor in December 1941 meant the cancellation of the Municipal Council's planned lavish centenary celebrations – the Shanghai treaty port died at 99½ years of age. Of all the treaty ports in China, none were as large, rich and cosmopolitan as Shanghai – not even close. Between the wars Shanghai was consistently the fourth- or fifth-largest city globally (after London, New York, Paris and, sometimes, Berlin), and by far the most densely populated, with approximately three and a half to four million people. Things were different in Shanghai; people thought differently in Shanghai, or so it was said repeatedly.

For those 99½ years foreign observers, visitors and (mostly critical) Chinese from outside the city talked as if people in Shanghai thought differently to the rest of China. Not just the foreign Shanghailanders, but also the Chinese from across eastern and southern China who had settled in the city, were said to exhibit this peculiarly Shanghai way of thinking. It has been a long-lasting notion. The idea of a 'Shanghai mind set' didn't die with its treaty port status. Deng Xiaoping placed Shanghai pretty much at the back of the queue when it came to Reform and Opening Up in the

1980s; he knew what happened when you stop sedating a ravenous tiger and open the cage door! But what exactly is this 'Shanghai Mind'?

Enter Arthur Ransome

The Shanghai mind set was perhaps first and best quantified by the English author and journalist Arthur Ransome. The legendary editor of the *Manchester Guardian*, C.P. Scott, had sent Ransome to China in January 1927, where he reported for the *Guardian* and the *Baltimore Sun*. Ransome travelled out by ship in December 1926 and would return via the Trans-Siberian Railway six months later. His newspaper reports and articles on China appeared between January and August 1927, and covered the massacre of the left by Chiang Kai-shek's Kuomintang (Nationalist Party) in Shanghai that year. Inevitably, as a journalist, Ransome got a book out of his sojourn in China (some things never change!) – *The Chinese Puzzle*, published in 1927.[155]

Today Ransome is really only known as the author of the *Swallows and Amazons* series of much-loved children's books – and then really only in Britain. Nowadays few remember that Ransome upped and left his wife and children in 1913 to study Russian folklore in Moscow, worked as a foreign correspondent in World War One, and covered the Bolshevik Revolution, becoming sympathetic to the communist cause and close to both Lenin and Trotsky. In Moscow Ransome met the woman who would become his second wife, Evgenia Petrovna Shelepina, Trotsky's personal secretary. He was nearly forty; Evgenia was a decade younger and towered over her new beau at six feet three inches tall. For a journalist trying to understand Russia in 1917, having a love affair with Trotsky's secretary would surely facilitate access. But it was a genuine relationship; they married in 1924 in England and spent the rest of their lives together.

---

155   Arthur Ransome, *The Chinese Puzzle*, (London: George Allen & Unwin, 1927).

Evgenia Petrovna Shelepina

In *Memoirs of a British Agent* the British diplomat and intelligence officer R.H. Bruce Lockhart, who worked hard to destabilise the fledgling Bolshevik government, described Ransome as 'a Don Quixote with a walrus moustache, a sentimentalist who could always be relied upon to champion the underdog, and a visionary whose imagination had been fired by the Russian revolution.'[156] They were exciting times and Ransome did share intelligence with London, but he was also considered to be a little close to the Bolsheviks for decent English society. Evgenia, travelling with Ransome to London, was suspected by British Intelligence (suspicions that seem to be confirmed by more recently declassified files in Moscow) of smuggling diamonds, reportedly concealed in her bloomers, to various Communist International (Comintern) agents in Europe. London ultimately decided Ransome was probably loyal, if perhaps a little misguided in his politics and love life. But the Ransome who arrived in Shanghai several years later was not yet the lovable yachtsman who wrote exciting tales for children about John, Susan, Titty and Roger Walker and their seaborne adventures, but rather was a still passionate socialist not overly well disposed to the freebooting capitalists he encountered in the Shanghai International Settlement.

---

156   Robert Hamilton Bruce Lockhart, *Memoirs of a British Agent, Being an Account of the Author's Early Life in Many Lands and of his Official Mission to Moscow in 1918*, (London: Putnam, 1932).

The Shanghai mind

Ransome stayed in and around Shanghai from January 1927 through to the spring of that year. The five months or so during which he observed the city led him to the conclusion that there was a specific 'Shanghai Mind'. Describing the readership of the largest local English-language newspaper, the *North-China Daily News* he wrote: 'The Chinese naturally turn to these papers and judge England and England's policy by what they find there. It is impossible to persuade them that what they find is an expression not of the British but of the Shanghai mind.'[157] Ransome was quite clear about where Shanghailander loyalties lay: 'The Shanghailanders hold that loyalty begins at home and that their primary allegiance is to Shanghai . . . Shanghailanders of English extraction belong, if they belong to England at all, to an England that no longer exists'.[158]

The idea that Shanghai and its community of Shanghailanders were somehow apart from both China and their home countries was echoed at around the same time by the Sinologist and former Chinese Maritime Customs Officer L.A. Lyall: 'The British residents in Shanghai are the spoilt children of the Empire. They pay no taxes to China, except that landowners pay a very small land tax, and no taxes to England. Judges and consuls are provided for them; they are protected by the British fleet, and for several years they have had in addition a British army to defend them; and for all this expenditure the British taxpayer pays.'[159]

Ransome's notion of the Shanghai Mind is at the heart of *The Chinese Puzzle,* his book collecting his China reportage. Former Prime Minister David Lloyd George, who was out of office, but still leader of the Liberal Party, had apparently enjoyed Ransome's China reporting and suggested to C.P. Scott at the *Guardian* it be published as a book. He even offered to write a foreword; something Ransome jumped on as a very good idea to help sales. Ransome wanted to get it printed as soon as possible – while his China travels, as well as the bloody events on Shanghai's streets of

157 Arthur Ransome, 'The Chinese Puzzle', *Guardian*, May 2, 1927.
158 Ibid.
159 L.A. Lyall argued this line for some time and it is included in most detail in his book *China*, (London, Ernest Benn Limited, 1934).

spring 1927, were still fresh in readers' minds. Unfortunately Lloyd George refused to write the foreword until he had read the final proofs, which delayed publication. Though the publishers still managed to get the collection out before the end of the year, and with Lloyd George's foreword, this was generally seen as disastrous for a book on fast-moving contemporary events. Ransome rather missed the boat as the situation in China moved remorselessly on with Chiang Kai-shek's suppression of the warlords and the successful Northern Campaign to unify China. While Chiang had been the villain of the piece in April 1927, massacring the left in Shanghai, by the end of the year he was now more often perceived by the foreign press, and foreign offices in European countries, as the good general crushing bandit armies and bringing China together as one nation under the Nationalist government while ensuring China's hinterlands were peaceful for trade from Shanghai. When it finally appeared, *The Chinese Puzzle* sold very poorly.

Still, in the book, Ransome expanded on the term 'Shanghai mind' and referred to the International Settlement and its inhabitants as a 'hermetically sealed glass case', a quote that would be used regularly by journalists and commentators when looking to criticise Shanghai. Ransome did make the very good point that China was often misguided on official British government and Foreign Office policy towards the country because it listened first to the often very divergent British Shanghailander opinion and subsequently understandably confused the two. It was also the case, as some critics of *The Chinese Puzzle* pointed out, that (to paraphrase) Bolshevik-loving, questionably patriotic Arthur Ransome was not exactly in tune with official British foreign policy either. Still, it is hard not to draw parallels between the Shanghailanders Ransome encountered and today's cadre of multinational 'China Experts' in Shanghai (and, in these post-imperial days of course, in Beijing and elsewhere too) who express varieties of opinions on China that may or, more likely, may not represent the foreign offices of their home nations and so often completely muddy the waters for many reading their op-eds or having to listen to their presentations.

The Shanghai mind responds

Shanghailanders didn't take Ransome's characterisation lying down. The maligned *North-China Daily News* was among the first to reply to Ransome, declaring his article 'the most objectionable misrepresentation of the spirit of this British community that we have yet seen printed. Mr Ransome has not made the slightest suggestion of Shanghai's international status or character and has not hinted that there are thousands of persons here of a score of different nationalities who share with British residents the same mental outlook.'[160]

The *North-China* was very angry and referred in its own pages to the *Manchester Guardian* as a 'pink paper' (i.e. socialist, if not indeed fully Bolshevik, inclined) and accused Ransome of being a 'piscatologist', i.e. fishing for stories that supported the left-leaning position of the newspaper. The *North-China* accused Ransome of suggesting that Shanghai was a 'Far Eastern Ulster'.[161]

The *Manchester Guardian* was also flooded with letters and telegrams from 'Angry of Bubbling Well Road'. It reprinted a few rejoinders, most of which were of the 'Chinese don't understand concepts of law and order' and 'London has been far too indulgent of the Nationalist government' variety. Still, while thinking that Ransome basically had Shanghailanders nailed, one has to have a certain sympathy for one letter-writer, Mr John Tallents Wynyard Brooke of Bowdon, Cheshire (recently returned to England after twenty years as an architect in Shanghai) who pointed out that: 'We in Shanghai are becoming accustomed to the attacks of touring journalists who spend a month or two in China, and perhaps a day in Shanghai, and then go home to write books on China.'[162]

One thing all agreed on – be it Ransome critiquing the city for the *Manchester Guardian* or the legion of proud Shanghailanders poring over their morning *North-China Daily News* – was that

---

160 'The Shanghai Mind', *Manchester Guardian*, May 27, 1927. The article includes various responses to Ransome's article on Shanghai including a letter from the *North-China Daily News*.
161 Ibid. Of course essentially that is exactly what Ransome had done.
162 'Letters', *Manchester Guardian*, May 5, 1927.

Shanghai was unique and critical to the trading success of the Yangtze Delta and a vast hinterland. That hasn't changed. It's also true that contemporary Shanghailanders and Shanghainese feel strongly that their port city is China's most advanced, modern, stylish, and best, while the capital city in the north continues to either sneer down its scholarly nose at vulgar Shanghai or look concernedly over its spectacles at a city that might not always be quite so Party-respectful as the Beijing bosses would like. Perhaps today we can talk of a Shanghai mind, with Chinese characteristics?

After Shanghai

In 1929, a year or so after his return from China, Arthur Ransome began writing his phenomenally successful *Swallows and Amazons* series with his gang of children sailing, camping, fishing, exploring and engaging in piracy pretty much without any adult supervision. The books – there were twelve in all with one left unfinished at his death – made him quite rich and able to indulge his passion for yachts. In 1941 he wrote the tenth *Swallows and Amazons* adventure

entitled *Missee Lee*.[163] Set in 1930s China the children are on a round-the-world trip when they encounter Chinese pirates. Missee Lee is the leader of the pirates but turns out to be a frustrated academic who was sent to Cambridge for her education, only to have to return to China to be a pirate chief when her father died. Ransome claimed that he based the character on Soong Ching-ling, the wife of Sun Yat-sen. Ransome had met Madame Sun briefly in Shanghai in

---

163   Arthur Ransome, *Missee Lee*, (London: Jonathan Cape, 1941).

1927, admired her, and meant his character of Missee Lee as a compliment.[164]

Arthur Ransome died in 1967 in Manchester aged eighty-three; Evgenia died a few years later. They lived most of their lives together at Low Ludderburn, just east of Lake Windermere in the Lake District. They are buried next to each other at St Paul's Church, Rusland, in the Lake District.

---

164 Christina Hardyment, *Arthur Ransome and Captain Flint's Trunk*, (London: Jonathan Cape, 1984), pp. 170–171. Soong Ching-ling's feelings about this characterisation of herself as a reluctant pirate queen are unrecorded.

Red Sojourners at the Zeitgeist Bookstore: Irene Weitemeyer, Agnes Smedley &

Roger Hollis (1929)

Agnes Smedley (1939)

'But these days will be the best in my life. Never have I known such good days, never have I known such a healthy life, mentally, physically, psychically.' [165]

165 Agnes Smedley in a letter to her friend Florence Lennon, May 28, 1930, commenting on her relationship with Soviet agent Richard Sorge. Quoted in Janice R. MacKinnon & Stephen R. MacKinnon, *Agnes Smedley: The Life and Times of an American Radical*, (London: Virago, 1988), p. 147.

Evenings at the Zeitgeist

In the late 1920s the small Zeitgeist Bookshop by the banks of the Soochow Creek was a gathering place for those of a left-wing disposition. It was a place where the Chinese left might meet with the foreign residents of the city who were supportive of their aims and generally pro-Soviet. Among the regulars at the bookshop's social gatherings were an American journalist and left-wing activist Agnes Smedley; and a young Englishman working for British American Tobacco who had recently arrived in Shanghai in November of 1928, Roger Hollis. Their friendship and their evenings at the Zeitgeist were to eventually become notorious as possibly where Soviet Intelligence recruited their 'Fifth Man', the one who rose to the very top of British Intelligence, the one that was never caught. Did the greatest ever betrayal of British Intelligence begin on the North Soochow Road?

A small, narrow shop, poorly lit

In the 1920s the North Soochow Road was a rather higgledy-piggledy assortment of shops, small lodging houses and godowns adjacent to the often malodorous and *sampan*-congested Soochow Creek. In the early 1930s, the city's great property magnate Sir Victor Sassoon would clear a large swathe of these buildings for his enormous apartment complex known as the Embankment Building, with its own swimming pool, artesian well, central heating throughout, and electric elevators; indeed it was to be the largest apartment building in Asia. But that was a little later.

In the 1920s this remote end of the northern bank of the Soochow Creek was rarely visited without good reason. Already the International Settlement had settled into two distinct halves – south of the Soochow Creek and north. South was the heart of the Settlement, its administrative, judicial, diplomatic and commercial

Soochow Creek (c. 1920)

centre, with the best theatres, cinemas, hotels and cathedrals; to the north of the creek was the rather raffish district of Hongkew and then the long sweep east down through the Settlement's industrial district of Yangtzepoo. Hongkew abutted Chinese Shanghai at Chapei. The North Soochow Road ran along the length of the creek's embankment beginning at the junction with the Garden Bridge, close to the Astor House Hotel. It continued right the way along, westwards, to the northern edge of the Settlement north of the creek at the junction of North Soochow Road and North Thibet Road. Continuing along the side of the creek, now in Chinese-administered Shanghai, the street was named Kwang Foh Road. It ran all the way along the creek to the relatively deserted area around the Cantonese Cemetery and the adjacent shunting yards of the Nanking-Woosung Railway.

Walking along North Soochow Road from the Garden Bridge in 1929, a stroller would have passed a range of different businesses and shops. The Hongkew Medical Hall, really a large pharmacy store, was next door to the offices of the Shanghai Tramways Corporation. A long line of shops running westwards included a charity clothing store for White Russian émigrés, the Eastern Produce and Jewellery Company, the Havana Cigar Depot, the Broadway Drapers and Outfitters, and a chemists called Mactavish & Lehmann's. At No. 130 was a small, narrow shop, poorly lit, no more than twelve by eighteen feet, that sold books, magazines, periodicals and small works of art, both paintings and, on occasion, sculpture.[166] The store was called the Zeitgeist Bookshop. Further along the street after the Shanghai General Hospital at No. 190, North Soochow Road became increasingly darker and less populated. Beyond that, and stretching all the way across the border with the Settlement and into Chinese Shanghai, was a succession of mostly Japanese-owned silk filatures, one of the city's major industrial activities and notorious for child labour, abysmal wages, union trouble and terrible health and safety conditions.

The Zeitgeist Bookshop had opened its doors for business around a year earlier in 1927. We know this because the SMP took a particularly keen interest in its activities and stock right from the start. The British-run Special Branch in Shanghai was divided into six sections: S1 dealt with general enquiries as well as Russian, Japanese and Jewish affairs; S2 with Chinese liaison; S3 with film censorship; S4 with Indian affairs and gathering information on subversive activities among the Settlement's British Indian population (and the SMP's own Sikh employees who it felt it could not always trust); S5 dealt with newspapers and translations, as well as books and publishing within the Settlement in general; and S6 dealt with boarding houses, shipping matters and general licence applications. S5 was immediately keen to know more about the new Zeitgeist Bookshop.

Plainclothes officers visiting the shop incognito reported a large number of publications concerning the relatively new Union Of Soviet Socialist Republics, various Marxist tracts, a range of left-wing journals and other ephemera that fell under the descriptors of the day as 'progressive' by the left, and 'Bolshevik' by the right, in a range of languages including Russian, German and English. Alongside these was artwork by Russian and communist-leaning German artists. To the eyes of the officers of S5, the entire stock of the Zeitgeist was seditious material. Naturally Special Branch was also interested in the shop's proprietor, a woman from Göttingen

---

166   According to a description by George Hatem who visited in 1933 in Edgar A. Porter, *The People's Doctor: George Hatem and China's Revolution*, (Honolulu: University of Hawaii Press, 1997), p. 40.

in Northern Germany called Fraulein Irene Weitemeyer (some-times spelt Wedemeyer or Wiedemeyer, among other alternate spelling). Weitemeyer, who was known by her friends and comrades simply as 'Isa', ran the store with her younger sister.

According to Special Branch's files, in 1925 Fraulein Weitemeyer had been in her home country of Germany where, in her youth, she had met and married Wu Shao-Kuo, though whether this was ever a legally recognised marriage in Germany was unclear. Wu was of interest to Shanghai Special Branch due to the fact that he was a confirmed member of the newly established Chinese Communist Party. Together Weitemeyer and Wu had travelled to Moscow and spent all of 1926 and early 1927 at the Sun Yat-Sen University. Officially the institution was called the Sun Yat-Sen Communist University of the Toilers of China and was operated by the Com-munist International (the Comintern). The Comintern was the Soviet organisation dedicated to promoting revolution globally and to training revolutionaries in the Soviet model. Shanghai Special Branch was of the belief that the Zeitgeist Bookshop was a key hub in the chain of communication between left-wing elements in Shanghai, the Chinese Communist Party (at that time based in Canton) and the Comintern in Moscow.

Graduating from the Sun Yat-Sen University, Weitemeyer (still only in her early twenties) and Wu moved to Shanghai to open the Zeitgeist. While in Moscow they may have had a child. If they did then the child did not accompany them to China. The Zeitgeist happened also to be the headquarters of the Shanghai branch of the Friends of the Soviet Union. Just in case there was any remain-ing question as to where the sympathies of the Zeitgeist lay, it was noted that the store was also the Shanghai representative of the International Publishers of New York, the Comintern's publishers.

Welcome comrades

Several evenings a week the Zeitgeist would stay open late for lectures, book readings, political discussion groups, or small art exhibitions. These events attracted many on the radical left, including the writer Lu Xun, and not a few left-leaning foreign sojourners or those just passing through town.

A typical evening at the Zeitgeist would start with arrivals turning up at about 7 PM. Fraulein Weitemeyer herself would greet them at the door and usher them in. Weitemeyer was Jewish with a shock of flaming red hair and freckled milk-white skin. The all-seeing eyes of Shanghai Special Branch would make notes of the regulars at these events, a list of names as cosmopolitan as the International Settlement itself. Andrei Sotov, the head of the Telegraph Agency of the Soviet Union (the TASS News Agency) in Shanghai would regularly attend with his wife and perhaps one or two staff from the Soviet Consulate, located close by. Other regulars included the South African journalist and Trotskyist Frank Glass. Glass was a well-known fixture on the Shanghai media scene in the 1920s, having spent time in Moscow (where he married an American, Grace Simons, herself a politically committed communist and journalist in China) before moving to China and working variously for the American-funded *Shanghai Evening Post and Mercury* and the *China Press* as well as the *Shanghai Times*.[167] Later, despite his radical politics, he worked as an assistant editor on J.B. Powell's highly regarded *China Weekly Review* and was a popular commentator for the American-owned XMHA radio station. Glass soon fell out with Weitemeyer and stopped attending events at the Zeitgeist due to his involvement in the Trotskyite Communist League of China.[168]

Another regular was a Japanese man called Hotsumi Ozaki, a newspaper correspondent for the Osaka *Asahi Shimbun* who, while still living in Japan in the early 1920s, had become a Marxist and joined the Japanese Communist Party. Ozaki had recently entered into a relationship with an outgoing American woman who was

---

167 The *Shanghai Times* was an English-language newspaper supportive of Japanese policies in China and largely funded by pro-Tokyo sources. However, many foreign journalists worked for the paper during their time as freelancers in Shanghai.

168 Glass wrote for the league in many publications, using the pen-names John Liang, Myra Weiss and Li Fu Ren.

Agnes Smedley (1914)   *Hotsumi Ozaki*

always the first to arrive and the last to leave any socialist gathering
– Agnes Smedley.

Smedley had arrived in China in 1928 and moved to Shanghai's
French Concession in May 1929, six months after the young Roger
Hollis had pitched up in town. She was a known firebrand with a
particular dislike of the British Empire in India, against which she
had been highly vocal in campaigning. From the start of her sojourn
in China, which was to last until 1941, the SMP, Shanghai Special
Branch and British Intelligence in China monitored her closely.
Nominally her job was China correspondent of the *Frankfurter
Zeitung* newspaper. It has been claimed that Smedley worked for a
time at the Zeitgeist Bookshop, either in a paid or (more likely)
voluntary capacity.[169]

All of these radical sojourners who had gathered at the Zeitgeist
are of interest and have been written about to differing degrees.
They formed a nucleus that fostered and supported the emergent
Chinese Communist Party in Shanghai through the bloody and
repressive late 1920s. Smedley, Ozaki and others were also involved
in the 'Sorge Ring', an intelligence-gathering operation run by the
Soviet spy Richard Sorge that was highly active across Asia, particularly in Shanghai and Tokyo, before World War Two.

169 See M.J. West, *The Truth About Hollis: An Investigation*, (London:
     Duckworth, 1989), p. 26.

However, it is that young man with Smedley, quiet and some-what shy, who is also of interest because his time in Shanghai has been far less studied (at least publicly) and was, possibly, to have the most far-reaching consequences of any of the other Zeitgeist regulars in the decades to come. One night in the summer of 1929 Agnes Smedley arrived at the Zeitgeist with her new friend – an Englishman called Roger Hollis. As on many summer evenings, the cramped Zeitgeist was packed, the crowd spilling out on to the street to escape the claustrophobic heat inside the shop. Here, on various occasions throughout 1929, young Roger Hollis met and socialised with everyone. How those contacts affected the rest of his life has been the subject of intense speculation in intelligence and espionage circles ever since.

Mr Roger Henry Hollis of BAT

Roger Henry Hollis was just twenty-two years old when he arrived in Shanghai in November 1928. The year before he had moved from England to Hong Kong to work briefly as a journalist before taking

Roger Henry Hollis

a job with a more secure career path. He joined British-American Tobacco (BAT) in Shanghai, the largest foreign cigarette firm in Asia where smoking was just about universal (for males and increasingly for 'modern' females). His career path was not to his conservative family's taste. His father, George, had been vicar of Headingly, near Leeds, before becoming principal of Wells Theological College in Somerset. Roger had at-tended Clifton College in Bristol before going up to

Oxford's Worcester College in 1924. Annoyingly for his father, Hollis left two years later without completing his degree. He became a clerk with the Chartered Bank in London; a bank with long associations to the Far East. The boredom of clerking combined with a degree of wanderlust prompted him to opt for the journalism job in Hong Kong and then the move up to Shanghai with BAT.

Quite how Hollis met Smedley in Shanghai is unclear, though it was probably quite soon after she arrived in the Settlement in spring of 1929. As a well-informed man Hollis would have been aware of Smedley's reputation – the British newspaper had long followed her agitations against the Raj. We do not know if Hollis ever visited the Zeitgeist prior to meeting Smedley. If he did then he could simply have encountered her when she arrived and was visiting the shop.

After several visits to the Zeitgeist with Smedley, Hollis appears to have ceased his bookshop browsing on the North Soochow Road. But he had not left Shanghai; he just stopped attending meetings at the bookshop. He appears to have had no more overt contact with Smedley, Irene Weitemeyer, or any of the regulars at the Zeitgeist. Yet Hollis remained in Shanghai for another year or so, working with BAT. Did he fall out with Smedley and the Zeitgeist crowd? Did he find something objectionable or politically not to his taste on the Zeitgeist shelves? Did he not agree with one of the evening speakers? Weitemeyer, Smedley and their Comintern associates must have been aware of the interest Shanghai Special Branch paid them. Did someone suggest that Hollis perhaps not drop by any more for fear of drawing the attention of anyone observing events at the Zeitgeist Bookshop?

Hollis's social circle in Shanghai after his Zeitgeist days would be diplomats and businessmen, and he seemed to suddenly start playing a lot of golf.

Then, in 1930, BAT transferred Hollis north to their Peking office where he worked for nearly six years, though next to nothing is known of his time there. He appears to have had few friends in Peking, attended few formal events, nor joined any clubs or societies, played on no sports teams or been listed in any directories or social lists – highly unusual in the foreign colony of Peking unless deliberately intended. He did write several letters home reassuring his parents that all was well and that he had attended some picnics, including one with the family of the visiting British consul at Dairen. Perhaps he did, but there are few letters and little verification of these social activities.

British Army Captain Anthony 'Tony' Stables was stationed in Peking in 1928 and appears to have first met Hollis during his sojourn in Shanghai. Hollis and Stables shared a rented flat for some time in Peking. Speaking at a later date, Captain Stables stated he had assumed Hollis was left wing due to his known association with Agnes Smedley and another well-known Comintern agent, the German Arthur Ewert (sometimes spelled Ewerts) in Shanghai. However, Stables admitted he had been bemused by Hollis's relationships with Smedley and Ewert, as he appeared traditionally conservative in his social and political views.

Hollis returned to England on leave in 1934, travelling by the Trans-Siberian Railway. He spent a few days in Moscow seeing the sights; later he would claim to have spoken to no one during his time in the Soviet capital, to have found it dirty and drab, and then boarded the train home.[170]

Back after his furlough in 1935 he contracted tuberculosis in Peking and sought treatment. Hollis had suffered intermittently with TB and it had got progressively worse during his time in China. There are few records of this but then TB had a stigma attached to it in the 1930s and so Hollis may have wished to keep knowledge of his condition secret. At any rate his doctor advised him to leave Peking. Back in England he took a post with the Ardath Tobacco Company, an associate of BAT. After eighteen months or so with Ardath he made a life-changing career decision and joined MI5's F Division (tasked with counter-subversion).

During the Second World War and afterwards Hollis rose steadily through the ranks and, in 1953, was appointed deputy director general under Dick White (who was said to resemble the

---

170   The Peking picnics and Trans-Siberian Railway details from West, *The Truth About Hollis*, pp. 27–28.

British film star David Niven).[171] In 1956 White moved to head MI6. Hollis took over the top post at MI5 and served as director general until 1965, when he retired.

Hollis's intelligence career appeared unblemished, until 1963, when the Cambridge spy Kim Philby fled to the Soviet Union. Rumours circulated that Hollis himself had tipped off Philby that he was about to be arrested for treachery. Hollis was accused also of not having alerted John Profumo, MP and war secretary in Harold Macmillan's cabinet, that he was becoming embroiled in a Soviet spy ring through his friendship with Stephen Ward and affair with Christine Keeler. Keeler was already in a relationship with the Soviet naval attaché to London and intelligence officer, Yevgeny Ivanov. Hollis's silence allowed Profumo to become involved with Keeler to a level that ultimately meant the end of his political career in disgrace.

After the revelations around the now infamous Cambridge spies – Kim Philby, Anthony Blunt, Donald Maclean and Guy Burgess – it was hinted that Hollis was the supposed 'Fifth Man'. In 1987 the former MI5 operative Peter Wright published his highly con-troversial book, *Spy Catcher*, which was banned in Britain.[172] In the book Wright alleges that Hollis was a long-time Soviet agent, separate from the Cambridge ring and so undetected during those investigations. Rather than being recruited at Cambridge in the 1930s along with the others, Hollis had been recruited while in Shanghai in 1929 by Agnes Smedley at Irene Weitemeyer's Zeitgeist Bookshop on the North Soochow Road.

The Fifth Man from Shanghai

Was Roger Hollis recruited for Moscow by Smedley and others while spending time with them in the Zeitgeist Bookshop? It seems

171 Peter Wright, *Spy Catcher: The Candid Autobiography of a Senior Intelligence Officer*, (New York, Viking, 1987).

172 Copies of which were widely circulated in the UK despite the ban – this author, a student at the time, bought a paperback under the counter in Tottenham High Road in North London. Such was the atmosphere at the time that the newsagent looked decidedly nervous and I felt sure I would be arrested upon leaving the shop. I wasn't.

possible. If this was the case then the Zeitgeist Bookshop is one of the most infamous spots anywhere in the history of British Intelligence.

Firstly it's worth examining standard Soviet Intelligence operating procedure in England among young men of Hollis's class in the 1920s and 1930s.

Hollis was an Oxford man, completely distinct from the Cambridge spy ring, though he would later know all its members through his work with MI5. It has been suggested that Hollis could have been recruited while at Oxford, but this seems unlikely for a number of reasons. Firstly, he never finished his degree. Soviet Intelligence's usual working pattern was for recruited students to complete their degrees, the better to access the higher echelons of the British establishment as 'sleepers' or 'long-term penetrations'. With a good degree their chances of success in gaining employment in the elite universities, journalism, government, the foreign office and, of course, the Secret Intelligence Service (SIS), was far higher. Remaining at Oxford would have helped Hollis maintain the widest range of social contacts who might prove useful in some way. Secondly, it was not normal Soviet Intelligence practice to recruit at an elite British university and then have that agent move away from the centre of British power. The aim was for the agent to penetrate the establishment, not remove themselves from it selling cigarettes along the Yangtze. Thirdly, the point of recruiting young men of left-wing sympathies within the universities was then to have them renounce, or at least distance themselves significantly, from their initial radical politics and establish more acceptable political credentials, not to frequent a notorious left-wing Shanghai bookshop on the arm of an activist.

A brief flirtation with left-wing politics at Oxford or Cambridge was forgivable to the Foreign Office or the intelligence services if they soon assumed the correct ideologies and attitudes of the ruling class of which they were part. To be one of that generation of upper-class intellectual young Englishmen in the late 1920s and 1930s and to have some vaguely left-wing sentiments was deemed fairly normal. For the later Cambridge spies the world after the carnage of the Great War, the seemingly utter failure of capitalism and the Wall Street Crash of 1929, the rise of fascism in Italy, Germany, Austria and Spain, and the belief that only the Soviet Union stood solidly against Hitlerism, pushed them towards Moscow. Hollis had known the terror of the Great War as a boy, and the British General Strike of 1926. Hollis then found himself in Shanghai barely a year after the bloody events of 1927, the slaughter of the Chinese left and the deadly suppression of the Chinese Communist Party in the city. These events still reverberated strongly in the Settlement in late 1928 and 1929.

If Hollis had been recruited before Shanghai, Soviet Intelligence would not have encouraged him to make open contact with any Soviets or notable radicals in Shanghai. Such meetings would immediately bring their recruit to the attention of the local intelligence services reporting to London, rendering the agent useless. On the other hand, to recruit Hollis as a deep-cover long-term penetration agent was still possible as, despite some evening flirtations at the Zeitgeist, he never actually joined any radical organisations in China, something that would have been revealed in a standard background check conducted by sis.

Hollis was several years older than the majority of the Cambridge spies (though Blunt was admittedly only a couple of years younger than Hollis, Blunt was not recruited till later, after Hollis's time at Oxford). Hollis left Oxford in the spring of 1926, while it is believed the Soviets began actively recruiting radically inclined young men at the universities around 1933/1934. Kim Philby and Guy Burgess were recruiting fellow Cambridge graduates around 1938, a dozen years after Hollis had left Oxford.

If not recruited in England then we need to look at Hollis's contacts, friends and actions when in Shanghai in 1929.

Hollis moved to Shanghai after a brief stint as a journalist in Hong Kong. It was standard Soviet practice to encourage its long-term penetration spies to work for right-wing or establishment media – Kim Philby for *The Times* or Guy Burgess for the bbc, for instance. However, Hollis's short stint in journalism appears to have been more about obtaining an income after arriving in Asia (he did not have independent means). A job with bat in China had no immediate espionage potential, but was a popular choice for young Englishmen looking for the opportunity to live and work in China.[173]

In Shanghai Agnes Smedley had quickly befriended Hollis. It is clear that she was a recruiter for the so-called Sorge spy ring. Sorge himself was probably one of her many lovers, as was the Japanese journalist and Zeitgeist regular Hatsumi Ozaki. Indeed, Smedley introduced Ozaki to Sorge who subsequently recruited him to his ring. Ozaki was eventually to become Sorge's major agent in Japan.[174] Smedley undoubtedly recruited others, both foreigners and Chinese, to the Sorge Ring and to communist ideals in general.

Smedley was an overt and well-known radical leftist, nevertheless, but in Cambridge all the spies had seemingly moved swiftly away from left-wing politics once recruited, eschewing their student radicalism. This was, within the British elite, both a common and a forgivable sin. References from college tutors often referred to them having passed through their 'communist phase' or having shrugged off a case of the 'communist measles'. As was often said – 'Those who aren't revolutionaries in their twenties have no heart, those who remain revolutionaries in their thirties have no head.' After leaving Cambridge, Guy Burgess openly renounced his left-wing ideals, left the Communist Party and began to establish right-wing credentials – as instructed. The others did the same.

Richard Sorge arrived in Shanghai in 1930 working in part for Smedley's employer the *Frankfurter Zeitung*. Hollis's retreat from the Zeitgeist and distancing from Smedley began around the time of Sorge's arrival in Shanghai. If Hollis was recruited by Smedley at the Zeitgeist around the time of Sorge's arrival in the Settlement then that would explain his sudden cessation of involvement with the place and its denizens.

173   Perhaps most famously a young Graham Greene took up the offer of a China position with BAT. He began studying Mandarin at the School of Oriental Studies on Finsbury Circus where his teacher was a young man from Peking spending some time in London called Lao She, later to become one of China's greatest modern writers – see Anne Witchard in *Lao She in London*, (Hong Kong, Royal Asiatic Society China/Hong Kong University Press, 2012). Greene did not ultimately take up the position with BAT.

174   After arrest and torture both Richard Sorge and Hotsumi Ozaki were hanged as Soviet spies in Tokyo's Sugamo Prison on November 7, 1944.

Richard Sorge

In Shanghai, and then for his years in Peking, Hollis virtually dropped off the map. He may well have tried to join the Communist Party in Shanghai (others did) and been told, as more upper-class potential spies recruited in England often were, that perhaps they could do more for the cause from the outside. As with the spies back in England he retreated into non-political life, attracting no attention, concentrating on his career and eventually putting enough distance between himself and those trips to the Zeitgeist with Smedley to gain a position with MI5 in London.

In many ways Hollis's possible recruitment in 1929 by Smedley and Sorge on the North Soochow Road was textbook – a young man of some social rank, from a conservative family, seeking company and friendship, caught up in the politics of his time, intellectually curious and having not uncommon left-wing aspirations finds like-minded mentors. Once recruited he breaks all ties with known radicals and anyone associated with the Soviets, effectively disappearing for a time to another city where he lives in relative obscurity and anonymity before he returns to London, untainted, the son of a high-ranking cleric, a public-school boy, an Oxford man with some commercial experience of the Far East. Ripe material for MI5 and nobody remembering a couple of social events at a small bookshop in Shanghai a decade before.

The later days of the Zeitgeist

The American journalist and communist sympathiser Harold Isaacs arrived in Shanghai in 1930 and soon discovered the Zeitgeist. Isaacs's future wife Viola Robinson became good friends with Lu Xun. Like Frank Glass who knew the Zeitgeist in Hollis's days, Isaacs was a Trotskyist and, along with Glass, was involved in the Committee for the Defence of Leon Trotsky. This presumably did not go down well with Irene Weitemeyer.[175] Another slightly later regular at the Zeitgeist was Ursula Hamburger, who may actually have worked there for a time as she had some prior experiences in the book trade and spoke better English than Irene. In Lu Xun's brief memory of the Zeitgeist he recalled being introduced by Agnes Smedley to Ursula Hamburger during a 1932 exhibition at the store of German woodcuts by the Berlin artist Käthe Kollwitz.[176] Kollwitz was a friend of Smedley's from her Berlin sojourn between 1921 and 1928. Ursula Hamburger was born Ursula Kuczynsk in Germany and was a member of the German Communist Party. She left Germany after being fired for participating in a May Day rally and went to work in New York in a bookshop. She returned to Germany and married Rudolf Hamburger, a fellow Communist Party member. They moved to Shanghai in July 1930 (just as Hollis was in the process of relocating to Peking), met Agnes Smedley at the Zeitgeist Bookshop, who introduced them to Richard Sorge, who recruited her and gave her the cover name 'Sonja'.[177]

---

175   For more on Glass and the Shanghai Trotskyists see Baruch Hirson, *The Restless Revolutionary – Frank Glass*, (Johannesburg: Porcupine Press, 2003).

176   Elizabeth Emrich, *Modernity Through Experimentation: Lu Xun and the Modern Chinese Woodcut Movement*, (Leiden: Brill, 2014).

177   Ursula Hamburger is today better known as Ruth Werner. Rudolf Hamburger remained in Shanghai until 1937 working as an architect for the Shanghai Municipal Council. He designed the Victoria Nurses' Home, completed around 1933, which is an excellent Bauhaus-inspired building with some splendid ironwork adorning the interior staircases on Great Western Road adjacent to the Country Hospital (now the Huadong Hospital). I believe Hamburger was also involved in the 1935 design of the Middle School for Chinese Girls (now Shanghai No. 1 Middle School) on Singapore Road and was involved in designing an extension to the Ward Road Jail (later renamed Tilanqiao Prison).

Ruth Weiss and Xu Jun

At some point in 1932 or 1933 the Zeitgeist Bookshop moved premises, probably due to the general demolitions in the area for the construction of Sir Victor Sassoon's vast Embankment Building. It didn't move far, just to No. 410 Szechuan North Road, still in Hongkew. There the shop continued to attract a later generation of radical elements in China including George Hatem (known to the Chinese as Ma Haide), a Lebanese-American doctor turned communist advocate whose first Shanghai clinic was close by, and Ruth Weiss (known as Wei Lushi), an Austrian journalist and left-wing activist. Both arrived in the city in early 1933 and both were later to be eyewitnesses to the Chinese Revolution and to take Chinese citizenship shortly after the foundation of the People's Republic in 1949. Both Hatem and Weiss became close to Agnes Smedley in Shanghai. Hatem supposedly browsed the Zeitgeist's stock almost daily and was introduced to the Chinese Communist Party for the first time on a visit.[178] Hatem died in Peking in 1988; Weiss in 2006 at ninety-seven, the last surviving foreign witness to the birth of the PRC. Both Hatem and Weiss were close friends with the New Zealand labour reformer and left-wing activist Rewi Alley, who may well have been another Zeitgeist regular, possibly at the same time as Hollis, as Alley arrived in Shanghai in 1927.

---

178   According to Porter, *The People's Doctor*, p. 41.

Many of these Zeitgeist regulars lived close by the shop. It's unclear where Irene herself lived in the late 1920s (one source mentions an address in the French Concession[179]) but certainly later, once it was completed, Irene as well as Harold Isaacs and his wife Viola Robinson all appear to have lived in the new Embankment Building; George Hatem at his clinic nearby; Lu Xun at his residence on Ziang Teh Road in Hongkew nearby.

It seems Irene Weitemeyer left Shanghai in 1933, returning to Germany in 1934. This is also the time that Ursula Hamburger, Agnes Smedley and Richard Sorge left Shanghai, at least for a time. The sudden need to depart appears to be connected to the Noulens Affair, the earlier arrest in 1931 in Shanghai by Special Branch of Hilaire Noulens and his 'wife' (their real names were Yakov Rudnik and Tatyana Moiseenko). The Noulens were key members of the Comintern apparatus in China and the seizure of a cache of documents concerning the activities of the Comintern and the Chinese Communist Party led to a subsequent trial in late October 1931 of the couple by the Chinese authorities in Nanking. The Noulens became a left-wing *cause célèbre* both in Shanghai and around the world but it also led to the partial destruction of the Comintern in Shanghai and necessitated the hasty departure of more than one Zeitgeist Bookshop regular from the city.

Irene Weitemeyer appears to have died in West Germany in 1978; her husband Wu Shao-Kuo died in China in 1973.[180]

Roger and Agnes

As far as is known, and in accordance with Soviet Intelligence's operating procedure, Hollis never made contact with Agnes Smedley again – not in China and certainly not once he had returned to England and joined MI5. She in turn never mentioned him in any correspondence or memoirs.

179   Thomas Kampen, 'Irene Weitemeyer in Göttingen, Moscow and Shanghai – A Summary', sourced from Academia.edu. Kampen notes a Frenchtown address in the memoirs of a Chinese secretary.

180   Details of Irene Weitemeyer's life are in part from the excellent research conducted by Kampen, ibid.

Yet his past was to come back to haunt him. While Hollis was rising up through the ranks of the British secret service, Agnes Smedley continued to be an open and avowed radical. After the start of the Sino-Japanese War she famously spent a great deal of time with the Communist-controlled Eighth Route Army and the new Fourth Army. Smedley never joined the Chinese Communist Party (in fact her application was turned down over concerns about her seeming lack of discipline and questions about her louche personal life), though she tirelessly promoted the Party in her journalism and writing. She achieved international notoriety during her stay in the communist stronghold of Yan'an after the Long March and her interviews with the communist General Chu Teh (Zhu De), about whom she wrote a flattering and uncritical biography.[181] In May 1941 she returned to America, campaigning for support for China in the fight against Japan, publishing her influential book *Battle Hymn For China*,[182] and living at Yaddo, a bohemian writers' colony in upstate New York.

Smedley was not a conventional Stalinist. Whittaker Chambers, a former Soviet spy himself, denounced her as a member of the Communist Party of America – but she was not and never had been a member of any communist party. Indeed Smedley had long been critical of the USSR and Stalin, despite her collaboration with the Soviet-controlled Sorge Ring in China, which she saw as anti-fascism work. The FBI placed her on their security watch list in 1946. The House Un-American Activities Committee (HUAC) began its investigations in 1947 under J. Parnell Thomas. At first it concentrated on Hollywood, calling such luminaries as Bertolt Brecht (who gave evidence and then swiftly left for East Germany) and a succession of scriptwriters who became the 'Hollywood Ten'. On January 1st, 1948 it was reported that Smedley was being investigated by HUAC regarding her involvement in communist espionage in China and Japan in the 1930s. America was now entering the particularly vicious period of 'McCarthyism'. Smedley expected to

---

181 Agnes Smedley, *The Great Road: The Life and Times of Chu Teh*, (New York: Monthly Review Press, 1956). The text is somewhat incomplete and was published after Smedley's death.

182 Agnes Smedley, *Battle Hymn of China*, (New York, Alfred A. Knopf, 1943).

be called to testify any day. Unwell, in November 1949, she moved to England. Her health deteriorated due to a duodenal ulcer and on May 6th, 1950 she checked into a private hospital in Oxford for an operation on her stomach. She died on the operating table. Her ashes were removed from Britain and buried at the Babaoshan Revolutionary Cemetery in Peking in 1951.

But questions have always remained – was she planning to return to the United States and tell all? It was highly convenient that she died on the operating table during a routine and seemingly non-life-threatening operation. She chose Oxford, a city Roger Hollis had a long and intimate connection with since his youth; a city in which he maintained a house and had great influence in. In America the 'convenience' of her death before perhaps revealing the extent of the Sorge Ring and where those trails could lead was noted.

Rumours have swirled around Hollis (code name 'Drat' within MI5) for decades now and continue to surface every now and again as speculation about a 'Fifth Man' continues. MI5's former Principal Scientific Officer Peter Wright, who died in 1995, was convinced of Hollis's recruitment by the Russians while in Shanghai. His investigations (elaborated on in *Spy Catcher*) cited a number of reasons for suspecting Hollis. One key reason Wright believed was Hollis's friendship with Smedley in Shanghai at a time she was in a relationship with Richard Sorge.[183] Wright also claimed that the Fluency Working Party, an interagency committee (chaired by Wright) set up by SIS to examine all the hitherto unproven allegations about Soviet penetration of British Intelligence unanimously concluded that Hollis was the 'best fit' for various Soviet defector testimonies about the 'Fifth Man's' identity. Wright's Fluency Committee submitted its findings shortly after Hollis's retirement in 1965, but further investigation was not sanctioned by his successor Martin Furnival Jones. There are of course many critics of Wright's

183   Other key reasons, according to Wright in *Spy Catcher*, included Hollis's long-term friendship with the left-wing journalist suspected of ties to Soviet Intelligence, Claud Cockburn, and particularly Hollis's apparent obstruction into the investigation of information obtained from several Soviet defectors including Igor Gouzenko, who defected to Canada in 1945.

investigations, analysis and conclusions including a later director general of MI5, Dame Stella Rimington, who believed Wright was 'obsessed' with the Hollis/'Fifth Man' issue.[184] For his part Wright believed to the end of his life that 'Hollis's friends had bitterly resented the accusations and for ten long years both sides had feuded like medieval theologians, driven by instinct, passion and prejudice.'[185]

We may never now know the truth about Roger Hollis, Agnes Smedley, the Sorge Ring and what happened at the Zeitgeist Bookshop in 1929. It's hard to get a sense of the young Roger Hollis. His early life is shrouded in some mystery and he never wrote about himself in detail. Later descriptions of him as tall, with thick eyebrows and always in a pinstriped suit make him appear austere, remote, disliking small talk. But these are memoirs of MI5 officers faced with their director general, and DGs of MI5 are not known for their tactile chumminess. In photos he does smile sometimes, revealing a more human side. Certainly tracing Hollis's China years is difficult. We have no definite addresses for him in Shanghai or Peking, just a forwarding address (R. Hollis C/O Chartered Bank, Peking, China) or office addresses at BAT. Interviewed by the Fluency Committee in the mid-1960s, Captain Tony Stables, Hollis's old flatmate in Shanghai, was confused about his politics – left-wing friends like Smedley and Ewert had given way to golf and conservatism. A natural political progression or camouflage? He did maintain friendships with some left-wing contacts in China – Arthur Ewert in particular – but these may have been more about simply wishing to discuss current affairs with interesting people. However, veteran espionage writer Chapman Pincher also noted that Ewert was an 'inveterate talent spotter' for Soviet Intelligence.[186] Much has been made of Hollis's visit to Moscow in 1934 when travelling back to England on furlough, but the Trans-Siberian is one of the great train journeys of the world and many

184 Stella Rimington, 'Spies Like Us', *Guardian*, September 11, 2001.

185 Wright, *Spy Catcher*, p. 3.

186 Chapman Pincher, *Treachery: Betrayals, Blunders and Cover-Ups: Six Decades of Espionage Against America and Great Britain*, (New York: Random House, 2009).

foreigners in China took the opportunity of travelling home this way.

Quite possibly Hollis's meeting Smedley in Shanghai was nothing more than an intellectually curious young man looking for company and a social circle in a strange town who decides that perhaps that circle is a tad racy or a little too left wing for him, drops it and moves on. Hollis was one of many intellectually curious young men to be invited to events by Smedley. Or perhaps Hollis, like many others, was a single man who enjoyed a brief romantic flirtation with Smedley. Many others also did that – though none of them rose to become director general of MI5. Yet Peter Wright firmly believed that something more happened in Shanghai in 1929; something more serious and clandestine that had ramifications for British Intelligence and the Cold War spy game for decades to come and it happened at the Zeitgeist Bookshop on the North Soochow Road, on a summer's evening in 1929.

For my part, I believe it plausible that Hollis was recruited in Shanghai in the late 1920s. That Smedley and the Sorge Ring recruited him swiftly during his initial visits to the Zeitgeist seems likely given his political leanings at the time. That they understood that he was a certain type and from a certain class and would, like the Cambridge spies later, be capable of penetrating the highest echelons of the British establishment as a deep-cover agent also seems plausible.

In Shanghai, Hollis evinced an interest in left-wing issues and causes and regularly visited the Zeitgeist in the company of Smedley and others of an overtly pro-communist bent. Then suddenly he didn't and returned – first in Peking, and then back in England – to the more conventional opinions and politics of his social class. He remained in deep cover, probably unknown even to the Cambridge spies, and, I believe, worked for the interests of the Soviet Union throughout his entire career at the very peak of the British Intelligence Services.

Weimar on the Whangpoo:
Lily Flohr (1941)

Atelier Balázs phot.

*'Lily Flohr, the popular vocalist, will be flattered to see you
tonight at the newly redecorated Elite Bar.'*

A life as film

The following is a partial biography of the singer and actress Lily Flohr.[187] Lily was born in Vienna. She was a child prodigy of the city's variety theatre, then became a silent-movie star in Berlin. She went on to become a pioneer of cinema in Romania, and then, like so many Jewish entertainers, was forced to leave Germany under the Nazis. She chose Shanghai, where she was known and loved by many Germans, both Christian and Jewish, who had known her before exile back in Europe. In Shanghai she continued her career, performing both in the smart nightclubs and cabarets of the International Settlement and, slightly later, in the Hongkew Jewish ghetto. She survived the war and, I believe, settled eventually in Australia.

I say this is a 'partial biography' because there is so much I don't know, or at least am not certain about, when it comes to Lily Flohr. Over the years (and it's at least twelve years since I first heard of her) I've sought out details of Flohr's life, both before Shanghai, during her years there, and after. But much has remained elusive. For instance, I am not sure what her married name was. It is a puzzle to me why she quit the movies around the time that silent films gave way to the talkies. I am not sure when exactly she left Germany and arrived in Shanghai – there is conflicting data. I am not sure how she left Shanghai or later secured Australian citizenship. Over time I've encountered other researchers looking into her life – those interested in musical theatre in Germany and Austria, others researching the glory days of the pre-Nazi UFA film studios and a few looking in detail at the society of the Shanghai Jewish ghetto during World War Two. We've traded information to build a more

---

187 Most references spell her name as 'Lily', although 'Lilly' and 'Lili' are also common in her Austrian, German and Shanghai periods.

complete picture – Vienna, Berlin, Bucharest, Shanghai, Sydney – but still Lily Flohr remains something of an enigma.

I was drawn to Lily because of how she seemed to operate across two worlds in pre-war Shanghai. I now feel that if I wait until I have her full and fact-checked story I'll never get around to publishing anything about Lily Flohr. But if I publish what I know then perhaps more information, contacts, leads, will come out of the woodwork. My hope is that this brief biographical sketch (written in the style of a movie treatment because I have always imagined her life as a big-budget bio-pic) will become quickly redundant, that I'll receive a flood of emails and letters telling me I'm wrong and surely I should have known this or that. Here's hoping – Lily deserves a better biography than this, but it's all I've got for now.

INT. THE SPOTLIT STAGE OF THE ELITE BAR –
SHANGHAI'S INTERNATIONAL SETTLEMENT – THE
OPENING NIGHT OF LILY FLOHR IN CABARET – JULY 1941

Lily, a former child protégé of Vienna's music hall and silent movie star of Weimar Berlin in the 1920s is living in Shanghai where thousands of Jewish refugees from Europe are gathered. After the 1934 Nazi laws forbidding Jews to appear on either stage or screen effectively ended her once glittering career, she has worked hard to rebuild it in Shanghai and is now a sought-after singer in the International Settlement's most fashionable supper clubs and cabarets. But Japan has invaded China, fire-bombed the Chinese portions of Shanghai, and encircled the city, though not encroached on the foreign settlements ... yet. These are the last days of the old Shanghai.

The Elite Bar, on the corner of Medhurst Road and the Bubbling Well Road in the heart of the International Settlement, is tonight packed with both established Shanghailanders and more recently arrived European refugees far away from home in Asia's most modern and cosmopolitan city. They are expectantly awaiting the appearance of Lily Flohr who will sing the old German and Yiddish songs of pre-war Vienna and Berlin as well as some favourites of

---

LILLY FLOHR

the popular Vocalist
will be flattered to see you

To-night

at the newly-decorated

ELITE BAR

The Management

175 Medhurst Road   Telephones
Corner Bubbling Well Road   34345,
(Central Mansions)   34346

---

the crowd in French and English. She sings in all these languages to suit the cosmopolitan tastes of the multinational Settlement.

Backstage at the Elite Bar – Lily is nervous. The situation in Shanghai is awful, frightening. Germany and Austria are at war with Great Britain and Soviet Russia. Japan has encircled the foreign concessions; those that can are leaving Shanghai on evacuation ships; others, the stateless Russian émigrés and Jewish refugees like Lily, with no papers and few options, wait in Shanghai. But as Lily sings from the small stage of the Elite her audience is transported back to the key moments of her life in Europe before the war, before she had to flee. She starts to sing. . . .

INT. THE INTERIOR OF A CONCERT HALL – VIENNA –
FEBRUARY 1912

An eight-year-old Lily Flohr waits in the wings watching her mother and father performing, waiting for her cue. Then out into the bright lights that obscure the thousand-strong-audience to a mass of indistinguishable shadowy heads wreathed in curls of smoke from the hundreds of cigarette ends she can see glowing. A round of applause ensues as little Lily Flohr walks centre stage and makes a curtsey. She starts to sing as a hush comes over the crowd. None of this fazes Lily in the slightest. She's a pro already.

Vienna's vaudeville is raucous and lively, a contrast to the city's more staid classical culture. Fakirs in turbans palm watches from gullible audience members, acrobats tumble, magicians saw their beautiful assistants in half, and comedians crack up the audience with their rapid patter in a mixture of German, Yiddish and Wienerisch dialect.

Lily appears with her family nightly. They alternate between the traditional Viennese music halls and concert rooms and the growing number of Yiddish theatres that serve Vienna's Jewish population, swelled by the seemingly never-ending pogroms to the east. The Flohrs are a theatre family, performers all and Lily's first memory is of being on stage.

INT. THE SPOTLIT STAGE OF THE ELITE BAR –
SHANGHAI'S INTERNATIONAL SETTLEMENT – THE
OPENING NIGHT OF LILY FLOHR IN CABARET – JULY 1941

Between songs Lily tells of how, as a young girl, she tired of vaudeville work, repeating the same roles night after night. It was hard grind: matinees, evenings, tours. After the disaster of the Great War Vienna was no longer the capital of an empire but a provincial central European city with unemployed, homeless and horrifically wounded men seemingly begging on every street corner. The city's grandeur seemed tarnished. Lily finds escape from the depressing streets and the routine of vaudeville life in a new medium – cinema.

Theatrical agents in Vienna looking for new talent scouted Lily. She tells the audience she was flattered, charmed and excited. She agreed to a contract with a German film studio – she was about to enter a thrilling new world. It was time for a young girl from Vienna to make the journey to Berlin to be transformed into a movie star.

EXT. THE UFA FILM STUDIOS ENTRANCE – POTSDAM –
JANUARY 1919

Germany is in ruins following defeat in the Great War – supposedly the war to end all wars. The German economy is devastated, poverty endemic; demobbed soldiers have become the massed ranks of the unemployed; revolution is in the air. As Lily turns up on set for her first film role the communist Spartacists are building barricades in the streets of Berlin. As filming progresses and a fantasy celluloid world is created in Potsdam, the Spartacists and the reactionary Freikorps battle in the city streets. Barricades are erected; shots fired, water cannons, baton charges, it is effectively a civil war. Former soldiers seeking to create a better, utopian world, are battling former soldiers intent on preventing the spread of Bolshevism from Red Russia to Germany. Lily is working on *Das Mädchen aus der Ackerstraße* (*The Girl from Acker Street*), a melodrama of seduction and sexual exploitation of proletarian women by bourgeois society. Lily's movie career is underway.

A general strike is called across Berlin on January 7th. Lily must travel on foot to meetings with her agents, her fellow actors, directors and to the studios. Half a million workers surge into central Berlin waving red flags. They urge the government to resign, the army and navy to desert to their side. Talks between the strikers and the government rapidly collapse. The Spartacists urge their supporters to fall back on the tactic of street fighting. The government strikes back, unleashing the Freikorps. The Freikorps are better armed – they clear the street barricades hastily erected across the city. One hundred and fifty-six Spartacists are killed; seventeen Freikorps. The bodies of the Spartacist leaders Rosa Luxembourg and Karl Liebknicht are found badly beaten and shot in the head. Liebknicht's body is delivered to the city morgue; they dump Luxembourg's in the city's Landwehr Canal.

INT. THE SPOTLIT STAGE OF THE ELITE BAR –
SHANGHAI'S INTERNATIONAL SETTLEMENT – THE
OPENING NIGHT OF LILY FLOHR IN CABARET – JULY 1941
Lily regales her rapt audience – many of them German and Austrian cinema fans who remember her glory years – with how the days were long and the work hard on those silent films, social melodramas such as *Das Haus in der Dragonerstrasse* (*The House in Dragon Street*) and crime dramas such as the series of films titled *Aus dem Schwarzbuch eines Polizeikommissars* (*From the Black Book of the Police Commissioners*).

Before talkies, film sets were raucous, argumentative places. Directors, set builders, costumiers, carpenters, electricians, all shouted while the actors gestured and showed their emotions to tell the story. Everyone worked at a furious pace. Yet Lily knew that she was part of something special and magical; an escape from the economic and social turmoil engulfing Germany; the poverty and desperation of the early 1920s. So Lily kept on working. She becomes a star on the screen and a key player in one of the most creative communities of the twentieth century.

INT. THE UFA STUDIOS – POTSDAM – OCTOBER 1921

Germany's film industry is booming even though the country remains mired in economic recession and with rampant inflation. Crowds flock to the cinemas to see their new idols. After a dozen silent films Lily Flohr has become one of Germany's biggest female movie stars. The street vendors sell postcards of her; the movie magazines feature her; she is recognised in the street.

Day One of Filming: Lily walks onto the set of *Fridericus Rex: Sturm und Drang (Storm and Stress)*, a giant multi-film project detailing the life of the Prussian King Frederick the Great. It is her biggest film yet. The movie stars the actor Otto Gebuhr, Frederick's close lookalike. It is directed by the talented Hungarian Arzén von Cserépy. The film, and its follow-up *Fridericus Rex: Vater und Sohn (Father and Son)* made a year later, were to be among Germany's

Lily on a postcard

most popular, yet controversial, silent movies. The films, coming in the wake of Germany's defeat in the war, appear to some to be urging a renewed nationalism. The right wing love the films; the socialists and communists boycott them.

Day Two of Filming: On a hot day Lily is filming in a giant wig, corset and full make up. It is boiling and uncomfortable, the melting panstick make-up has to be constantly touched up between takes, water gulped, sweaty hair re-fluffed. But the light is perfect. The movie is controversial but, for Lily, it is a leading role.

INT. THE UFA-PALAST AM ZOO CINEMA – BERLIN – JANUARY 1922

A smart and intellectual Berlin crowd gather for the premiere of *Fridericus Rex Parts I & II*. The film with its scenario of a formerly great and peaceful Prussia will play to packed houses across Germany for months,

The UFA-Palast am Zoo in the well-heeled Berlin suburb of Charlottenburg is Germany's largest and most extravagant cinema. The crowds outside are ecstatic. The film's stars, Otto Gebuhr, Albert Steinrück, Gertrud de Lalsky, Erna Morena, Charlotte Schultz and Lily, process up the red carpet, pose for the photographers and accept the praise of fans.[188] Champagne flows; a lavish party ensues with UFA's finest stars centre stage. Beyond, through the giant picture windows of the UFA-Palast am Zoo, Chinese lanterns with coloured bulbs sway in the trees of the Berlin Zoological Gardens.

Outside the theatre, in the cold and wet on Hardenbergstraße, an angry crowd has gathered to protest against von Cserépy's film believing that it endangers the fragile German Republic by glorifying a triumphant and vainglorious Prussian monarch. They fight with the police into the early hours of the following morning as the celebrations continue in the Palast Theater.

Throughout the city Lily's portrait stands out on billboards – from Moabit to Wedding; Neukölln to Alexanderplatz; along the Ku'damm and the Unter den Linden. As Lily rushes about the city calling at her agents, costumiers, hairdressers and beauticians in Schöneberg, Charlottenburg, Potsdam, and out as far as Köpenick,

188   It is worth noting that every one of the stars of *Fridericus Rex Parts I & II* that attended the premiere at the UFA-Palast am Zoo in January 1922 continued working in the Nazi-controlled cinema throughout the 1930s and war years. Lily's fellow silent stars in 1922 Charlotte Schultz and Erna Morena were both to appear in *Jud Süß*, the notorious 1940 Nazi propaganda film made at the behest of Joseph Goebbels, and considered one of the most anti-Semitic films of all time.

Lily on a silent film set

Lily constantly sees herself thirty feet high. Lily marries a rich Jewish businessman in Berlin.

INT. THE CRAMPED OFFICES OF THE INDRO-FILM
COMPANY – BUCHAREST – ROMANIA – MAY 1927

Another half dozen films follow in quick succession. Controversial as *Fridericus Rex* was it seems to have done nothing to harm Lily's career. At the height of her silent film fame Lily decides to star in and co-finance the largest film ever made in Romania to date – *Lia.* To please her, Lily's wealthy husband funds the entire production, forming Indro-Film, a company that will make only this one picture. Why she does this is not clear. To the best of my knowledge Lily has no links to Romania. Perhaps her husband does – I simply don't know. It is one of the aspects of her life I have yet to uncover. Anyway, off to Bucharest she goes.

Lily gathers together the cream of Romanian cinema – the country's leading director Jean Mihail, top screenwriter Mircea Filotti, and an all-star cast including the actors George Vraca, Aurel Costescu-Duca, and others, alongside Lily in the lead role.

Despite working with her friends and paying for the film, conditions in Romania are harsh and tempers fraught. Still, the film is a hit with the critics and a box office success in both Romania and Germany. *Lia* is perhaps Lily's answer to the politics of *Fridericus Rex,* the film she wants to make; the story she wishes to tell. *Lia* is a stirring tale of street-level poverty and the life of the poor contrasted with the opulence of Bucharest's elite and privileged salons.

INT. THE SPOTLIT STAGE OF THE ELITE BAR –
SHANGHAI'S INTERNATIONAL SETTLEMENT – THE
OPENING NIGHT OF LILY FLOHR IN CABARET – JULY 1941

Between songs Lily tells her audience how she returned home to Berlin after filming *Lia* in Bucharest. She went to work with the highly respected director Carl Boese and his new production company. The movie they made would be an important social commentary on Weimar Germany and also Lily's final movie, though she didn't know it at the time. It was a challenging time for her; a challenging time for Germany. The end of an era.

INT. THE CARL BOESE FILM STUDIOS – BERLIN – MARCH
1929

The set of Lily's final film, *Kinder der Strasse (Children of the Street)* is an adaptation of Heinrich Zille's classic cartoons of Berlin's 'common people' commissioned by the politically daring satirical newspaper *Simplicissimus.* The message here is a long way from *Fridericus Rex,* and more pertinent and immediate than *Lia* to a Berlin audience seeing their own lives and city on the screen.

Lily is working closely with director Boese, whose 1920 film *The Golem* had established him as an early master of German Expressionist cinema. *Kinder der Strasse* is socially concerned and overtly left wing. The film attracts an angry response from Germany's ascendant and increasingly vocal far right. Half a dozen years ago socialist protestors had demonstrated outside the UFA Palast am Zoo against *Fridericus Rex.* Now Lily watches National Socialists demonstrate against *Kinder der Strasse* in the same spot.

While filming *Kinder der Strasse* Lily visits the UFA Studios, now financially crippled due partly to the enormous cost of Fritz Lang's *Metropolis.* It is here that Lily witnesses a new invention – a sound stage – indeed Germany's first stage for talking pictures. Her fellow Viennese Josef von Sternberg (himself Jewish) is directing Marlene Dietrich, an actress approximately the same age as Lily but as yet largely unknown, in Germany's first 'talkie', *Der Blaue Engel (The Blue Angel)*.

Lily sees Dietrich performing *Falling in Love Again* for von Sternberg. She's impressed. Later she goes to a cinema and both sees and hears Dietrich on screen singing in *Der Blaue Engel*. Von Sternberg and Dietrich are symptomatic of the vast funds UFA are investing in the talkies; creating giant sound stages like the Tonkreuz at Babelsberg. Where once film sets were a noisy environment full of shouting, scraping and laughter, now they are like libraries, even whisperers are shushed, only the directors get to raise their voices and interrupt the work of the new microphones. Smaller independent producers either cannot afford sound or at an aesthetic level remain wedded to the silent cinematic art and are resistant to the change. For some reason, despite being just twenty-six, talented and famous, Lily 'retires' from the cinema.

Why? Was it really that Lily did not, or for some reason could not, see a future for herself in the German cinema once the talkies came? Was it a particularly strong Viennese accent? A little too Wienerisch? Perhaps a little too Yiddish-inflected, too slangy? Fine for cabaret perhaps, but not for the talkies? If so why not do what so many actors and actresses did in Berlin, as well as in Hollywood or London, and take elocution lessons?[189] Or did she share the opinion of many cineastes in late 1920s Germany (and elsewhere) that the talkies were debasing the finer art of the silent cinema? If so then she was moving against the tide of history. Just why Lily 'retired' from the movies remains unclear. Though no longer on

189 I am grateful to Sophie Fetthauer from the Institut für Historische Musikwissenschaft at Hamburg University who kindly corresponded with me about Lily and generously shared her knowledge. As a non-German speaker I asked the question about Lily's Vienna accent and talking pictures. Sophie did not think it a likely reason as, to her knowledge, there were other Austrian and Hungarian actors and actresses with accents, for example the opera and operetta soprano Gitta Alpár, who successfully made the transition from silent movies to the talkies.

screen she did continue to appear in cabaret around Berlin for the next few years.

INT. THE SPOTLIT STAGE OF THE ELITE BAR –
SHANGHAI'S INTERNATIONAL SETTLEMENT – THE
OPENING NIGHT OF LILY FLOHR IN CABARET – JULY 1941

Lily wants to entertain her audience but this show is about her life. And difficult moments must be faced and spoken of. Nineteen thirty-three: the Nazis. Under their exclusionist laws all Jews are banned from the cinema, the stage and the arts. Many great artists – directors, screenwriters, actors – Jewish and non-Jewish – leave Germany for Hollywood. For Lily too, Berlin after nearly fifteen years appears finished.

But Weimar is in full swing – this is the Berlin of Christopher Isherwood's *Berlin Stories*,[190] of cafés and cabarets, powerful gangsters, prostitutes and rent boys, and overnight black-market millionaires. Inflation is rising along with overt anti-Semitism and the Nazi Party. The Brown Shirts purge the streets; the Nazi's cultural commissars purge UFA and the Berlin studios. Cabaret becomes political. The Nuremberg Laws are enacted – to all intents and purposes Lily's career as an actress, singer and cabaret artist in Germany is over.

How does Lily's audience at the Elite Bar in Shanghai react to this? Fred Stern and Joe Klein, both of whom knew what Lily had experienced in Germany, ran the Elite. British, American, French ... any and all Shanghailanders could attend the Elite Bar. We can probably assume that many in attendance are cultured Germans, perhaps deeply ashamed of their country's descent into barbarism, intolerance and anti-Semitism.

---

190 Consisting of the two novellas, *Goodbye to Berlin* (1939) and *Mr Norris Changes Trains* (1935). Isherwood of course knew his Berlin cabarets and cafés well. Whether he ever knew Lily Flohr I do not know, but later, when he visited Shanghai in 1939 with W.H. Auden, he did recall meeting again a former Berlin cabaret manager Freddie Kaufmann who was living and working in Shanghai managing the Tower Restaurant and nightclub at the top of the Cathay Hotel. That meeting is briefly recalled in Auden and Isherwood's *Journey to a War* (London: Faber & Faber, 1939).

So Lily departed for Shanghai – to the one city on earth that took in the outcast, the stateless, those without papers, émigrés, refugees. Berlin's loss; Shanghai's gain. Those rejected and exiled came to this great and modern city of China – among them more than 30,000 stateless Jews fleeing Nazi persecution.[191]

EXT. THE ROOF GARDEN OF THE BROADWAY THEATRE – WAYSIDE ROAD – SHANGHAI – JUNE 1939

Lily Flohr's 'Shanghai Week' on the roof garden of the Broadway Theatre in June 1939 is supported by an opera singer and a tap dancer.[192] The Broadway, in the heart of what is rapidly becoming a Jewish ghetto in the Tilanqiao district of Hongkew, is a theatre that also acts as a cinema. They put on special Purim matinees for their largely Jewish patrons, as well as a regular programme of Jewish entertainers. Lily Flohr is the highlight of their year by a long, long way.

Lily gets her costumes from Salon Fufi, just down the street and run by another German Jewish refugee. After the show everyone heads to the Mascot restaurant nearby for dinner and drinks, where it's like old times again. The Mascot is run by three more German Jewish refugees – the 'Three H's': Heinz, Henry and Hermann. In Shanghai's hot and humid late June the Three H's open the windows out onto the street and hang out their new sign: *'Exquisite Kueche; Kalte Platten; Civile Preise!'*

Lily is carving out a career for herself in the vibrant cabarets and nightclubs of Shanghai's International Settlement. She is a long way from home, but not completely without friends. Many Austrians and Germans live in Shanghai and know her well. The Paris Cinema on the Avenue Joffre in the French Concession shows second-run and old German movies – *Fridericus Rex, Kinder der Strasse,* all have their loyal Shanghai fans. There are several Austrian

191   It is not entirely clear to me when Lily and her husband arrived in Shanghai; if indeed he accompanied her – I have no record of him in Shanghai. But then I have no record of them separating or divorcing either. Lily ceases to appear in the German press around 1934. However, she doesn't really appear in the Shanghai press until 1939. The years between remain a mystery to me.

192   It was a Shanghai curiosity that the Broadway Theatre was on Wayside Road and the Wayside Theatre was on Broadway.

and German Jews in the entertainment business. Viennese Joe Farren runs chorus lines and upmarket dancehalls at the Paramount and the Canidrome Ballroom; Sol Greenberg runs the Casanova; the Romanian Jewish Wiengarten Brothers run the Red Rose Cabaret; Sam Levy and Girgee Moalem manage the Venus Café; fellow Berlin émigré Freddy Kaufmann is the manager of the Tower nightclub at the top of the Cathay Hotel while Al Israel, his brother-in-law 'Demon' Hyde, and his wife Bertha run the Del Monte club out west by Siccawei. Fred Stern and Joe Klein at the Elite Bar booked her as soon as she arrived in town. Sometimes it feels like Shanghai's cabaret and nightclub business is almost entirely composed of German, Austrian and Romanian Jews.

Lily has also seen what needed to be done to be truly successful in Shanghai – she needed to be able to perform in English, the *lingua franca* of the Shanghailanders. Lily had thought Berlin an international city, but Shanghai audiences were seemingly comprised of every European nation, the United States, Japan and, of course, those modern and cultured international Shanghainese Chinese too.

So many talented Jewish artists in Shanghai – the violinist Alfred Wittenberg, the musicians Otto and Walter Joachim whose band plays the upmarket DD's Café on the Avenue Joffre, the singers Rose Albach-Gerstel and Monica Herenfeld, the comedian Herbert Zernick. Lily is especially good friends with Zernick's sometime partner Gerhard Gottschalk who runs the Tabarin Cabaret on Broadway. Gerhard is a comedian with a slender frame and features too big for his face – thick lips, jug ears. The more serious he looked the more the crowd roared. With Gerhard, Lily performed comedy numbers on stage once again at his supper club.

INT. THE SPOTLIT STAGE OF THE ELITE BAR –
SHANGHAI'S INTERNATIONAL SETTLEMENT – THE
OPENING NIGHT OF LILY FLOHR IN CABARET – JULY 1941

Lily is applauded. The crowd demand an encore; flowers are thrown onto the stage. Lily finally feels that she has found a new home and launched a new career. But things are about to change once again. . . .

The Japanese attack on Pearl Harbor is announced on the radio. The next day Japanese troops move into the International Settlement. Allied nationals are interned, the stateless Jews forced to live in a Japanese-managed 'Zone of Safety', the Hongkew ghetto. Shanghai is an occupied city, Japanese tanks and soldiers roam the European boulevards of the International Settlement and Frenchtown. Those who can secure berths on evacuation ships and leave town. The Japanese soon begin to intern nationals of the Allied nations. Shanghai is now a city where Lily must survive, once again, largely without work.

EXT. THE TEEMING STREETS OF THE HONGKEW JEWISH
GHETTO – SHANGHAI – JUNE 1942

Where Lily is living is unknown – it seems most likely that it is outside the Hongkew ghetto, the 'Restricted Sector for Stateless Refugees', but I cannot be sure of this. Not all Jews are required to live there; those who have passports from France, Portugal or Spain for instance (and I do not know what nationality Lily is claiming in 1942) opted to live in the relative freedom of the French Concession under the control of the Vichy administration, loyal to the puppet collaborationist French leader Marshal Pétain. Frenchtown has enacted some of Vichy's anti-Semitic legislation regarding Jews who are not now allowed to practise law or teach. But they are not rounding up Jews or forcing them into the Hongkew ghetto. Lily though is determined to play her part in opposing the Nazis.

She is involved in fund-raisers to help ease the worst hardships of the ghetto, to aid those Jews who turned up with no money or assets, whose skills are of little practical use in China, are too old, too young, too distraught and traumatised to look after themselves. With Gerhard Gottschalk she puts on benefit concerts for the Ward Road Hospital. Their comedic clowning is a ray of light at a dark time for many in the ghetto.

There is a performance of *Die Masken Fallen (The Mask is Fallen)*, an original opera about the lives of the Jewish refugees in Shanghai by two ghetto residents, Hans Schubert and Mark Siegelberg. Siegelberg has himself recently escaped from the Buchenwald

Shanghai ECHO

上海回論日報

Verwaltung		Ist taeglich ab 6 Uhr morgens im Strassenhandel erhaeltlich.
284/85		
Kwenming Road		Sonntag, den 5. Mai, erscheint unsere Sondernummer "7 Jahre Emigrantenpresse"
Tel. 50581		

TAEGL. NACHRICHTENBLATT · DAILY NEWSPAPER

DIE MASKEN FALLEN
von Mark Siegelberg und Hans Schubert.

Dr. Paul Brach, Journalist	Robert Weiss-Cyla	Kirsky	Fraunhofer	Fritz Heller
Christine, seine Frau	Lily Flohr	1. Kriminalbeamter	Lehmann	Gerhard Gottschalk
Susi, beider Kind	Klein Olly Gutstadt	2. Kriminalbeamter	Elsa	Jenny Rausnitz
Josef Brach, Paul's Vater	Victor Flamm-Geldern	Blumenreich	Stenotypistin	Marion Lissner
Dr. Forstner	Herbert Zernik	Heller	Kellner	Max Guenther
Dr. Huber	Erwin Frieser	Woegerer	Chauffeur	Robert Boer
Rokalsky, Journalist	Harsch Friedmann	Nigl	Die Stimme des Ungasistes Hitler	Fred Lang

Im 4. Bild singt Max Warschauer: „Al Tashlichenu" von Lewandowski

Regie: Robert Weiss-Cyla	Buehnenbild: Walter Kornitzer	Technische Leitung: Hans Cassel
Beleuchtung: Rosenbaum	Friseur: Fessler	Verstaerkungsanlage: Aeriale, Hahn

Zwischen dem 3. und 4. Bild ist eine Pause von 20 Minuten.

Die Moebel wurden in liebenswuerdiger Weise von der Firma "Old and New Arts",
20 Muirhead Road, zur Verfuegung gestellt.

ATELIER KOLM & H. KOHN	**" D E L I K A T "**
1074 BUBBLING WELL ROAD	Das fuehrende Restaurant in Hongkew
PHONE 62325	23, Chusan Road
FIRST CLASS JEWELLERY	I a Wiener Kueche · Hausgemachte Mehlspeisen
SELECTED DESSINS	

Announcing 'Die Masken Fallen'

Concentration Camp and somehow managed to make it to Shanghai. Lily plays the female lead – Christine. This is a role not without risk. The story line involves mixed marriages in China and contains direct criticism of National Socialism. The German Consulate in Shanghai has done all it can to stop performances, telling the organisers, and Paul Komor of the Jewish Émigré Committee in Shanghai, that if performances continue reprisals will be taken against the Jewish community left in Nazi-controlled Europe. The performances continue despite the threats.[193] Lily also appears in other shows including Bertolt Brecht's *The Threepenny Opera* as Polly Peachum. All have overt anti-Nazi lines and themes. The Nazis at the German Consulate led by the former 'Butcher of Warsaw', Gestapo boss Josef Meisinger, again threaten reprisals against the Jews in both Europe and Shanghai. But the performances continue.

EXT. AN AERIAL VIEW OF THE CITY OF SHANGHAI –
BOMBERS BEARING THE STARS OF THE USAAF CROSS THE

---

193 'Gestapo Threat Stops Jewish Play', *China Weekly Review*, November 28, 1940.

SKY – TO THE EAST OF THE SETTLEMENT PLUMES OF
BLACK SMOKE RISE WHERE BOMBS HAVE FALLEN – JULY 1945

Shanghai is dangerous as the Japanese defeat edges closer. In July American bombers appear in the sky. Two hundred and sixty-three bombs fall on Shanghai, mainly on the docks and wharfs of Pootung and Yangtszepoo, near to the ghetto. The ghetto is finally liberated on September 3rd. A ragged Nationalist Chinese army finally marches back into the city to be met by cheering crowds. With the US Army Air Forces' help, the liberation of the city from the Japanese is achieved. One ordeal is over, though with the war ended, a new one begins: a civil war for China's soul – where and what now for Lily?

INT. THE STAGE OF THE EASTERN THEATRE – JANUARY 1946

The war is over, the ghetto's restrictions lifted, Shanghai's stateless Jews await decisions on their emigration. The National Jewish Welfare Board and the new United Nations Relief and Rehabilitation Administration do what they can but the wheels of bureaucracy turn slowly. Still, visas and permissions do come through eventually; new homes are found. People begin leaving . . . for Australia, for the USA, for Canada, for Brazil. . . .

The Jewish Welfare Board organises one last, great celebration of Jewish culture in Shanghai – *The All Star Parade*. It is held at the Eastern Theatre on Muirhead Road, where Lily has performed at Yiddish culture nights and appeared in productions of Brecht singing songs by Kurt Weill. Close by are many Jewish businesses – Lily has her make up and nails done at Senorita Warshawski in her beauty parlour on the street; her coiffure is attended to by the hair stylists at the Salon Mosberg next door. Then Lily walks out to centre stage and to rapturous applause as top of the bill for this last fling of Jewish culture in Shanghai.

EXT. A TYPICAL SUBURBAN STREET – PEACE AND CALM –
SYDNEY – AUSTRALIA – THE 1950s

Shanghai falls to the communists in June 1949 and the remaining Jewish refugees of Shanghai scatter to the four winds. An era ends. Some time before this it seems Lily managed to secure a passport to a new life. I think she was still in Shanghai in 1948 as Gerhard Gottschalk, also still in Shanghai, thanks her in a card I have seen.

Lily made it to Australia – but of this process, this decision, this journey I know nothing. Many Shanghai Jewish refugees did go to Australia and most, as it appears Lily did, headed to Sydney. I have so many questions I have not been able to answer. Was she alone in Australia? Did she continue her career somehow? She would have been in her early fifties when she arrived in Sydney. Did Lily ever have children, did she stay married, divorce, marry again?

An Australian friend who knows of my interest in Lily sends me a photograph of a plaque from the Northern Suburbs Memorial Gardens, a crematorium in the Sydney suburb of North Ryde. It simply states:

Lily Flohr
Died 7th July 1978
Aged 84 Years

Is it my Lily Flohr? I think so but I can't be sure.

Lily is hard to access now. Her films are difficult to source. They're never really shown on TV or available on DVD. To my knowledge there haven't been any retrospectives of her work. Apart from one or two people working in German film archives or academic institutions I've never met anyone who has ever heard of Lily Flohr. But she was a star on the Vienna stage; she did make approximately twenty silent movies in Berlin and, in July 1941 she was flattered to welcome packed houses to her one-woman cabaret at the Elite Bar on the corner of Medhurst Road and the Bubbling Well Road in the International Settlement of Shanghai.

Murder in the Shanghai Trenches:
Eliza Shapera & Ameer Buchs (1907)

Hongkew Police Station

*'If a drunken man or licentious European reprobate
enters these quarters, the chances are ten to one
against him ever coming out.'*

Scott Road, Shanghai International Settlement

At 7.45 PM on Wednesday September 18th, 1907, a dishevelled young woman of apparently Russian or East European origin burst into Hongkew Police Station on Woosung Road and reported the murdered body of a white woman at No. 56 Scott Road. Sergeant John O'Toole grabbed PC Cornelius Hamilton and the two Shanghai Municipal Policemen set out to the address leaving the distraught woman under guard at the station.

When O'Toole and Hamilton reached Scott Road they found a large crowd gathered outside No. 56, including one Indian man, apparently drunk, shouting and screaming in the middle of the road. They ignored him and headed immediately inside the narrow detached house and made their way upstairs to the front-facing bedroom looking down onto the crowd below.

Sergeant O'Toole was just shy of thirty and had left Ireland and the Royal Irish Constabulary to join the Shanghai Municipal Police in 1900. Since arriving in the International Settlement, he had seen his share of dead bodies among the driftwood of humanity that somehow made its way to the great foreign-controlled centre of commerce for eastern China and the Yangtze Delta. For PC Hamilton, barely out of his teens and arrived in Shanghai from rural County Limerick just months before, this was his first murder.

Before them, on the room's only bed was the body of a dead European woman, sprawled across the mattress and with a pillow partly covering her face. O'Toole and Hamilton then went out into the corridor to check the back bedroom. Nobody was in that room, the window was ajar but all appeared to be in order. They heard a noise behind them, returned and found the drunk and ranting Indian man from downstairs had entered the house and come upstairs. He had removed the pillow from the victim's face. He had started to turn the body over when the policemen grabbed him. PC

Hamilton escorted the man off the premises and then detained him outside.

O'Toole felt for a pulse and found nothing. The woman was wearing a tattered nightdress and white stockings loosely tied with ribbons. The charge room at Hongkew Station had contacted the senior detective on duty and O'Toole was to secure the crime scene, touch nothing, and await the arrival of the designated investigating officer.

Detective-Sergeant Thomas Idwal Vaughan, a stocky Welshman, had joined the Shanghai Police in 1900 in the same intake as O'Toole, but had since made detective. He arrived at 8 PM and found a large crowd of excited and argumentative European women in the hallway of the building shouting in a language that he believed to be Russian. He called up to O'Toole, told him to come downstairs and clear them out of the house while he inspected the body.

Vaughan noted that the body was cold and lying on its left side. It smelt of putrefaction, which indicated the woman had been dead some time. The autumn weather in Shanghai was still mild, the room's window only slightly ajar and the room stuffy, which could have accelerated the decay. Her legs were bent at the knees, and just above the ankles, were tied tightly together with a towel. Around her neck was another towel, tied in a reef knot, and a twisted curtain that had clearly been used to strangle her. There was heavy bruising around her neck. Her arms appeared to have been forcibly pulled back behind her as if they had been held there as she was strangled. There were bloodstains on the curtain and towel, which had been left slack after her asphyxiation. The woman's face was black and swollen and she had heavy bruising around her left eye and further bruising under her right eye. Her false teeth had fallen out and were lying next to her on the mattress. The dental plate was broken. Next to the bed were three more bloodstained towels. The sheet covering the mattress was also bloodstained as were a pillow by her head and a beige shawl lying nearby.

Apart from the murdered woman, the bedroom and the other upstairs bedroom appeared to be untouched. Vaughan went downstairs to investigate the rest of the house. He found the downstairs back room, the house's living room, ransacked. A large travelling trunk, seemingly filled with clothing had been upturned and emptied and the clothes strewn about the room. A tray from inside the trunk had been removed and was lying on a small bed in the corner. Clearly the entire room had been searched and all the cupboard drawers and several boxes in the room opened and the contents thrown out. However, none of the heavier furniture had been moved, no crockery or glass was smashed and Vaughan concluded that while the ransacking had been thorough it had been conducted quietly.

Completing his preliminary examination Vaughan took hold of the corpse and lifted it up to check if there was anything underneath. He'd found no weapon that could have made the bruising around the woman's eyes. As he lifted the corpse he saw something drop onto the bed from inside the stocking – a handkerchief with one corner knotted. He picked it up and unfolded it to find two sovereigns, two American five-dollar gold pieces, a Korean fifty-cent coin and a small gold locket and chain.

The Shanghai Trenches

To the Shanghai Municipal Police, a call to Scott Road invariably meant two things – prostitution usually and trouble always. In 1907 Scott Road was the most notorious street in Shanghai. At its height the strip was home to an estimated 300 brothels, mostly small houses inhabited by two, or a few more, working prostitutes. Lanes ran in-between and behind the houses allowing both punters and girls to come and go in relative anonymity and making it virtually impossible for the police to pursue anyone through the alleyways and houses of the densely packed rookery.

In 1907, Chinese, Japanese and Korean women worked alongside, and in competition with, a rising number of European women, mostly from Eastern Europe, and many of them trafficked. Among them Jewish women were prominent, having being brought into Shanghai, via pimps and *souteneurs* working out of London and Marseille. Most of these women were originally from Odessa, Bessarabia, Moldo-Wallachia, Romania or other far-flung, and largely impoverished, regions of the Russian and Austro-Hungarian Empires. Many arrived via ships from Britain and also began to appear in the port cities of the British Empire such as Bombay, Singapore and Hong Kong. Others came via Marseille and popped up in Saigon, throughout French Indo-China and Shanghai. Three events had greatly increased the number of white prostitutes arriving in Shanghai in 1907 – the faster route to the Far East from Europe courtesy of the Suez Canal; the horrific anti-Semitic pogroms that flared up throughout Bessarabia and the Russian Empire in the early years of the century; and the 1906 earthquake in San Francisco, which saw an influx of working girls from the United States arrive in the Settlement.

Shanghai's main centres of foreign prostitution divided along two very different streets. In the heart of the Settlement, several blocks back from the bustling Bund waterfront, was Kiangse Road, home to several high-class foreign bordellos run by American madams and stocked with American (and occasionally French and British) girls. The so-called 'Line' was expensive and relatively exclusive with an all-white clientele and centred on the most notorious bordello of all, (former San Francisco and Yokohama madam) Gracie Gale's No. 52. However, most of the trafficked women from eastern Europe, and those Chinese prostitutes willing to service foreign men, were concentrated in the poorer districts to the north of the Soochow Creek, just outside the Settlement's full authority and on Scott Road – known as the 'Trenches'. In 1910 one visitor to the Trenches recorded that, 'if a drunken man or licentious European reprobate enters these quarters, the chances are ten to one against him ever coming out.'

Scott Road ran north from the junction of Szechuan Road and Dixwell Road along the side of Hongkew Park. The Hongkew docks and wharves were not far away, making the area convenient for visiting sailors while the Settlement's most easterly district, Yangtsepoo, with more docks, was also close by. Though the Municipal Police would attend murders and other crime scenes in the area, as Scott Road was technically outside the Settlement's borders, they did not subject the road's bars, opium dens and brothels to the same regulations as those within the Settlement.

They had tried to keep order – in 1906 a number of gambling sheds near Scott Road were destroyed but by the end of the year new sheds had been erected and gambling was in full swing again. It was a badlands, a virtual no man's land legally and little more than a slum. By 1907 the tenement houses and lanes along Scott Road had become home to much of Shanghai's underworld, a multiracial cluster of criminality on the margins of the city, men and women on the run, drug pushers and gun runners, gamblers, armed-robbery gangs, pimps and prostitutes.

Immediately Detective-Sergeant Vaughan entered the bedroom at No. 56 he had, despite the facial swelling and injuries, recognised the dead woman as Eliza Shapera, a Russian Jew who'd lived on Scott Road for some time.

Scott Road was well known to the Hongkew police; they knew Eliza Shapera too, as a woman involved in the prostitution business of the Trenches. When Vaughan entered Scott Road he was entering a netherworld maze where the Municipal Police's writ ran thin and the local population was antagonistic to any sort of authority. He had a pretty good idea what sordid worlds the investigation of Eliza Shapera's murder would open up and was also aware that public co-operation in the Trenches, an area with its own alternative codes and loyalties, would be zero.

'I have seen two women fight with the dead woman.'

Sergeant O'Toole had brought the woman who had come to the Hongkew Station to report the murder to the front lower room ready for Vaughan to question. The detective, coming in from having surveyed the ransacking in the living room, recognised the young woman as Minna Nedal. He didn't know where she was from exactly but did know from previous arrests for prostitution that she was a subject of the Austro-Hungarian Empire and also Jewish. He began to question her. Nedal claimed she'd been living at No. 58 Scott Road with Eliza Shapera for over a year, that Shapera was married though her husband had left Shanghai some time ago and not returned. She had no idea when he was due back, if ever. Nedal claimed to have gone to Yangtsepoo on Monday evening to the house of some friends there to celebrate the impending Rosh Hashanah holiday, the Jewish New Year. She had stayed for two nights, returning to Scott Road at 7.30 PM that evening. She had found the front door locked and didn't have her own key.

She'd then gone to No. 53 Scott Road, a friend's house. With the Chinese houseboy from there she'd returned to Eliza's and tried the back entrance on the alleyway that ran behind the buildings. She entered the house and found that the living room, which she also claimed was her bedroom, had been ransacked. She had gone upstairs and found Eliza dead in her bedroom. She had then rushed straight to Hongkew Station, getting there a quarter of an hour later at 7.45 PM and told Sergeant O'Toole of the murder. Vaughan now had a timeline for the killing, an infuriatingly long one. Eliza could have been killed anytime between Monday night, when Nedal left for Yangtsepoo, or 7.30 PM Wednesday evening when she returned.

As he was questioning Nedal, Vaughan heard a scuffle in the corridor outside and the Indian man burst in again, with Constable Hamilton attempting to restrain him. With Hamilton holding him back the Indian man shouted at Vaughan, 'I have seen two women fight with the dead woman.' The Indian gestured at Nedal. Vaughan asked the man to calm down and explain exactly what he had seen but the man simply pointed at Nedal again, insisting he had seen her fighting with the dead woman. Vaughan told him to leave the house and wait outside. The Indian man left and then promptly disappeared into the crowd. With the large mob still milling around on the street, and no other officers or constables at the scene except O'Toole and Hamilton, Vaughan could do nothing to follow the man.

Vaughan instructed O'Toole to clear the street and start looking for any witnesses and Hamilton to secure the house and not let anyone else enter.

The Protocols of Shanghai

Extraterritoriality: Every Shanghai policeman's complication. Within the Shanghai International Settlement foreigners were not subject to Chinese laws and Chinese punishments, but only to their own judges, courts and penalties. The British, French, Germans, Americans and others had all established their own judicial systems to deal with their wayward citizens and subjects. A further judicial layer was the so-called Mixed Court, established to try cases involving Chinese residing in the Settlement or cases where the defendant was of questionable nationality. In the Mixed Court the Chinese magistrate was 'assisted', in turn, by foreigners – American, British, and German. The system was messy, inconsistent and full of loopholes. If an American murdered a German and the only witnesses were British and French then the case would go before the American court. However, the American court could not compel the British or French witnesses to appear. The Americans could go to the court of the witnesses' nationality and request that court to take evidence for the witness, but this was cumbersome. In Shanghai's melting pot this convoluted system rendered an efficient and effective court system virtually impossible.

As soon as he had recognised Eliza Shapera and Minna Nedal Vaughan knew he had a case that would probably be clear in its motives – robbery-murder by a client of Shapera's, or perhaps a fight over money between the two prostitutes. But he also knew he had to work within the rules of extraterritoriality that governed the Shanghai Settlement. From Scott Road Vaughan went straight to the Russian Consulate, a couple of miles away towards the centre of Shanghai where the Soochow Creek flowed into the Whangpoo River. The imposing consulate sat on the northern, Hongkew, side of the creek opposite the Astor House Hotel. Shapera was a Russian subject and so protocol determined that the Consulate be informed.

At that time of night the consul-general was at home but Vaughan found the vice-consul, Leonid Brodiansky on duty. The Russian Consulate's doctor, who had the right to view the body *in situ*, was away from Shanghai on business but Brodiansky authorised a Dr Voelkers to examine the body on the consulate's behalf. Voelkers accompanied Vaughan back to Scott Road, and examined Eliza Shapera, pointing out several recent scratch marks on her shoulders Vaughan had not noticed before. The detective-sergeant then called the municipal mortuary and an ambulance was despatched. Eliza Shapera was taken to the Shanghai Municipal Morgue at 9.45 PM.

Before leaving for the night Vaughan placed Minna Nedal under caution and had her transferred to Hongkew Police Station for the night, informing the Austro-Hungarian Consulate of her detention.

The 'Mohammedan'

On Thursday morning Vaughan arrived at Hongkew Police Station to be met by Detective-Inspector John McDowell who would now be the ranking officer on the Eliza Shapera murder investigation. McDowell had joined the force in 1898 and was a highly experienced detective working out of Hongkew Station. McDowell told Vaughan to interview Nedal again while he went to find the excited Indian from the night before. The police files referred to him as a 'Mohammedan'. McDowell knew the Trenches well and began a house-to-house inquiry. Just two doors down, at No. 58, he found a Chinese woman, Lien Yow, living in the upper bedroom. She knew exactly who the Detective-Inspector was looking for.

McDowell knew a working girl when he saw one and clearly to him Lien Yow was one of Scott Road's many Chinese prostitutes who serviced the sailors and other Europeans who frequented the strip. The idea of a young Chinese woman, who wasn't a prostitute, living alone on Scott Road in 1907 was simply unheard of. She claimed to have known the Indian, whose name she told McDowell was Ameer Buchs, for about one month and that he sometimes stayed with her overnight. McDowell guessed their relationship to be one of pimp and prostitute. Lien Yow had no idea where Buchs was at the moment and didn't know when, or if, he would return. She was aware of the murder two doors down, claiming to know Shapera and Nedal only slightly.

Lien Yow described Buchs as an Indian who drank a lot and always wore straw-soled slippers, loose trousers and Chinese-style jackets – the same clothes he had been wearing when he'd burst in on Vaughan and Nedal the evening before. She claimed that on the

Monday previously Buchs had taken her for a carriage drive to a dancehall in Siccawei on the other side of Shanghai, across the Settlement and then further out to the south-west of the city's French Concession. They had returned at 1 AM on Tuesday morning; Buchs was drunk and went straight to sleep. On Tuesday Buchs had left the house but Lien Yow did not know when as she had been asleep. He had returned at 8.30 PM and stayed the night with her. On Wednesday morning he had left the house at 8 AM and not returned till 7 PM. He had sat with Lien Yow drinking beer and then, hearing shouting out on the street, had left the house returning an hour later saying that the Russian woman at No. 56 had been murdered. She asked him for details; he didn't know how she had died but did say that the body smelt. He told her 'not to meddle in the affair and mind her own business.' He then stayed in the house for the rest of the evening drinking.

McDowell left No. 58 to continue his search. He didn't have long to wait. On Scott Road it was now 7.30 PM and dark with both working girls and the flotsam and jetsam of the Trenches emerging for their night's business. McDowell headed along the strip and found Buchs, seemingly drunk and excitable, walking towards him wearing what appeared to be pyjama trousers and a Chinese jacket with black straw slippers. McDowell arrested him. Buchs protested, struggled and told McDowell, 'I savee who killed this woman. I have see two women beat her.'

Buchs claimed to have returned from his trip to Siccawei with Lien Yow at 1 AM Tuesday morning and heard Minna Nedal, another woman and Eliza Shapera shouting and fighting inside No. 56. He went and banged on the door but the women refused to open it. He broke the glass in the front-door window and swore at them in Russian asking them what they were arguing about. He could see one of the women holding Shapera's hair, forcing her head down, while the other woman, Nedal, hit her. McDowell escorted Buchs back to No. 58 and Lien Yow's room, which he then searched finding whisky and beer that belonged to the Indian.

McDowell then brought Buchs into Hongkew Police Station and took his full statement. Despite Buchs being drunk, somewhat unstable and obviously a pimp, nevertheless McDowell believed his story. If Buchs had seen Minna Nedal at No. 58 early on Tuesday morning then her alibi of being at a Rosh Hashanah party in Yangtsepoo was questionable to say the least. By now it was early Friday morning and McDowell decided to release Buchs. He then formally arrested Minna Nedal and arranged for her to be brought before the Austro-Hungarian Consular Court at a special session on Saturday morning.

It had been a long day. Despite exhaustive house-to-house enquiries by O'Toole and Hamilton along Scott Road nobody was admitting to hearing or seeing anything. Although No. 56 was a narrow house with the adjoining residences having upstairs front windows not more than ten feet from the open window of the bedroom in which Shapera had been murdered, nobody at either No. 55 or No. 57, both known brothels and homes to working prostitutes, admitted to having heard anything, or having seen Shapera enter or leave the house on Wednesday.

Detective-Sergeant Vaughan had been busy too. He'd been canvassing known associates of Eliza Shapera along Scott Road all day. Several Russian women had told him that they thought Shapera always kept around $200 in the house and had recently shown them a bank passbook with $900 in savings recorded. Vaughan returned to No. 56 and searched the house again. He found the passbook but there was no sign of any money on the premises at all.

Before Herr Kobr

The Austro-Hungarian Consular Court convened Saturday morning, presided over by Vice-Consul Miloslav Kobr. Herr Kobr conducted a preliminary hearing *in camera* with both McDowell and Vaughan in attendance. Ameer Buchs's claims against Nedal were heard though she vehemently denied being in the house on either Tuesday or Wednesday until she returned home and found Eliza's body. She claimed never to have fought with Eliza, nor to know who the other woman was whom Buchs claimed was pulling Shapera's hair while Nedal had supposedly hit her. However, she was unable to produce any of her 'friends' in Yangtsepoo with whom she had supposedly been enjoying the Rosh Hashanah party and refused to reveal the address. The hearing lasted all morning and went on into the afternoon with Nedal continually protesting her innocence. At the end of the day she was remanded back into the custody of Hongkew Police Station. But there were now doubts about Buchs's claim and, as he left the court to return to Scott Road, McDowell arrested him.

McDowell may have been inclined to believe Buchs's story, despite recognising the man as a 'loafer', a pimp and a drunk, but nobody else on Scott Road had even hinted that they'd heard a fight in No. 56 in the early hours of Tuesday morning, or seen Buchs in the street outside. Several claimed the glass in the door had been smashed for several months and not repaired.

Police records showed that Buchs had become known to the police a couple of years previously as a witness to a murder in the Pootung district of Shanghai, the area of docks, wharves and godowns across the Whangpoo River opposite the Bund. His testimony then had ultimately proved unreliable. Over the following week McDowell and Vaughan began to investigate Buchs and his claims more closely.

By the end of September they had enough evidence against Buchs to bring him to court – this time His Majesty's Police Court in Shanghai, as Buchs was under British jurisdiction being an Indian subject. While the case against Buchs was being prepared another lead came to light, one that with Buchs in custody and new information appearing meant Herr Kobr at the Austro-Hungarian Consular Court ordered the release of Minna Nedal.

Loafers

Detective-Sergeant Maurice Fitzgibbon had been recruited to the Shanghai Municipal Police from his home in Limerick, Ireland in 1900. He worked out of Hongkew Station and was assigned to the Eliza Shapera murder case. While McDowell and Vaughan had concentrated on Nedal and Buchs, Fitzgibbon had arrested two indigent Chinese men – Lee San-foh and Sung Ling-ling. Both were described as 'loafers' in the records. They had formerly been house servants on Scott Road but had been discharged by their employers and remained hanging around the district. Fitzgibbon had heard that the men had been seen in the vicinity of No. 56 on Wednesday. His sources told him the two unemployed men had been seen in the notorious gambling sheds near Scott Road with money to bet.

In any robbery of European households in Shanghai, Chinese servants and former servants were immediately suspected. The captain-superintendent of the SMP, Clarence Bruce, a former commandant of the British Army's Weihaiwei Regiment in Northern China, had only been appointed the force's boss in 1907 but felt confident enough to write in his first annual report to the Shanghai Municipal Council that in the 'majority of cases minor robberies can usually be traced either to servants or ex-servants'. Going so far as to murder a householder was extreme, but not unknown. Eliza Shapera was unusual among Europeans in Shanghai, even the poor and criminal, in not having any domestic servants.

However, since the start of the investigation McDowell had worked on the assumption that, if Shapera was not killed by Nedal and her mystery accomplice as claimed by Buchs, then the killer or killers must have entered No. 56 by the back door. McDowell and Vaughan had returned to Scott Road and inspected the small passageway that ran behind Nos. 56, 57 and 58 and the passages than ran between the detached houses. In the yards of the houses were the building's privies and cookhouses. The side passage between Nos. 57 and 58 was open and led from the street to the rear passageway behind the house, which allowed access to both Nos. 56 and 57. However, the rear passage between Nos. 57 and 58 had a five-foot-high wall separating the properties. Conveniently though, leaning against this wall was a bamboo ladder making it easy to climb from No. 58 over the wall and onto the cookhouse roof of No. 57, jump down and then enter No. 56 from the rear passage. Tiles on the cookhouse roof of No. 57 were broken indicating someone had recently entered the backyard of the house this way and the policemen found freshly broken tile fragments scattered in the passage linking No. 57 to No. 56. Buchs could have accessed the house from No. 58, killed Shapera and then returned. It was a neat theory but the problem was, given the easy access to the rear of No. 58 from Scott Road, so could anyone else.

Fitzgibbon arrested both Lee and Sung and brought them before the Mixed Court on Saturday 28th September with Magistrate Pao Yi and the German Assessor Dr Hans Schirmer sitting. The judge and assessor believed the men had a case to answer and both were remanded into custody while further enquiries were made. It seemed the murder of Eliza Shapera could be as simple as a robbery gone wrong.

Means, Motive, Opportunity

Fitzgibbon's further enquiries went nowhere but McDowell and Vaughan had been busy with Buchs and now believed that they could prove he had the means, motive and opportunity to murder Eliza Shapera. Buchs was living at No. 58 and so could access the rear of No. 56 without being seen. He knew Shapera, could watch the house and know when she was alone – the means. He had probably heard the same gossip Vaughan had about the $200 she kept about the place. McDowell had visited a local Chinese general store and discovered that earlier in the month Buchs had signed chits (promises to pay) for $102.80. The shop assistant he questioned, Kwang Ling, hadn't been authorised to extend credit to Buchs as his boss thought the Indian unreliable, but he had done so anyway. Buchs owed the money and had not been able to settle the bill – the motive.

And Buchs had opportunity. Asked about his whereabouts on the Wednesday Shapera's body was discovered, Buchs claimed that he had gone to an Indian food store in the French Concession to collect food he had ordered on Tuesday evening. He claimed to have arrived there at 1 PM and remained for six hours meaning he would have returned home to Lien Yow's about 7 PM, as she had stated. However, the Indian shopkeeper told Vaughan that Buchs had left at 4 PM. This left the hours between 8 AM and 1 PM and 4 PM and 7 PM on Wednesday unaccounted for.

Buchs claimed he had gone to the house of some fellow Indians on Hongkew's Sawgin Road for a bath, a winding road that ran alongside the fetid and stinking Sawgin Creek. McDowell and Vaughan visited the house on the street that was well known to them as housing generally undesirable and indigent Chinese and foreigners – just a few months before, a major gang of Chinese armed robbers had been arrested holed up in a house on Sawgin Road. The Indians at the house denied that Buchs had come there for a bath, indeed they denied ever knowing him. His alibi was shot through with holes he couldn't explain.

Means, motive, opportunity. McDowell prepared the prosecution case for Rex v. Buchs at the HM Police Court before Police Magistrate J.C.E. Douglas. The British Police Court was part of the British Supreme Court for China and Korea. It dealt with minor criminal cases and committal hearings involving British subjects.

Infuriatingly, while Douglas decided there was indeed a case to answer and agreed to a committal hearing, the court's appointed doctor felt Buchs should go to a hospital first for psychiatric tests to assess his worthiness to be tried. The case was postponed for a week.

Monday 21st October, 1907 – Rex v. Ameer Buchs

Buchs was declared fit to attend his committal hearing to decide if he should be put on trial for murder before a jury in HM Supreme Court. John Charles Edward Douglas was a fearsome magistrate to come before. Barely in his thirties, he was the son of a Royal Navy admiral, had been educated at Radley School and Merton College, Oxford and had spent several years presiding over the Shanghai court.

Formalities first. The British Court needed formally to know that the Russians had been made aware of the death of one of their own. They had, and they had ordered no inquest but left it in the hands of the SMP. Douglas decreed that Buchs's testimony before the Austro-Hungarian Court would not be accepted as evidence in the British Court: 'A statement made by a man in a criminal action in another Court was not evidence against when tried by HM Supreme Court'.

Detective-Sergeant Vaughan was sworn in and retold his story of arriving at the crime scene and examining the body, and of Buchs's outburst accusing Minna Nedal, that the Minna Nedal case had gone nowhere and neither had the case against Lee and Sung. Vaughan outlined the holes in Buchs's alibi – that he had not been at the Indian food store for as long as he'd claimed, that the men on Sawgin Road did not know him and that the glass he claimed to have smashed when witnessing the fight in No. 56 had been broken months before. He also explained to the court that Buchs had large debts with local merchants.

Vaughan and McDowell had noticed that Buchs customarily wore Chinese-style straw-soled slippers. They had returned to No. 58 and confiscated a pair that they knew to be his from Lien Yow's rooms. They had then gone to the crime scene at No. 56 and found scuffmarks on the bottom of Eliza Shapera's bed. McDowell measured the marks and determined they came from Chinese slippers of exactly the same length and breadth as Buchs's. Vaughan produced drawings of the scuffmarks and Buchs's slippers as evidence.

McDowell then entered the witness stand and produced diagrams that explained how Buchs, living at No. 58 with Lien Yow, could have used the access routes across the back passages and the cookhouse roof to enter No. 56. He produced the fragments of broken tile found in the passage showing someone had scrambled across the roof and down to the passage behind No. 56.

Douglas retired to consider the evidence.

Douglas summed up the case as he saw it. The police knew Buchs wasn't always where he said he'd been, but they didn't know where he had actually been at those times. The marks on Shapera's bed were from the type of shoes Buchs habitually wore, but then so did hundreds of thousands of other people in Shanghai. Dr Voelkers had been unable to state with any certainty the time that death had occurred. Douglas did admit that Buchs had lied, his alibis were worthless, that he had falsely accused Minna Nedal. He further agreed that someone had effected an entry across the cookhouse roof and the rear passage of the building and that Buchs had been in the vicinity of the house at the time of the murder. However, there was no hard evidence that it was he who had entered No. 56 and killed Eliza Shapera.

Magistrate Douglas concluded, 'There is the strongest case of suspicion against the accused, but, on the evidence being forthcoming, the decision as to whether there is a *prima facie* case to answer is in the negative.' The accused was discharged. Buchs walked free from the court and disappeared back into the swamp of the Trenches.

Who Killed Eliza Shapera?

Eliza Shapera was probably a trafficked woman herself – lured from the Jewish shtetls of Russia, brought to Shanghai by white slavers in the late 1880s and forced to work as a prostitute in the Trenches. She had probably known nothing but the sordid and debauched world of Scott Road since she was a young woman. She had no known husband – late nineteenth- and early twentieth-century propriety demanded women claim they were married and often traffickers bigamously married multiple women to reduce the suspicions of immigration and port authorities regarding single women. Perhaps Eliza still sold her body, but by 1907 she was most probably the madam to the much younger, and probably also trafficked, Minna Nedal.

What happened on the 18th September 1907? Was it simply a case of two Chinese 'loafers' chancing on an open back door and the possibility of some loot, finding a woman inside who would fight to keep her money and killing her for $200? The police investigation of the two Chinese men arrested went nowhere and they were eventually released.

Did Minna Nedal, and perhaps another younger prostitute, fall out with Eliza over money or a customer? Perhaps, but while Nedal's alibi collapsed there were never any witnesses, except Ameer Buchs, to confirm she was in Scott Road that night. No trace of the third woman fighting at No. 56 that evening, as he claimed, was ever found. Nedal adamantly refused to admit to being on Scott Road, but couldn't account for her whereabouts. The most likely explanation is that she was with a client and did not want to admit to prostitution or implicate her customer.

And what of Buchs? Who was he? We know little of him except that he was a Muslim from India. In 1907 the Shanghai authorities were becoming concerned about the rising number of indigent Indians in the Settlement. It was perhaps alarmist, the vast majority of Indians in Shanghai were either employed by the police themselves or worked as watchmen, with a few more as servants and storekeepers. However, some Indians, through impoverishment or desire, slipped into the city's underworld. Buchs seems to have been one of these.

He was a drunk, he had come to the police's attention before during a previous murder investigation, he was probably living off immoral earnings as Lien Yow's pimp and maybe had other girls working for him too. His alibis all collapsed, he lied about his whereabouts – it seems he most probably lied about the supposed fight in the early hours of 18th September. Did he dislike Shapera and Nedal being in competition with his girls? Did the two Jewish women refuse to work for him? He certainly seemed quick and determined enough to implicate Nedal in Eliza's murder. Revenge? Or did he simply need money and decide that he would take Eliza's savings and kill her to stop her talking? His lies to the police about Sawgin Road and visiting the food store in the French Concession and the broken glass were amateurish and easily disproved. If he was in his right mind he must have known his tales would not stand up under police scrutiny. Buchs was unstable, dangerous, a loose cannon, a chronic drunkard – perhaps that's why Lien Yow was so eager to confess her relationship with him to McDowell, why the Indian men on Sawgin Road denied even knowing him. He was a liability.

After the conclusion of the trial of Ameer Buchs all the main characters fade away from history. Neither Minna Nedal nor Ameer Buchs are ever recorded again in Shanghai police records. PC Cornelius Hamilton left the SMP in 1917; John O'Toole served until 1932 when he retired from the force. Thomas Vaughan left the SMP in 1927 and John McDowell left a few years after the Shapera case in 1910.

After the First World War the Trenches got a new lease of life with a massive influx of White Russian refugees from the Bolshevik Revolution flooding into Shanghai. Many turned to prostitution, taxi-dancing, gambling and running nightclubs to make a living. An American was shot and killed in the Trenches in 1920. A rival strip of clubs and bars flourished nearby, just outside the Settlement's control on Jukong Alley and things didn't improve. The Shanghai Municipal Council and the Chinese authorities tried to suppress the Trenches but they just kept on flourishing and were still going strong by the time of the Japanese invasion of Shanghai in 1937.

Eliza Shapera's final resting place is unknown. Indeed her entire life remains surrounded in mystery – where she was born, when exactly and how she came to leave Russia and arrive in Shanghai. She was strangled in 1907, and her death remains one of old Shanghai's unsolved murders.

Bobby Broadhurst Teaches Shanghai to Dance:
Florence Broadhurst (1926)

'I'd always been told that I was born before my time.'

Getting Out of Mungy

Florence 'Bobby' Broadhurst was born in July 1899 at Mungy Station, near Mount Perry in Australia's rural Queensland. It was pretty remote territory – a couple of hundred miles out from the state capital of Brisbane, Mount Perry had only two hundred residents at most; Mungy Station just a couple of dozen. There was a railway line to Bundaberg, plenty of cattle, a few hopeful gold prospectors still in town, and some low-yield copper workings on the outskirts. Mungy was never going to be big enough or anywhere near exciting enough to satisfy young Florence Broadhurst.

Florence launched her show business career at just sixteen after winning a singing competition in 1915. The prize was to sing *Abide with Me* with the Australian operatic soprano Dame Nellie Melba, who raised massive sums of money for the Australian war effort with her concerts. Florence was invited on tour with Dame Nellie but fractured her skull in a car accident, was hospitalised and so couldn't join her. When Florence recovered she began appearing at wartime fundraisers herself where she was reportedly a popular contralto. She sang at a Smart Set Diggers[194] concert in Toowoomba, Queensland, which led to her being offered a place on a tour through the Far East with the newly formed 'Globe Trotters' song-and-dance troupe in 1922. The Globe Trotters featured a couple of comedians, a duo of female impersonators, a pianist and Florence Broadhurst as the troupe's singing act. All the troupe were involved in sketches, comedy routines, Pierrot dances, and putting over a bit of patter. The troupe was formed by comedian Richard (Dick) Norton who'd successfully toured the Far East vaudeville

---

194   The Smart Set Diggers were formed to entertain ANZAC troops during World
       War One and did tour France and Belgium as well as appearing in London.
       They kept on going for a couple of years after the war but eventually broke
       up and formed into myriad new troupes, such as Dick Norton's Globe
       Trotters.

Bobby Broadhurst on tour in India, 1920

circuit with the Bandmann Opera Company (more a theatrical revue and variety company than strictly opera), an international touring company which had a base at the Empire Theatre in Calcutta. Norton saw great potential for touring variety shows throughout the major European colonial communities in Asia.

The Globe Trotters left Brisbane in December 1922, sailing for Java in the Dutch East Indies and then on to Singapore, Malaya, the Kingdom of Siam and India, where they spent most of 1923. The tour went on into 1924 with appearances in Hong Kong, Japan and China. Broadhurst sang a repertoire of popular Australian Edwardian-era songs including *The Enchantress*, *My Dear Soul* and *Sink, Sink, Red Sun*. The Globe Trotters were relatively popular, though played to as many half-empty houses as full ones. The fact was that the market was saturated with touring companies from Europe, America, Australia and talent from émigré (largely Russian) communities in Asian cities such as Shanghai. A selection of the venues played by the Globe Trotters gives an indication of a typical Far East variety tour between the wars. The venues ranged from the exclusive, like the Royal Bangkok Sports Club, to traditional theatres and cinemas, like Pathé Theatre/Cinema in Batavia,

the Empire Theatre in Calcutta, the Palace Theatre in Karachi, the Royal Theatre in Hong Kong's Kowloon, Gordon Hall in Tientsin, to hotel lounges, like the Yamato Hotel Lounge in Dairen among others.[195] Usually the Globe Trotters stopped in town for just one or two nights; sometimes, in larger places more receptive to their acts such as Shanghai or Singapore, a week or more.[196]

Broadhurst came back to Australia with some adventurers' tales. She claimed an Indian maharaja in Delhi fell in love with her and, to prove it, shot a tiger in her honour; that she had performed for the King of Siam; that she was trapped in a house in Nanking during an uprising and had to be rescued by the Royal Navy.[197] Whatever the full truth of these anecdotes,[198] after visiting Peking, Tientsin, and Dairen, the Globe Trotters' 1924 tour of China was dramatically cut short in Shanghai due to the political turmoil.

But Florence Broadhurst, with a few other Globe Trotters, opted not to return to Australia and instead formed a smaller troupe called the Broadcasters. This troupe visited Bali, Japan, Malaya, Siam and

195   Batavia is now Jakarta and the Dutch East Indies are Indonesia. The original Royal Bangkok Sports Club Clubhouse is long gone. The Empire Theatre in Calcutta is now (I believe) the Roxy Cinema on Chowringhee Place. The Palace Theatre in Karachi later became a cinema specialising in screening comedies. I am not sure if the building still exists. The Royal Theatre in the Kowloon district of Mong Kok was replaced with a shopping centre after a fire in 1978. Gordon Hall in Tianjin still stands on Jiefang North Road and the Yamato Hotel is now the Dalian Hotel in the city of the same name.

196   'Five Years Abroad: An Interview with Miss Florence Broadhurst', *Bundaberg Daily Times*, July 23, 1927.

197   Ibid.

198   And I have no other sources than Florence herself for them as told in the article above.

Singapore before sailing back to China. They performed in Manchuria in northern China, the treaty port of Tientsin, the ancient capital Peking, and then finally reached the Shanghai International Settlement in 1926.

Right away Florence liked Shanghai and decided to stay on in the International Settlement. This was not a radical decision for an entertainer in 1926 – Shanghai was the entertainment Mecca of the Far East with more nightclubs and opportunities than any other Asian city. Florence parted company with the Broadcasters and got a gig as a dancer and singer working with the Carlton Follies. The Follies danced at Louis Ladow's prestigious and very well known Old Carlton Café on the Ningpo Road, down near the Bund.

The Old Carlton Café

'Dark' Louis Ladow was a legend among Shanghai's *demi-monde* and nightlife crowd in the 1920s. He was an octoroon, (i.e. one-eighth black), and a former inmate of California's Folsom Prison. When he was released Louis left America and sailed to Yokohama in Japan (then itself a treaty port) before moving on to China and finding a home in Shanghai in 1922. That home was the Carlton Café, a rather ramshackle wooden building on the Ningpo Road, not far from the Bund. Ever since opening the Carlton Café, Dark Louis had been teaching Shanghai to swing, promoting everything from Negro ragtime acts and Creole waltzes to Hawaiian ukulele sextets and a White Russian chorus line in skimpy rose-coloured outfits who sang the popular ballad *The World is Waiting for Sunshine* in reportedly impenetrable Russian accents. He had recruited Danish-American band leader Whitey Smith for his house band in what was essentially, according to Whitey, 'a small restaurant downstairs with a few rooms on the second floor. Later he remodelled the upstairs into the Old Carlton.'[199]

Still, the Carlton Café lit up brighter than any other joint at night and Louis mixed the meanest drinks in the Settlement – the

199 Whitey Smith, *I Didn't Make a Million,* (Manila: Philippine Education Company, 1956). It has since been reissued by Earnshaw Books in Shanghai with a foreword by Andrew Field.

On the town

house specials were vodka cocktails spiked with absinthe for a little extra kick.

Florence took the stage name 'Bobby' Broadhurst in the Carlton Café cabaret. When she wasn't performing at the Carlton she appeared around town at various other cabarets and nightclubs. But Florence had plans beyond just sticking it out in the Carlton Café chorus line. In 1926 she was twenty-eight years of age and reckoned her hoofing days in the chorus line were nearly over. Good timing perhaps as the Carlton Café's days were coming to an end too. Dark Louis's fortunes took a downturn as the Shanghai economy and confidence in the Settlement took a big hit after the bloody strikes and violent suppression of the Communist Party in 1927. Louis had over-expanded: just as Shanghai investors got a dose of the jitters Louis moved into larger premises and went upmarket. The Carlton Café's Shanghailander big spenders felt their purse strings tightening and opted to stay home. Louis lost it all and died in penury, much mourned by the city's *demi-monde*, in 1928. When he lost his club they said he died of a broken heart.

The Broadhurst Academy

Florence decided to establish the grandly titled Broadhurst Academy and Incorporated School of Arts. This appears to have been basically a private school, offering classes in violin, pianoforte, voice production and the banjolele, an instrument that is a mix of a ukulele and a banjo, which Florence had learnt to play on tour with the Globe Trotters. It is quite possible that Florence was both the first and last teacher of the banjolele in Shanghai – she claimed to make students proficient in just six lessons, which probably wasn't very difficult. There were additionally classes in modern ballroom dancing, classical dancing, musical culture and journalism.

Florence ran the academy from premises at No. 38 Kiangse Road at the junction with the Nanking Road, on the second floor over Admiral Lane, a row of houses that ran off Kiangse Road. That particular corner was a busy one. Weeks & Co. Ltd – outfitters, milliners, carpet and furnishing warehousemen, fancy goods dealers – occupied the ground floor next to the offices of Brewer & Company, who sold canned baby milk.

Florence appears to have taught most of the music and dancing classes herself. Her youthful singing and then time with the Globetrotters and Broadcasters as well as at the Carlton Café had ensured she was a more than capable exponent of both the Charleston and the Tango, modish dances everyone in Shanghai wanted to learn. For the more classical styles of dancing she called upon the city's sizeable stock of un- or at least under-employed White Russian classically trained dance teachers. Professor Kaurnitz Bulueva taught piano while his wife, Madame Bulueva, taught classical dance.[200] Florence also roped in her friends and people she met around the artistic salons of Shanghai to both bolster her academy and its curriculum.

One such hire was Jean Armstrong, an Australian freelance journalist from Sydney who shared lodgings for a time with Florence. Florence persuaded her to make a little extra money teaching

---

200 I know nothing about this talented couple of Russian émigrés in Shanghai. This may be because the spelling of their name in the local newspapers and records is erratic from entry to entry, and is perhaps totally wrong.

ESCAPES BANDITS—Jean Armstrong, of Sydney, Australia, was spared by Chinese, bandits who captured a ship plying between Shanghai and Hongkong, killing many of the crew. (International Newsreel.)

journalism and short-story writing at the academy. Jean had been making her way around China having a series of adventures, writing them up and selling them to the British newspapers. Armstrong had the good fortune (for a journalist looking for a story anyway) to encounter river pirates on a voyage from Hong Kong to Shanghai. She claimed that the white passengers were spared but that the Chinese passengers and crew were forced to 'walk the plank'. The pirate leader reportedly had only eight fingers and wore steel blades attached to each of his remaining digits. Armstrong made it to Shanghai where she swiftly penned the story complete with gory details and sent it off to International Features Services who sold it to dozens of newspapers, accompanied by a picture of Miss Jean Armstrong smiling defiantly.[201]

Broadhurst also hired a young man called Daniel Melsa, a Polish-born child violin prodigy. Born Isek David, Melsa lost his father and sister in the 1905 anti-Semitic pogroms in Poland. With his mother he went to Berlin where friends arranged for him to attend the famous Klindworth-Scharwenka Conservatory. He won the conservatory's top prize for violin in 1909 and came to the attention of the American ambassador in the city who bought him a Carlo Bergzoni violin. He made his debut as a soloist in 1912 in Berlin, took the audience by storm and then played to sold-out venues across Europe and the United States.[202] Melsa spent most of the war years in London and New York but in the 1920s began travelling further afield. Australia was keen to hear him, the circuit there was profitable and, of course, between Europe and Australia was

201 'Perils of a Pretty Summer Tourist Among the Shanghai River Pirates', *Hamilton Evening Journal* (Ohio), August 21, 1926.

202 The early years of Daniel Melsa's life are described in an appendix to Israel Zangwill's 1908 play *The Melting Pot* (which popularised the term) about a Jewish family fleeing the pogroms and settling in the United States.

Daniel Melsa

the Far East. Certainly he played concerts in Singapore and seems to have come to China around 1926 *en route* from Australia.[203]

Why Melsa took time off from his world tour to work as a violin tutor at Bobby Broadhurst's Academy on Kiangse Road, Shanghai, is not quite clear. Perhaps he merely wished to take a break in a pleasant city for a while; others have suggested he was exhausted from constant touring and Florence's offer gave him a chance to relax for a few months at least.[204]

But it is Florence who clearly drove the academy with the force of her personality. She comes across as a dynamo – dancing in multiple troupes, establishing the academy, teaching a good percentage of the classes while also being an active member of the Shanghai British Women's Association (by virtue of being an Australian) which had been established to support the troops back in Europe during the Great War but carried on afterwards performing good works around the Settlement. She popped up regularly in the society pages of the *North-China Daily News*, *China Press* and the other Shanghai English-language news-papers – all of which, of course, did the academy no harm in terms of free publicity.

203   Melsa certainly appeared in Peking in 1926. Sidney David Gamble, then in Peking amassing his treasure trove of pictures of China during that period, recorded in his diary that he saw Melsa perform in the city.

204   Melsa, with his actress wife Joan Carr, did return to London finally and settled there. He regularly appeared on the BBC Home Service radio and at the Proms and found time to write a book called *The Art of Violin Playing*. Melsa died in 1952 at home his home in Hendon, North London, at just fifty-nine years of age.

Everyone moves on. . . .

But Florence Broadhurst didn't stay in Shanghai long – just over a year. It seems that the dreadful events of the Shanghai Massacre in 1927, and the subsequent economic slump in the city, convinced her that it was time to move on. She opted to catch a ship to London, married a wealthy British stockbroker, Percy Kann, and reinvented herself as Madame Pellier, French couturier. She opened a dress salon serving the rich and famous at No. 65 New Bond Street in 1933 called Pellier Ltd, Robes & Modes.

After a decade in London Florence separated from her stock-broker husband and started another relationship, with an engineer, called Leonard Lloyd-Lewis, with whom she had a son, Robert. She remained in Britain during World War Two working for the Australian Women's Voluntary Services. In 1949 the couple and their son returned to Australia, with Florence now successfully reinvented as an English lady. She appears to have been financially comfortable and to have lived the life of a society hostess and amateur landscape painter working out of a studio in Sydney's Paddington district, reportedly producing two hundred paintings of the Australian landscape in under four years.

However her second husband left her for a much younger woman. Undaunted, she at the age of sixty launched a wallpaper business, which is still going strong under the name Florence Broadhurst Wallpapers Pty Ltd. Many of her designs were inspired by her time in Shanghai and travels in Asia – Japanese florals and bamboos, fans, cranes, etc. In the 1960s and 1970s Florence's hand-drawn hand-printed and silk-screen wallpapers designs were being exported around the world and still are today – along with branded jewellery, pillows, home furnishings and bed linens, pyjamas and luggage – all under the Florence Broadhurst signature.

Florence was found murdered in her Paddington apartment at the age of seventy-eight in 1977. An intruder appears to have beaten her to death with a piece of wood. The case remains unsolved.

Man's Fate and the Shanghai of the Absurd:
André Malraux (1933)

'Asia today is a tourist attraction.
In those days (1921) it still had a mystery.' [205]

205 From *André Malraux – Past, Present, Future: Conversations with Guy Suarès*,
(London: Thames and Hudson, 1974).

Storm in Shanghai

André Malraux's *La Condition Humaine* is perhaps the best novel about Shanghai ever written. Published in 1933 in French, it was translated into English a year later and published in London as *Storm in Shanghai* and simultaneously in America as *Man's Fate* (which, despite *Storm in Shanghai* being arguably a more catchy title, is how the book has been titled in English on both sides of the Atlantic ever since). It was an international bestseller and won the prestigious French literary prize, the *Prix Goncourt*. The novel is set during the failed communist and trade union uprising in Shanghai in 1927 and its subsequent bloody suppression. With Malraux's two previous Asian novels – *Les Conquérants* (*The Conquerors*) in 1928 and *La Voie Royale* (*The Royal Way*) in 1930, *La Condition Humaine* forms a trilogy on revolution in Asia. *Les Conquérants* is set in Canton during a wave of anti-foreigner strikes, while *La Voie Royale* is set in Angkor, Cambodia and deals with treasure hunters.

There's a clear autobiographical element to *La Voie Royale*. In 1923 the twenty-two-year-old Malraux and his new wife Clara sailed from France to Indo-China and the French protectorate of Cambodia. Malraux hoped to gather antiquities (on the cheap) from Angkor Wat, the sprawling twelfth-century Buddhist temple situated in the old capital of the Khmer empire. The idea was to sell the antiquities to French museums and collectors, netting him a decent profit and securing his future. For Malraux, treasure hunting in Indo-China appeared to be a free-for-all sanctioned by the French government, who were themselves responsible for removing quantities of antiquities from Angkor Wat back to Europe. Many of these artefacts are today housed in the Guimet Museum in Paris. Malraux, Clara and Malraux's friend Louis Chevasson headed inland in search of hidden temples. However, Malraux had no official permissions – he was arrested and charged with stealing a bas-relief from the Banteay Srei temple at Angkor. He contested the charge but lost. He was angry with the French government in Indo-China and became involved with various anti-imperialist movements, co-founding the Young Annam League as well as a newspaper, *L'Indochine,* that supported Vietnamese independence. And then it gets even more murky. . . .

Malraux told some people that after his misadventure in Angkor he had crossed over from Indo-China into China and visited Canton, giving him the material and direct experience to write *Les Conquérants.* He even suggested to some that he had visited Shanghai in 1927 – again indicating that *La Condition Humaine* was drawn from his own experiences. But this wasn't true. Malraux and Clara were back in Paris by 1926 when he published what was to be his first major publication, *La Tentation de l'Occident* (*The Temptation of the West*), a work in the form of a series of imaginary letters exchanged between a young Chinese man visiting Europe and a young Frenchman about to travel to Asia in the 1920s. In the letters they compare various aspects and differences in the two broad cultures – a tried and tested format in literature, from Montesquieu's *Lettres Persanes* (1721) and Oliver Goldsmith's *Chinese Letters* (1760) to Goldsworthy Lowes Dickinson's *Letters From John Chinaman* (1901).

When quizzed around this time, Malraux dismissed the question of whether or not he had ever visited China or Shanghai, claiming that for him *La Condition Humaine* was a metaphysical novel and so the Shanghai of the story was no more important than, so he suggested, St Petersburg was to Dostoyevsky's *Crime and Punishment.* Later Malraux changed his tune and did claim to have visited China briefly in 1931 (which would still have been after all the events described in the three Asian novels). But then, spinning around once again, in a letter to the Japanese novelist Akira Muraki, he denied ever having visited Shanghai at all. Finally, in one last spin, when Malraux arrived in China in 1965, as the French minister of culture, he suggested that he was now 'returning' to China! So, did he or didn't he visit Shanghai?

'Fiery and sincere'

André Malraux was a self-declared 'mythomaniac'. He was also a voracious and wide reader and certainly did read everything about China he could get his hands on, especially about the demonstrations and strikes in Canton and the uprising in Shanghai. But, it is often argued, if he had never visited Shanghai then his quite detailed descriptions of the city's topography, various districts and several specific locations in *La Condition Humaine* would surely have appeared to Shanghailanders as inaccurate or wrong. However, it seems generally not – people who knew the city well (and had no personal connection to Malraux, nor anything to gain by congratulating him on his portrait of the city) almost universally praised *La Condition Humaine*. Shanghailander society darling, the *New Yorker* correspondent Emily Hahn, gave Malraux her official seal of approval. In an article rounding up the most recent books (good and bad) on China in 1933, Hahn praised the book:

> Fiery and sincere, it is very convincing in spirit. Mr Malraux may not have known much of Shanghai, and many of the details are wrong, but these are of no importance. For the first time I saw the Chinese as people possibly like myself instead of excuses for romantic longings, or as mysteries sinister and profound. . . . In vain did Chen live and toil and die; useless were Kyo's sufferings.[206]

But did he, or did he not, visit Shanghai? It seems Malraux did at least call in at Shanghai in 1931, two years before he published *La Condition Humaine*. He arrived by steamer, visited only for a couple of days, but clearly got a sense of the city, enough for him to portray Shanghai in all its resonant glory.

The first thing to note is Malraux's description of Shanghai as modern. His rendering of the city as exploding with electric lights, drowning in neon, humming with overhead telephone wires and paralysed by traffic jams, would not have surprised readers in 1933 when people were familiar with images of contemporary Shanghai

206 Emily Hahn, 'The China Boom', *T'ien Hsia Monthly*, October 1935.

and its modernity. After World War Two, the Chinese Revolution and the firm coming down of the Bamboo Curtain during Maoism, the notion of any Chinese city as modern would have been surprising to Western readers. While today, thanks to a raft of historians having talked up the 'Shanghai modern' notion of the International Settlement and French Concession as the most technologically advanced metropolis in Asia in 1927, one can assume a familiarity with Shanghai's renaissance. But, during those long decades when the city languished under the dustsheet of a disapproving and puritanical communism, this notion of Shanghai as modern was largely lost.

La Condition Humaine offers a contemporary rendering of Shanghai as a symbol of modernity – in the dramatic opening passage as the revolutionary Chen waits, poised tensely, to perform an assassination, he hears the honking and roar of Shanghai's night-time traffic outside the bedroom window; the German Shanghailander Hemmelrich works in a thoroughly modern 'gramophone shop'; the reactionary Ferral of the Franco-Asiatic Consortium drives a Voisin, at the time by far the most modern, expensive and, frankly, downright cool French car ever produced. Malraux's Shanghai is *trés moderne*, connected, electrified, a cauldron of modern products and ideas – it dances to hot jazz gramophone records, it sits on trolley buses in traffic jams on neon-lit streets, it receives telegrams, reads Marxist tracts and it convulses in a revolutionary spasm with machine guns.

Certainly there are some clunkers in Malraux's description of Shanghai, most notably a courtyard house of a style unknown in Shanghai but common in Peking. There are also some silk mills located where, in reality, there were none. But many of the locations are well and accurately described – the Laoximen District and old town of Shanghai as well as the Boulevard des Deux Republiques that ran round the old town forming a border between this Chinese enclave and the French Concession. The Black Cat bar feels genuine and there were at least two such named bars in the city in the early 1930s. Certainly some scenes seem based on the Astor House Hotel, where Malraux almost definitely, though briefly, stayed in 1931.

The philosophies of *La Condition Humaine*

Malraux's Shanghai is modern philosophically too. *La Condition Humaine* embraces two major currents of thought that preoccupied French intellectuals throughout the nascent revolutionary movement: existentialism and absurdism. Basically existentialism argued that you, as an individual, are solely responsible for giving your life meaning, and for living your life passionately and sincerely in spite of any amount of despair, angst, alienation and tedium. In this way you may just about achieve freedom. For many intellectuals, drawn to leftist revolutionary causes, existentialism chimed sympathetically; the passion and the romance of the rebellion alongside the liberation and progressiveness of the cause. In *La Condition Humaine* the half-French, half-Japanese revolutionary Kyo Gisors and the Russian Comintern agent Katov each confront their own existential dilemma; while Chen, the Chinese revolutionary, validates his brief time on earth through serving the cause as a terrorist, the ultimate existentialism that still resonates in our world today. The major French existentialist thinkers, notably Jean Paul Sartre and Simone de Beauvoir, were each to follow similarly tortured paths of justification through communism (at times in its Maoist variant).

In 1927 Shanghai, failure dogs all Malraux's characters. Ultimately they are left with no way to give their lives meaning other than in the choice of the manner of their own deaths. Kyo is faced with the failure of his ideology, his marriage, his relationship to his scholar father, as well as his inability to defeat the Kuomintang who he sees as reactionaries. He is left only with the ability to determine the manner of his final exit. Similarly Katov, who watches his revolutionary endeavours fail utterly, is left only to become a 'sort of hero' by giving away his cyanide capsules to those more frightened of torture and death than himself. Noble perhaps; but also, ultimately, futile.

The second philosophical strand that runs through *La Condition Humaine* is also particularly redolent of 1930s Shanghai – absurdism. Here, again, Malraux is ahead of his time just as his subject matter, the city of Shanghai, was ahead of its time. The absurdist notion that any attempt to seek meaning in life will ultimately fail because no such meaning exists, was perhaps easier to understand from the perspective of the European generation of writers and thinkers who saw the mud and the blood of the trenches of the 'Great' War. It is also familiar from a slightly later generation – Camus's publication of *L'Ètranger* (*The Stranger*) in a Nazi-occupied Paris in 1942 and *La Peste* (*The Plague*) in 1947 with French collaboration and Nazi genocide still so recent and raw. But Malraux is writing at a time when hope was more ascendant than at any other time since the *Belle Epoque*. Of course those hopes would ultimately be unrealised – Bolshevism as progressive in the long term, the success of a left-leaning Kuomintang in China, a more liberal and inclusive capitalism in America ... all these failed to materialise. They would also degenerate horrendously as the decade aged – Soviet Stalinism, European fascism, the Great Depression, the Japanese Militarist onslaught, and then Chinese authoritarianism. But in 1927, and still arguably in 1933, hope existed and all was still to play for.

The absurdist strain in *La Condition Humaine* is strong and, given the descent into barbarism, brutality and mass murder of the uprising of 1927, understandable, if not unavoidable. Chen, his body mangled from his own bomb, lies dying on the Boulevard des Deux Republiques not knowing if he has managed to assassinate Chiang Kai-shek or not; Katov goes before the firing squad surrounded by the apparent death of socialism; the opium dealer and gun-runner Baron de Clappique relies on the absurdity of the casino and games of chance to save himself through a big win at the tables (he declares gambling, 'suicide without dying'); Ferral, Malraux's most Conradian character, considers committing suicide (that most absurd of absurd gestures?) while fretting about which final woman will be the most satisfactory one for him to sleep with before dying – his mistress Valerie whom he has failed to 'own', a French whore, or a Portuguese brunette? Decisions, decisions. . . .

Ultimately the revolution descends into the final absurdity of mass slaughter and failure; Shanghai becomes a city of, largely pointless, death. Most of the main characters die while the existentialist search for the meaning of the self becomes absurd as only the selfish survive. Only Clappique, Malraux's most parasitical and

Shanghai massacre of April 12, 1927; the setting for 'La Condition Humaine'

undesirable character, escapes Shanghai – dressed up as a sailor on a departing tramp steamer.

But *La Condition Humaine* also presages a third philosophy, one which, like existentialism and absurdism would evolve into an aesthetic movement – though rarely linked to Malraux or his Shanghai novel. It was a movement that was to emerge most vividly in France as the 1930s wore on; that would embrace both the romanticism and style of the period as well as the more tawdry elements of what the English poet W.H. Auden would dub the 'low, dishonest decade'.[207] French poetic realism was to gain ground as the 1930s advanced and, though seemingly Franco-centric – differing from German expressionism, American *noir*, or the British 'kitchen sink' drama – seems oddly appropriate to Shanghai in many ways.

La Condition Humaine is at heart an early example of French poetic realism – a fatalistic view of life that is nevertheless romantic. Its characters live on the margins, are invariably powerless in the greater scheme of things, lead lives of repetitive toil, have strained finances and suffer intense disappointments. Invariably after a life of repeated failure (as the Chinese would have it, 'eating bitterness') they are offered one last solitary chance at love. They take it, but it

207 From Auden's poem September 1, 1939, first published in *The New Republic*, October 18, 1939.

always fails. Such are Kyo, Chen, Clappique, Ferral, and the tragic figure of Hemmelrich, burdened by poverty and a family that is a millstone round his neck – failure all round, no happy endings here. *La Condition Humaine* is often discussed in terms of the existential/ absurdist spectrum, but feels to me more like classic poetic realism; a genre that attracted most attention in its celluloid form.

However – and despite several attempts – *La Condition Humaine* is yet to be filmed. Sergei Eisenstein tried and failed early on. MGM cancelled their planned Hollywood version a week before filming began. Bernando Bertolucci offered the Chinese government an adaptation of the novel, but they preferred his idea of a film about Pu Yi, the last emperor. Perhaps a stylist like Eisenstein could have perfectly realised *La Condition Humaine* on the screen through his perceptive montage. Hollywood could have perhaps made an edge-of-your-seat thriller out of the book. In his memoir *Adventures in the Screen Trade*, William Goldman ruminates on the problem of adapting novels to the big screen and the demand for great opening scenes in films that are often lacking in literature. He does come up with one example however: 'As I sit here I can only think of one first-class modern novel that begins at full speed, and that's Malraux's *Man's Fate*.'[208]

Of course there is so much more to the book than its great opening. Maybe Bertolucci (a self-declared Marxist) could have interpreted its characters, though the lush grandeur of *The Last Emperor* (1987) or *Last Tango in Paris* (1972) seem more to his Italianate aesthetic than the intensely interior *La Condition Humaine*. How much more appealing the book would have been to the scenic vision of a Jean Renoir, a Jean Vigo or a Marcel Carné? How much more suited to a cast of the likes of Jean Gabin, Simone Signoret or Michélle Morgan? – the regular repertory company of 1930s French poetic realist films.

Poetic realism was also about being trapped within locations for one reason or another – the thief who cannot leave Paris (Carné's 1938 *Hôtel du Nord*), the prisoner in gaol (Renoir's 1937 *Grand*

---

208 William Goldman, *Adventures in the Screen Trade: A Personal View of Hollywood*, (New York: Warner Books, 1983).

Illusion), the gangster who can never leave the Casbah of Algiers (Gabin in the 1937 *Pépé le Moko*). Malraux's Shanghai, both the foreign concessions and the surrounded Chinese city, is an island nobody leaves except in disgrace and surreptitiously – or by death.

Shanghai's Most Charming Gangster:
Elly 'The Swiss' Widler (1940)

'All Shanghai is agog with the news of Swiss-subject Elly Widler's alleged involvement in the removal of $2,000,000 worth of copper from a Commercial Express warehouse.' [209]

209 'Shanghai A Free City', *China Digest*, Vol. 58 No. 6, December 1940.

The red gold robbery

It took four hours for Elly Widler's 'Swiss' crew to clean out the godown of the Commercial Express and Storage Company on the Szechuen Road. They arrived after midnight on September 2nd, 1940, chloroformed the White Russian gate keeper, backed up half-a-dozen flatbed delivery trucks stolen from Hongay's coal depot two hundred yards up the road and started to pick the place clean. The Swiss gang loaded copper ingots, known in the late 1930s as 'red gold', worth US$2 million (about US$12 million in 2018 money) onto the back of the trucks and drove them away to who knows where. By 5 AM, when someone raised the alarm, the SMP arrived to find that Shanghai's largest-ever heist had happened on their watch. Elly Widler's boys – Swiss by name and Swiss by nature – left the place spotless. The commissioner of the SMP, Kenneth Bourne, was furious and demanded Widler's head.

Never had so much been stolen in one robbery in Shanghai; probably never in China. Elly Widler, already one of Shanghai's more colourful characters, had made himself a criminal legend. It was an open secret in Shanghai who had committed the heist. The newspapers wrote about it obsessively, Widler's audacity was the

Elly Widler's 'wanted' photograph in the 'China Weekly Review'

talk of every Blood Alley bar, Badlands casino and exclusive Shang-hai club. Some said it was Elly himself who had tipped off the police. Ever the self-publicist with an ego the size of the South China Sea, he delighted in topping the Shanghai criminal league ladder. The Chinese newspapers called Elly and the Swiss gang '*ming huo*', 'daring robbers', and people speculated on the true amount stolen, pushing the total up and up ever higher.

For days nobody had the faintest idea where Elly or any of his gang were. However, in 1940, the Shanghai International Settle-ment and Frenchtown was *gudao*, the 'Solitary Island', surrounded by the Japanese and with all ships entering or departing by the Whangpoo River searched by the Japanese River Police. Getting out of town was no simple proposition. Elly was lying low, some-where within the foreign concessions of Shanghai. . . .

'Elly the Swiss'

There are many fantastic stories about foreign adventurers in China at the end of the nineteenth century and the early twentieth. Elly Widler's has to be in the top five at least.

Elly was the second son of David Jaffa, who'd been born in Constantinople, Turkey in 1855 when it was still the Ottoman Empire. Tales of the Jaffa/Widler clan abound but it seems David Jaffa moved to Jerusalem at some point, trying to do business trading with various Swiss-based companies. However, the anti-Jewish laws in Ottoman-controlled Palestine, which limited his freedoms, frustrated him. He changed his name to David Widler, dropped his religion and declared himself Swiss – whether Switzerland ever knew anything officially about their new citizen is unclear!

Around 1905 Widler senior got fed up with Palestine and relo-cated to China with his two boys – Naoum 'Ned', and Elly. There's a tale that says he left Palestine and bought a plantation in, or near, Singapore but that the business was ruined by the Krakatoa erup-tion. But that was in 1883 and the dates don't really match up. Whatever the route – the Widlers were settled in China before World War One. Rumour has it that David set up a travellers' inn at Kalgan in Hebei province where a railway line had just been established, opening the interior of northern China to trade. Kalgan, in the late nineteenth century, was a crazy town of about 70,000 – bandits, robbers, Russian tea merchants, camel trains heading for or just departing Peking, and assorted adventurers both foreign and Chinese. A British diplomat passing through at the time noted:

> The Police in Kalgan wore white arm bands bearing the word 'Police' in both Chinese and English while Chinese, Mongol and Russian (and other European) business people spoke a sort of bastardised pidgin Mongol to communicate. Russian tea agents had European style houses and there was a Russian Post Office with a Russian Post Master too, as well as a Greek and a Russian Orthodox church. There were some English and Swedish missionaries, a Russo-Chinese bank, a post of the Imperial Chinese Telegraph Administration that connected China to the telegraph lines in Siberia.[210]

The Widler family inn seems to have been a place thieves could bring stolen goods to sell and trade. Of course that too may just be a rumour – there are other tales that say David was simply a humble merchant and philanthropist. Whichever, sometime around 1907 or 1908, David Widler died.

His two sons, Ned and Elly, set out to make their own fortunes. Ned reportedly became a noted photographer running the Pluto Photography Studio on Shanghai's Bubbling Well Road where, it has been claimed, he took portraits of visiting maharajas, the Burmese-Chinese 'Tiger Balm' King Aw Boon-Haw and, so it is said, even travelled to Tokyo to photograph the Japanese emperor and his family. The stories about maharajas and Aw Boon-Haw are probably true; an emperor sitting for a portrait is a bit of a stretch.

Elly followed his older brother Ned to Shanghai, gaining a job as a clerk in 1908 with Moller Bros., Merchants, Ship Agents and Ship Owners in their building at No. 9 Hankow Road close to the

Bund. But the routine life of an office clerk in Shanghai did not suit Elly for long. And so he left the International Settlement soon after arriving and went in the other direction, heading back into the Chinese hinterlands.

On the run

By November 1940 Elly was hiding somewhere deep in the Badlands, that area of western Shanghai that had once been the peaceful and pleasant Western External Road Areas (*huxi* to the Chinese) just beyond the Settlement boundary. Now the streets around Avenue Haig, Columbia Road, Edinburgh Road and the far reach of the Great Western Road were a lawless morass of illegal casinos, opium dens, nightclubs, *shabu* (methamphetamine) shacks and brothels.

Initially the SMP had raided Elly's luxury penthouse apartment in the Broadway Mansions, right by the Garden Bridge, overlooking the Soochow Creek. Elly had long resided there, running scams, controlling his 'trading empire', planning heists and living in some splendour. Elly was in his early fifties; his beautiful Russian girlfriend was barely twenty. Elly had lived virtually his entire life in China; he'd never been to Switzerland; yet he'd remodelled his

The Widler family at home; Elly far left rear, grinning (1920s)

Broadway Mansions apartment to look like it was a luxury chalet in a wealthy Swiss canton – cuckoo clocks, a roaring log fire, cow bells, wooden ornaments, fondues and *bündnerfleisch* for his whole gang of Swiss and French outlaws on Fridays! The police had kicked the door down and found the penthouse vacated.

Elly was at his bolt-hole in the Badlands, beyond the reach of the SMP. A giant nightclub and casino in the Badlands on Avenue Haig, the Six Nations covered an entire block and, except for the famous Farren's joint, was the largest club in the district of sin. Elly and his Swiss gang moved in, set up cot beds and poured themselves large glasses of *kirsch* to celebrate life beyond the (not so) long arm of the law.

'Just a normal Swiss businessman'

Elly liked to call himself 'just a normal Swiss businessman'. That was stretching the truth. At first he set up a fur-trading business in Daqianlu. The town had a population of barely 5,000 but was known as the 'Shanghai of Tibet'. It was where a half dozen trade routes converged out of China and into Tibet – tea, Yachao wickerwork, and all manner of skins and furs were traded there. Although China had ruled Daqianlu, on the border between far-western China and the Tibetan province of Kham, since the eighteenth century, the streets felt more Tibetan than Han.[211] Comparisons to Shanghai may have been a bit far fetched. Beyond a branch of the China Inland Mission and a house occupied by the consular agent representing British interests, there wasn't much for the assortment of Chinese, Tibetans, Russians, other merchants and one Swiss fur trader to do.

So Elly based himself in Chungking, visited Daqianlu regularly, bought up fox and other furs from local hunters, took them back to Chungking and then shipped them down the Yangtze to Russian and Jewish furriers in Shanghai. For a few years Elly was constantly moving between Tibet, Chungking and Shanghai. He pocketed a

211 Gary Tuttle and Kurtis Schaeffer, *The Tibetan History Reader*, (New York: Columbia University Press, 2013), p. 497.

very decent mark-up over what he paid the local trappers in Daqianlu. It was a profitable business and Elly put the proceeds into opening the Cosmos Club in Chungking.

It's highly doubtful if Chungking had ever had, or has ever since had, a dodgier nightclub than the Cosmos. Elly brought jazz, gambling, opium smoking in public and Russian prostitutes to Chungking. For Elly, what the Cosmos provided, apart from a pleasant venue to relax in when he got back from long trips to Daqianlu, was a focal point for anyone with money in Chungking. With the profits from the Cosmos nightclub he set up a savings trust promising big interest payments for those who chose to trust their money to 'Elly the Swiss'. Many did, foreigners and Chinese. After all, who doesn't trust the Swiss with money?

And there were other opportunities. In the chaos of 1920s China, as warlords rampaged across the country with their private armies grabbing territory the size of European countries, they needed arms and had the money to pay for them. When they came to Chungking many of the western Chinese warlords found their way to the Cosmos. Elly worked his Shanghai contacts and started dealing guns and ammunition to the warlords in the Cosmos. The money rolled in in even greater amounts – furs, nightclub profits, and now gun running.

In 1923, two warlords fought a series of battles not far from Chungking. Elly sold guns and ammunition to both armies simultaneously. The losing warlord, General Yang Sen of the Sichuan Clique's Second Szechuan Army, took umbrage and sent his men to seize Elly in his office out the back of the Cosmos Club, taking him hostage. Yang Sen was a Taoist master with numerous wives, concubines and children, and not shy of a bit of duplicity himself. When it came to warlord manoeuvrings, last week's ally was this week's nemesis. But he didn't approve of Elly selling guns to his foes. Yang Sen hastily convened a court martial to try Elly for treachery. None of the foreign consuls in Chungking – not Swiss, French or from anywhere else – would represent or recognise Elly as their problem.

Barefoot, with a rope around his neck and his hands tied behind him, Elly was led at the head of Yang Sen's mercenary army for two hundred miles into Yang's Sichuan province stronghold at Wanxian.[212] Holding the rope was Yang Sen's powerful Chinese executioner, his head-chopping broadsword slung over his back. Along the way Elly was taken for several days to the remote camp of General Lan Da Ju Ban ('Big Natural Feet'), a thirty-year-old female warlord in command of 6,000 men and whose bodyguard was her sixteen-year-old sister who always held a Mauser pistol by her side.

Yang Sen then kept Elly in a jail cell for six months until some generous foreign diplomats (none of whom could actually work out who was ultimately responsible for Elly) managed to secure his release on the grounds that, even if he wasn't their national, it was bad form to leave a white man in the hands of a Chinese warlord. Some said the diplomats hadn't had to negotiate too hard. Yang Sen was reportedly glad to get rid of him[213] – Elly had taken over the jail, organised the other prisoners into a gang that had then made a small fortune from dealing opium, cigarettes and women of dubious occupation brought into the prison. The gang terrorised the warden into staying in his office all day! Others said that the deal was 200 Mausers plus ammunition in return for Elly.[214]

Free, Elly decided to head to Shanghai once again. He didn't stop in Chungking on the way to say farewell – nobody who ever invested in his savings trust ever saw their money again! Elly immediately set about telling his tale of captivity and within a few months of his release had a best-selling book in Shanghai.[215]

---

212 Now Wanzhou District of the Chongqing Municipality and the border between that Municipality and Sichuan Province.

213 Yang Sen went on to become the Governor of Sichuan Province and eventually a loyal general to Chiang Kai-shek and the Nationalist Army. In 1949 he moved to Taiwan. Naturally for a bloodthirsty former warlord he finished out his days as the Republic of China's Olympic Committee chairman and chairman of the Taiwan Mountain Climbing Association. He died in 1977, leaving behind twelve wives and at least forty-three children.

214 The latter story about the Mausers is probably the true version of events. Warlords regularly used prisoners to raise money or secure additional arms while they weren't overly worried about conditions in their prisons.

215 Elly Widler, *Six Months Prisoner of the Szechwan Military*, (Shanghai: China Press, 1924).

'A man fighting against the odds'

Hiding out in Shanghai in 1940, Elly appealed to the Swiss consul general, Emile Fontanel, arguing that he hadn't stolen the copper ingots but only removed them on orders of the Japanese Army, and who could say no to them! Widler wrote to the local English-, French- and German-language newspapers telling the people of Shanghai they should believe him, that his mother had been given a medal by Queen Victoria (there is absolutely no evidence for this), that he was 'a man fighting against the odds ... chivalrous, generous, courageous.'[216]

Elly demonstrates a bulletproof vest to the SMP

Actually many would have agreed with him. Elly was a charming gangster. There were few inhabitants of the Shanghai *demi-monde*, the Badlands casinos, clubs and bars, who hadn't regularly been stood a drink by stand-up Elly the Swiss. Elly had somehow secured a cache of German bulletproof vests in his various business dealings. The SMP actually needed bulletproof vests as the city's crime rate spiralled in the 1930s and guns became everyday items. But could you trust 'Elly the Swiss' to sell you decent goods? So Elly took the police over to Hongkew Park, donned a vest and told the nearest copper to shoot him in the chest. The policeman obliged, fired at

216 'Widler's Request is Rejected', *China Weekly Review*, November 16, 1940.

a range of about twelve feet, and Elly went down hard in the Hongkew dirt and stayed down. But then he rolled over, got up to his knees, showed the police the bullet lodged in the vest, took it off and revealed his bruised chest. The Municipal Police bought the whole consignment and toasted the deal with bootleg champagne Elly had on ice in the boot of his car. Even the Shanghai coppers liked Elly.

Life was good – business was up, heists and robberies were plentiful in wealthy Shanghai. Things went bad a few times – Elly's brother Ned died in 1936, of poisoning, with foul play suspected. The police looked into it, there were a lot of suspects, though none were ever prosecuted. Elly got rich, trading guns to warlords, bulletproof vests to the SMP, occasionally still acting as a conduit for Daqianlu fur traders to the best furriers in Shanghai, though he never went near Chungking again. Elly got a young girlfriend and rented the most sumptuous pad in the newly completed Broadway Mansions.

Widler's Six Nations Club

As Shanghai falls, so Elly falls. . . .

The end of Shanghai was the end of Elly's run of luck. He robbed the Commercial Express godown in September 1940. For a year he hid out in some style at the Six Nations Club in the Badlands and then, on December 8th the Japanese attacked Pearl Harbor and, at the same time, occupied the International Settlement of Shanghai.

Elly still claimed that he'd had the permission of the Japanese military to remove the Commercial Express copper. He remained a free man, still claiming Swiss nationality (and now neutrality) until the spring of 1942. Emile Fontanel, the Swiss consul, was never convinced of Elly's claim to Swiss nationality but represented him anyway. Fontanel denied the Japanese had ever provided him with evidence that they had sanctioned Elly's heist. If he did have 'permission' then it was from corrupt elements in the Japanese army looking for a cut. Unsurprisingly none came forward.

Then, somehow, Elly got on the wrong side of the Japanese army. They locked him up in the notorious Bridge House interrogation centre on the Szechuen Road. Elly may well have been struck by the irony that Bridge House was just a stone's throw from the old Commercial Express godown he'd robbed in September 1940.

Unlike many others less fortunate, Elly managed to survive the depredations and tortures of Bridge House – there are rumours he even drove his guards demented with his antics and they kicked him out the door and sent him on his way into occupied Shanghai. He managed to somehow get out of Shanghai to the United States at the end of the war; though it's unclear whether or not his young wife, who was a stateless White Russian, was able to remain with him or what became of her. Elly died in 1962 in Manhattan. He lived a pretty good life and his post-war days were said to have been quite comfortable though nobody in New York was quite sure how he came by the funds to keep himself so comfortable – but then not one single copper ingot from the Commercial Express heist in Shanghai was ever recovered.

A Showgirl, Bloody Saturday and
the Shrapnel Swing:
Terese Rudolph (1937)

*'War, Quake, Plague: Then Chicago Girl
in Shanghai Loses Clothes.'* [217]

217   Headline, *Chicago Tribune*, September 5, 1937.

Bloody Saturday – August 14th, 1937

That sultry summer of 1937 the local newspapers reported that Shanghai had been expecting to be hit by a typhoon of 'violent intensity'. The typhoon passed, but what did strike Shanghai was a man-made typhoon of bombs and shrapnel that brought aerial death and destruction such as no city on earth had ever seen before. It was all a terrible mistake, though nobody in the International Settlement or French Concession was to know this for some days. The Japanese – already in occupation of Peking and Tientsin since early July – had moved south and begun to shell the Chinese portions of Shanghai to the north of the Soochow Creek – Chapei, Paoshan and Kiangwan. But they had stayed clear of the foreign concessions knowing that any attack on them would mean war with Britain, France and America, something Japan was not yet ready for.

The Chinese were fighting back, hunkered down around the North Railway Station. The Japanese camped out in Hongkew Park. In the Settlement Shanghailanders gathered on rooftops to watch the shelling and firestorms that raged across the creek to the north. The biggest threat was the Japanese battle cruiser and flag carrier, *Idzumo*, moored on the Whangpoo directly in front of the Japanese Consulate, just across the Garden Bridge Hongkew-side. On Friday August 13th Generalissimo Chiang Kai-shek, from his war room in the Nationalist capital of Nanking, ordered the Chinese Air Force to attack the *Idzumo*. It was a risky strategy – the typhoon had left low-lying rain clouds which meant that the planes had to bomb at far lower altitudes than they'd been trained for. The *Idzumo* was a large ship but the Whangpoo is a tight target, the Settlement close by to one side; the warehouses, godowns and fuel dumps of Pootung to the other – any error of judgement would be disastrous.

And so it proved to be. After several bombs missed the *Idzumo* and smashed into warehouses Pootung-side, the next one hit the Settlement almost in its symbolic heart – just off the Bund, on Nanking Road. The first bomb weighed 2,000lb and hit the Palace Hotel at precisely 4.27 PM. It passed straight through the roof and plummeted downwards through the building. The hotel's tea lounge, restaurant, lobby and bar were all destroyed. Many of the dead and injured were found later, still in their rooms. Part of the Palace's façade had been blown away and had begun to collapse. The second bomb struck seconds later, bearing directly down on Nanking Road. It glanced off the side of the Cathay Hotel's ferroconcrete structure, cracked the canopy covering the entranceway and ex-ploded into the tarmac. Shrapnel hit the clock on the front of the Cathay, which stopped at 4.27 PM exactly. The bomb left a gaping crater right outside the front doors. Always a busy intersection, the street instantly became a mass of burnt-out cars and charred corpses. Flames licked from a gutted Lincoln Zephyr parked near the hotel's entrance.

A second group of off-target bombs fell at 4.43 PM. This time they struck at the corner of Thibet Road and the Avenue Eddy, right outside the Great World amusement palace. It was the French Concession's busiest junction. The pavements around the enter-tainment complex were, as ever, thronged with the curious. The first bomb detonated shortly before hitting the ground, sending out a spray of deadly eviscerating shrapnel that killed people over seven hundred yards away. The second bomb hit the asphalt street and created a huge crater, ten feet by six, adjacent to a traffic control tower. The bombs that exploded outside the Great World were even more deadly than the first wave in Nanking Road. There was a greater concentration of people in the area and these bombs, being made of shrapnel, accounted for the higher casualty rate at the Great World. The shrapnel spread across a wide arc, reaching as far as the racecourse on Bubbling Well Road where stray pieces of red-hot metal caused the immediate cessation of a cricket game underway at the time.[218]

218 The old racecourse being located where Renmin (People's) Park is today.

The *Idzumo* remained untouched and simply increased its shelling rate into Chinese Shanghai. Nobody knew quite what had happened. Were these Japanese or Chinese bombs? Rumours ran rife. That Chiang Kai-shek had ordered the attacks to hit the concessions to force the Europeans and Americans to fight Japan; that the Japanese had disguised planes to look like Chinese Air Force bombers to drive a wedge between Chiang and the treaty-port powers. For the next twenty-four hours at least Shanghai became a city of death and panic; of Shanghailanders looking to evacuate while tens of thousands of terrified Chinese from north of the Soochow Creek streamed across the Garden Bridge seeking sanctuary. Nobody knew if the four bombs that fell were to be the last or just presaged the start of an all-out Japanese attack on the foreign concessions.

That day, at 4.27 PM, Terese Rudolph was in the Cathay Hotel preparing for her stage show later that night. She was the star performer of the hotel's nightly cabaret. Hearing the explosions, looking out upon the bloody carnage of the Nanking Road she was understandably terrified. . . .

Beginnings

Terese Rudolph was a dancer, showgirl and world traveller. In 1937 she was working in Shanghai, performing in various nightclubs and with a semi-regular gig as the star of the nightly cabaret at Sir Victor Sassoon's Cathay Hotel on the Bund. She was well-known in Shanghai, courted by other nightclubs and cabarets, though everyone knew that Sir Victor paid top dollar for his acts. Terese's career seemed set in the International Settlement. She had travelled a long way to become a star in Shanghai.

Terese Rudolph was born in 1913 in Budapest, Hungary. She emigrated to America with her family in 1925 when she was twelve years old. The Rudolphs, like so many other Hungarian emigrants to America before them, settled in Chicago. By the time Terese arrived in America her vowel sounds had already been formed and so she never quite lost her original Hungarian accent.

Terese's mother thought that the performing arts might be a way for her daughter to escape a life of drudgery in the factories of East Chicago. And so Terese was enrolled to study dance with Laurent Novikoff, who had once partnered the most famous of all ballerinas, Anna Pavlova. Novikoff had graduated from Moscow's Bolshoi Ballet in 1906 and opting not to remain in Russia after the Bolshevik Revolution, joined Diaghilev's *Ballets Russes* just before the First World War. In the 1920s he left Diaghilev to join Anna Pavlova's company and toured the United States. In 1929 he took the job of ballet master at the Chicago Civic Opera Company. Terese could not really have asked for a better teacher. Her mother was keen she become a dancer and was what might be called a 'stage mother'. Terese later recalled that her mother attended every rehearsal and performance. Skipping classes or rehearsals was never an option; mother was always there encouraging her to try harder, work harder.

In 1930, Novikoff hired Terese, aged just seventeen, as a ballerina with the Chicago Civic Opera Company. She danced several seasons with the company's ballet until, in 1932, it missed a season due to poor finances and Terese found herself out of work in the midst of the American Depression. She decided to try her luck on the vaudeville and revue circuit. In the mid-1930s she appeared in various cabarets across the United States and Canada, billed as a 'premiere danseuse' or sometimes as a 'Hungarian Dancer'. Whichever act she performed she was a smash all across the country – ballet, traditional Hungarian folk dancing, or a little acrobatics thrown in for entertainment, all were crowd pleasers. Talent agents looking to book acts to travel out to Shanghai and the Far East noticed her. She signed on for an Oriental tour.

Shanghai . . . and beyond

Terese arrived in Shanghai in early 1937 and, almost from the start, was the 'feature act' at Sassoon's Cathay Hotel. Her mother never stopped supporting her, even from afar. Doing her best to ensure she had as long a career as possible she told the newspapers she was delighted her 'twenty-one-year-old Terese was headlining in Shanghai'[219] – Terese was by 1937 just over twenty-four.

When the bombs fell on the Cathay Terese was rehearsing on the mezzanine floor of the hotel. Terrified at the carnage she saw she felt sure this was just the start of something far more terrible to come. Too afraid to return to her lodgings she packed a bag with only the clothes she had in her dressing room at the Cathay, ran down the Bund to the jetties and boarded the first liner she could secure passage on, the Dollar Line's *President Jefferson*. It happened to be heading out of the war-torn and still smouldering city filled to bursting with refugees, mostly American, heading to Manila in the Philippines.

If Terese had so far been on a lucky streak in her life – emigrating to America, becoming a ballerina, finding success in vaudeville, securing one of the top gigs in Shanghai at the Cathay, then in August 1937 it appeared that her lucky streak had well and truly ended.

The *President Jefferson* to Manila took several days across a turbulent and typhoon-whipped East China Sea. It was a rough passage of crying babies and seasick passengers but, in August 1937, Manila should have been a safe haven away from the bombs and warring Chinese and Japanese armies in Shanghai. Terese was not the only American on the *President Jefferson* – in fact 376 evacuees, mostly American women, often with their children, being sent by their nervous husbands to safety, had managed to board the liner. One fellow passenger of Terese's, a Mrs O'Toole of Washington DC, the wife of a warrant officer in the Fourth Marines stationed in Shanghai, told the press awaiting the refugees in Manila that on Bloody Saturday Shanghai was, 'Hell on earth ... bombs fell everywhere . . . shrapnel fell indiscriminately, killing and wounding many people. Everyone was terrified.'[220]

Even evacuating the city had been dangerous and potentially deadly. To get to the *President Jefferson* the scared evacuees had to take a tender from the Bund jetty down to the anchorage at

219 'Dancer in Shanghai', *Chicago Tribune*, August 16, 1937.
220 'Says Shanghai "Hell on Earth"', *Record-Argus* (Greenville, Pennsylvania), August 20, 1937.

Woosung. The tender was filled with mostly female evacuees, more than a few of whom were expectant mothers (one gave birth aboard the *President Jefferson*) crowded into the tender. Normally the trip fourteen miles downriver to the Woosung anchorage was relatively sedate, but in August 1937 this was most definitely not the case. The tender's captain was eager to get past the *Idzumo* (still firing its huge guns directly into Chapei and Paoshan) and get downriver as fast as possible. This meant the voyage was a rough one – Mrs O'Toole recalled everyone on board being terrified the tender would roll over and pitch them all into the muddy and fast-moving river at any moment.

But just as the *President Jefferson* finally pulled into Manila Bay a massive earthquake hit the city. Many of the evacuees from Shanghai thought they had sailed into another war. In fact the island of Luzon had been rocked by two quakes in quick succession at 8 PM of 7.5 magnitude each, which were felt up to 200 miles away in the summer hill resort of Baguio. The epicentres of the quakes were just miles from central Manila. Remarkably very few people had been killed or injured, but there was massive devastation to the city's buildings and infrastructure, forcing thousands to camp outside. Despite the low casualty rate, the city's power grid had been completely knocked out. Manila, and its population of over 600,000, was in total darkness except for occasional fires raging in some outlying districts of the city. Further smaller tremors continued to terrify an already panicked populace, many of whom were now homeless. The earthquakes were the worst to hit the island of Luzon in over forty years.

The US Navy stationed in Manila tried to ease the fears of the Shanghai arrivals with a rousing welcome despite the conditions. The navy band came to the dockside to play for the passengers. But as the refugees from Shanghai disembarked, the second quake hit the city. The lights in the Customs House went out, plunging everyone into darkness and chaos. Refugees started uncontrollably screaming; others reportedly fainted. Manila's main street, Escolta, was a sea of shattered plate glass; the Great Eastern Hotel on Makati Avenue had sunk four inches and hotel guests were wandering around outside in their pyjamas. Cinemas and theatres had been turned into emergency hospitals and the streets were swimming in water where mains had broken. The whole southern half of the city across the Ayala Bridge was now totally without power or water. Several church steeples had toppled and crashed to the ground below. Manila appeared to Terese to be in a worse state than the Shanghai she had just fled.

At 10.33 PM a third large quake, of magnitude six, hit the city, cracking the exteriors of office and apartment buildings. Elevators jammed, trapping people; any remaining plate glass in Manila shattered; fires extinguished reignited. One of the Shanghai refugees from the *President Jefferson* told the press gathered to greet them in the Customs House and now trapped with them, 'Looks like we left a war to find an earthquake.'[221] The city's hotels were in complete disarray, as staff could not get to work, and they were all now overbooked with Filipinos rendered homeless by the first quake. The Shanghai refugees had to be housed with volunteers who had private homes with space.

And onwards. . . .

Manila was a chaotic scene. Terese knew nobody in the city and obviously finding a new gig was impossible for the foreseeable future. There was nothing else to do but to move on again as soon as she could. She managed to find space on a steamer bound for the British Crown Colony of Hong Kong in the hope it would be both Japanese army- and natural disaster-free. But Terese's streak of bad luck hadn't ended yet. . . .

Arriving in Hong Kong a couple of days later after sailing back across a South China Sea still plagued by typhoons and rough seas Terese found the colony in the grip of typhoid and cholera epidemics. The colonial government had enacted emergency measures and was attempting to inoculate thousands of people every day. Long queues snaked around hastily prepared inoculation centres as people waited for their jab. The situation was chaotic – Terese's

221 'Manila Shaken by Heavy Earthquake as Refugees Arrive', *Daily Independent* (Murphysboro, Illinois), August 20, 1937.

steamer of refugees from the Luzon earthquakes was joined in Victoria Harbour by boats from Shanghai still evacuating people from the Japanese attack.

More ships from Manila arrived as increasing numbers of Filipinos fled the quake's devastation. Kowloon train station was packed with refugees – from the bombing in Shanghai and from neighbouring Guangdong province where the typhoid outbreak was most severe, running rampant with little in the way of inoculation. Hong Kong's Happy Valley racecourse had been converted into a reception centre, initially sheltering a thousand homeless people – the number was to rise rapidly. The British authorities estimated that they had registered 20,000 refugees but that perhaps another 30,000 had arrived in the city from Guangdong, Shanghai and the Philippines and all remained without inoculation. They were expecting the total entering the colony to reach at least 100,000 within a few days. Terese had arrived in the midst of epidemics compounded by a refugee crisis, a situation that even had the Hong Kong government been at all prepared for, was being rendered daily worse by Chinese from cholera-ridden Guangdong and the influx of refugees from the Shanghai war and the Manila earthquakes. A triple whammy of devastation – disease, war and natural disaster – was stretching the capabilities of Hong Kong to breaking point.

Within days the cholera epidemic had reached nearby Macau. An outbreak in Formosa saw yet more refugee ships leave for the British colony. Inoculation was a slow process and Britain appealed for extra serum supplies to be flown swiftly to Hong Kong as their own ran out. It wasn't enough; eighty per cent of victims died. Singapore flew in 250 litres of serum, enough to inoculate a quarter of a million people. Evacuees from Shanghai were given jabs on their ships before disembarking. The colony's authorities eventually had fifty treatment centres operating across the territory but serum supplies remained dangerously low.

With refugees arriving from Shanghai and Manila as well as Macau, southern China and Formosa, Hong Kong was full to bursting and people were dying in scary numbers. So Terese decided to make one last voyage . . . back home . . . via Hong Kong, up the China coast to Shanghai.

Home again. . . .

Shanghai was still war-ravaged; the scene outside the Cathay Hotel still chaotic though the bodies had been removed, the burnt-out cars hauled away and smashed glass swept up. The clock outside the hotel's foyer still read 4.27 PM. The Fourth Marines were sandbagged in along the southern bank of the Soochow Creek in case the Japanese Imperial Army attempted to invade the central Settlement. British soldiers had set up heavy artillery on the racecourse; French soldiers were fanned out along the Quai de France, the French portion of the Bund, to protect their concession. Evacuation panics kept breaking out; rumours of all British, American and French non-essential nationals being evacuated swirled around the city. Thousands of Shanghailanders crowded outside the Dollar Line offices on the Bund, around the nearby offices of P&O and Messageries Maritimes, trying to secure berths on ships that were already full and whose arrivals, let alone disembarkations, remained uncertain. The Scandinavian nations had already ordered their nationals to evacuate. The flagship of the US Asiatic Fleet, the USS *Augusta,* was moored three miles upriver; Royal Navy and French Navy ships were moored on the Whangpoo waiting for the order to evacuate their respective nationals. The city was tense – cinemas closed, shops opening for only a couple of hours a day, banks limiting withdrawal amounts, all police, fire service and ambulance crews on alert, the Settlement's hospitals still full to overflowing. British, French and American troops had been rushed to the city to protect the foreign concessions; out-of-control fires and gas main flares continued to ravage the Chinese portions of the city as Japanese and Chinese snipers traded shots across the rooftops.

Terese's nightly cabaret at the Cathay was closed indefinitely – though the hotel never closed its bar! It was clear that there was no future for Terese any more in Shanghai and she used her last few dollars to purchase a ticket home to America.

Terese managed to secure a berth on the Dollar Line's *President Hoover* but the chaos was still in full flow. Somehow all Terese's trunks got left behind on the Bund at the jetty and didn't get loaded

REPORTED MISSING in Shanghai when Cathay Hotel was bombed, Terese Rudolph, dancer, escaped, arrived here on President Hoover. —Photo by San Francisco Examiner.

onto the tender to take them down to the waiting liner at the Woosung anchorages. Then, despite the *President Hoover* flying a large Stars and Stripes flag, the Chinese air force accidentally strafed and bombed the liner. Thankfully she wasn't sunk. However, one of Terese's shapely dancer's legs was scratched by glass from a smashed porthole. She must have been at the end of her tether.

Terese finally got back to San Francisco on September 14th. She took a train to Chicago and went straight to the home of her mother (also named Terese) on East 61st Street. Her picture was snapped dockside in California – despite war, bombs, earthquakes, cholera, lost luggage and three weeks at sea on cramped evacuation ships, Terese still managed to look fantastic when she walked down the gangplank at San Francisco, every inch the successful showgirl . . . and she still had a sense of humour. Terese told the newsboys she'd invented a new dance in Shanghai, the 'Shrapnel Swing'.

And she had . . . and she performed it at numerous nightclubs over the next year. The Shrapnel Swing aimed to replicate the effects on a person of being under bombardment. The dance had four basic movements – 'Warbirds Approach' as the dancer gazes skywards at the approaching menace; then 'Fear' as she realises these are enemy planes about to attack; next comes 'Stunned' and the shock of the falling bombs and finally the climax which the newspapers could not quite decide how to describe beyond 'Death'.[222] Quite what American audiences made of the Shrapnel Swing we cannot be sure, but at least Terese Rudolph had made it back to America from Shanghai in one piece.

It's the "Shrapnel Swing"--From Shanghai's Smash Hit

Anyone who remembers the wild-west six-shooting bullies who made their victims dance may appreciate war's new contribution to the arts—the "Shrapnel Swing," just in from China. Created by Terese Rudolph, American dancer, after her experience in the Shanghai warfare, "Shrapnel Swing" depicts the emotions of a person under fire. In the first episode, upper left, Miss Rudolph portrays "Warbirds Approach." Then, in center, "Fear," followed by "Stunned." The climax below is "Faint"—or, perhaps, "Death." Miss Rudolph was dancing at Shanghai's Cathay hotel at the time of the bombardment.

222 'It's the "Shrapnel Swing" From Shanghai's Smash Hit', *Reading Times* (Pennsylvania), October 13, 1937.

After Shanghai

After Shanghai Terese Rudolph was soon back in the nightclub business, touring again across America's nightspots through 1938 and up till America entered the Second World War in 1941. Terese (who was known as 'Teri' or 'Terry' to her friends) joined the American United Service Organisations entertaining the troops during the war. She appeared in America alongside an act called the Gloria Lee Girls. Then she was sent abroad and ended up in Paris for the city's liberation in August 1944.

After the war Terese returned to America. In 1947 she appeared at the Copacabana in Miami Beach[223] and danced in a revue at the Rio Cabana Club in Chicago, where *Billboard* magazine noted her as the star of the show.[224] By the summer of 1947 she was back in Chicago appearing at the Vine Gardens where *Billboard* reported, 'Blonde Terese Rudolph opens with a nifty toe bit, which featured plenty of spins and whirls to keep the eyes interested. She pulled off the padded slippers early to close with a boogie.'[225] Terese was top billing at the Vine Gardens supported by Jack Soo, described in *Billboard* as a, 'Chinese crooner, a good looking Oriental, with a big voice and a contagious smile.'[226] In fact Jack Soo had been born Goro Suzuki on a boat to America with his Japanese family in 1917. He'd grown up in Oakland, California, and then been interned in Utah along with the rest of the Japanese-American population in the Second World War. After the war he launched his show-business career, taking a Chinese name to avoid the lingering stigma of being Japanese.

Around 1949 Terese moved to Germany to run the American Army-owned Casa Carioca in Garmisch-Partenkirchen, an R&R resort for US army personnel in the Bavarian Alps. The Casa Carioca had an ice skating rink attached and she helped train the ice skaters in dance to improve their shows (though she didn't skate herself); the skaters were from all over – America, Scotland, Germany. Terese choreographed a cast of roughly thirty-five skaters backed by a

223 *Billboard,* February 22, 1947.
224 *Billboard,* June 28, 1947.
225 *Billboard,* August 16, 1947.
226 Ibid.

seventeen-piece live orchestra. The ice stage was under a removable dance floor and diners could enjoy dinner while watching the ice shows. Many of the skaters hired by Terese went on to become professional skaters appearing in the Ice Capades, Ice Follies and Holiday on Ice shows back in the States. Rudolph stayed in Garmisch-Partenkirchen running the Casa Carioca till 1968. After she left, the club fell under something of a cloud following allegations of embezzlement and in 1970 it mysteriously burnt down while investigators were looking for the accounts. . . .

Terese returned from Europe to live in Los Angeles where she remained in the business, training skaters for the Ice Capades. Though never an accomplished ice skater herself she was able to teach accomplished skaters presentation, stretch and body alignment.

Terese 'Teri' Rudolph died of a heart attack at ninety-two years of age in January 2005.

Manouche on the Route Vallon:
The Gypsies of Shanghai (1930s–40s)

'Pleese. No fadder, no mudder, no eat.'

The forgotten Shanghailanders

This chapter aims to correct an omission. Never in any history of Shanghai or its foreign concessions have I ever read any reference to the Roma, or gypsy, community in the city. But they were there and, while never great in number, they were noted in various contemporary newspaper articles and memoirs. I came across the Shanghai gypsies while researching the city's nightlife. Of course jazz had long been extremely popular in Shanghai and, around the mid- to late-1930s, 'Gypsy Jazz' came into vogue as a sub-genre. But not every musician playing Gypsy Jazz was Roma.

Along with the vogue for Gypsy Jazz ('Jazz Manouche' in the French Concession) went an international vogue for gypsy characters in movies and 'gypsy fashion'. The rather stereotypical and rarely overly authentic images of gypsies that appeared in popular culture across Europe emphasised music, dancing and sexual attractiveness, particularly of female Roma and the 'gypsy look' of large earrings, darkened skin, eyes and hair.[227] This trend arrived in Shanghai via movie and music magazines. For instance, the highly successful and acclaimed 1937 Julien Duvivier film *Pépé le Moko*, which played in Frenchtown cinemas to good reviews, featured a gypsy character (Inés) played by the French actress Line Noro.[228]

According to Shanghai's English-language newspapers the Roma community in the mid- to late-1930s was composed of approximately 300 people. They were usually referred to simply as gypsy or *cigany/tzigane*.[229] The majority of identified Shanghai Roma in the 1930s worked in the entertainment industry as either musicians,

---

227 Ginette Vincendeau, *Pépé le Moko*, (London: British Film Institute, 1998).

228 Sadly in the movie Inés, who is in love with the French gangster-on-the-run Pépé, is thrown over by him as he pursues Gaby (Mireille Balin), the French mistress of a businessman.

229 'Roma' is in fact the collective name for various groups that were previously known as 'Gypsy', as well as being politically correct today.

singers or dancers in the cabarets, restaurants and cafés of the Settlement, Frenchtown or the Western Roads entertainment district (after 1937 generally referred to as the 'Badlands').

Shanghai gypsies

With its large European population, including a sizeable number of White Russian émigrés as well as North Americans and, from the late-1930s, a growing number of Jewish refugees from across continental Europe, the Roma community has been largely overlooked. By their very nature Roma tend to live outside of mainstream society and, being usually transient, historians lack the bureaucratic resources that are available to those researching other, more settled and integrated, communities. However, those Roma working in the entertainment industry had commercial reasons to draw attention to themselves and their culture via the newspapers. Consequently, substantially more is known about them than Roma engaged in other occupations, about which we know virtually nothing. It is also the case that Roma communities globally have traditionally suffered from intolerance by mainstream society which has often led to at worst, acts of violence and forced exclusion, and otherwise a general lack of understanding of Roma culture and traditions. While foreign Shanghai's authorities practised no official discrimination or enacted any legislation against the Roma community specifically, it is nevertheless the case that there were issues of discrimination and prejudice by other Shanghailanders towards Roma-Shanghailanders.

Shanghai's Roma community appears to mostly have belonged to three large extended families of Russian Roma origin: the Petroffs, the Minersk and the Vishnevsky clans. There are thought to also have been other Roma in Shanghai not attached to these clans, though their numbers were small – perhaps only a couple of dozen at most. The majority of identified Roma in Shanghai appear to have worked in the entertainment industry while others were engaged in such activities as cooking, gem dealing and fortune telling (which the forces of law and order in the Settlement would term 'prognosticating for money'). The majority lived in the French

Concession in close proximity to each other on Route Vallon, Rue Bourgeat and Route Père Robert.[230]

Most were practising Roman Catholics and the majority were either from the Lovari sub-group ('tribe') of the Romani people (with their own dialect, influenced by Hungarian) or the invariably more traditional and conservative Kalderash (or Kelderasa) sub-group, originating mostly from Romania or the Ukraine.

Many of the gypsy families and extended families came to Shanghai from either Tsarist Russia (including what is now Ukraine) or Romania. The majority had joined the exodus of White Russians following the Bolshevik Revolution of 1917, and their route to Shanghai was similar – through north-east China down to Shanghai. The Russian and Romanian Roma were not classified as a separate ethnic group or nationality by either the Shanghai Municipal Council or the SMP.

Smaller communities of Roma survived in Harbin, the major White Russian enclave in China outside Shanghai, and also the treaty port of Tientsin. The Russian theatre director and writer Vladimir Ivanovich Nemirovich-Danchenko noted the presence of Russian gypsies in the city of Harbin around the time of the 1904–05 Russo-Japanese War: 'Conversations in numbers, dreams in multiplication tables, thoughts in arithmetic calculations. Such was Harbin before the war, and such it remains. Only now the pioneers have been joined by new arrivals who have rushed here from every corner of Russia with a sole goal – to snatch a large sum while avoiding the military courts and get away in time, in one piece. Armenians, Georgians, Germans, Jews, Russian *kulaks*, and even gypsies all rush into the mad hurly-burly, thinking in thousands at the least, without fear of the sums reminiscent of the vast distance from Earth to Mars.'[231]

Similarly gypsies were present in both Harbin and Tientsin as fortune-tellers. The Hollywood actress Natalie Wood was born Natalia Nikolaevna Zacharenko in San Francisco to Russian

---

230 'Shanghai Gypsy Community', *North-China Daily News*, June 17, 1940.
231 Quoted in David Wolff and Nicholas Riasanovsky, *To the Harbin Station: The Liberal Alternative in Russian Manchuria, 1898–1914*, (Stanford, C.A., Stanford University Press, 1999).

immigrant parents. Her mother Maria Stepanovna (née Zudilova) had grown up as a White Russian refugee in Harbin where she recalled having her fortune told regularly by a Russian gypsy.[232] Most Shanghai Roma are thought to have spoken Russian as well as Roma dialects and often good English and basic functional Chinese too.[233] While Tsarist Russia had not had any exclusionary laws against Roma such as those pertaining to Jews, there had been traditional distrust and discrimination against the indigenous Roma community (usually referred to as the *Russka Roma*). This accelerated after the formation of the Soviet Union, which came quickly to suppress all nomadic communities including the Roma. Hence their exodus to China following the revolution.

Gypsy troubadours

With the rise in popularity of Gypsy Jazz as well as more traditional forms of Roma music and dance, Shanghai's Roma community moved from the margins of the city's entertainment industry to become one of its central components. Initially this meant more work for Roma entertainers and troubadours, a high profile and secure income – where work previously had been highly erratic and fickle. Along with the new variants such as Gypsy Jazz and Gypsy Swing, there was traditional Roma music and dancing, while the larger Roma entertainment groups also included jugglers, magicians and comedians (who told jokes in English, French or

232 Suzanne Finstad, *Natasha: The Biography of Natalie Wood* (New York: Three Rivers Press, 2002). The Harbin gypsy told Wood's mother that her second child (Natalie) would be famous throughout the world and should 'beware of dark water'. Natalie Wood drowned in 1981 under mysterious circumstances.

233 From the memoirs and sources consulted it is not clear which Romani dialect/language(s) were spoken in Shanghai as they are usually just referred to as 'Romany' or 'Roma'. While all Romani languages are Indic in origin, there are generally agreed to be seven varieties divergent enough to be considered languages in their own right – Vlax Romani, Balkan Romani, Carpathian Romani and Sinti Romani are the largest currently. There are additionally a number of creole or mixed Romani languages that have developed in locations as disparate as the British Isles, Scandinavia, Armenia and Portugal. Most Russian Roma spoke one or other of the so-called Northern Romani dialects.

Night Club　　　　　**Restaurant**
272 YU YUEN ROAD

Good Bye Shanghai!

On the eve of our leave for Tsingtao we are
offering a Gala Farewell Soiree to our Patrons.

Entertainers :

E. Krasso, Miss Karja Schapiro, Ballan and
"Charlie", Hartmann's Gipsy Swing Band

Russian depending on their audience's majority language). Well-known Shanghai Roma entertainers included Shoora Petroff who was considered one of the city's best dancers.[234]

Though gypsies in Shanghai hailed from a variety of sub-groups including the Lovari and a few Machwaya, the costume favoured by all when performing was that most associated with the Kalderash – wide, bright skirts, wide sleeves, fringed shawls worn around the shoulders or hips.[235] The male 'gypsy costume' was Russian Cossack in style with blouson shirts and knee-high leather boots. For many Roma their entry into the entertainment industry appears to have occurred after arrival in China. For instance, the Lovari Vishnevsky clan, who came to have the largest gypsy dance band in Shanghai and to own a number of venues from the late 1930s until they left China in 1949, had undertaken various occupations in Russia, primarily the traditional male *Russka Roma* occupation of horse dealing. Quite simply the opportunities for dealing horses in Shanghai were limited; the opportunities for providing entertainment comparatively plentiful.[236]

Although, prior to the Japanese invasion of 1937, Shanghai was by far the largest market in China for gypsy entertainment, Roma entertainers travelled the country providing entertainment. The major destinations were port cities and treaty ports such as Tientsin and Tsingtao. In this sense they followed the established tour routes

234　'Shanghai Gypsy Community', *North-China Daily News*, June 17, 1940.

235　The Lovari sub-group speak their own dialect based on Hungarian and come mostly from Hungary, Romania, Poland, France, Germany, Italy and Greece. The Machwaya sub-group originates in the main from Serbia and the former Yugoslavia and throughout the Balkans.

236　Victor Vishnevsky, *Memories of a Gypsy*, (Maryland: Salo Press, 2011).

for foreign entertainment acts in China. Touring gypsy troubadours were popular in Harbin, Tientsin and Tsingtao as well as
Peking. These destinations are unsurprising. Harbin, as previously
noted had a large Russian population as did Tientsin (which had
included a formal Russian Concession until it was renounced and
'handed back' to the Chinese after the creation of the USSR), while
Tsingtao had a White Russian population, was a resort destination
for many Europeans from across China in the summer months,
and was also where many leading Shanghai and Peking nightclubs
and cabarets retreated for the summer when business was slower
and weather in the cities humid (and air conditioning still relatively
rare in many smaller venues). For instance, the Hungaria Club, a
popular and relatively long-established venue at No. 272 Yu Yuen
Road in western Shanghai's 'Badlands' was a nightclub-restaurant
that regularly booked 'gipsy musicians' and decamped for Tsingtao
every summer. In 1940 the Hungaria departed for Tsingtao as
normal holding a Gala Farewell Soiree featuring, among others,
Hartmann's Gipsy Swing Band.[237]

There had been roaming groups of gypsies in China since the
White Russian exodus. In September 1922 several American news-
papers carried articles from Peking recounting the arrival of a 'group
of gypsies' setting up tents and 'fortune-telling booths'. They
claimed to have come from central Europe but were actually from
Harbin but trying their luck in pastures new. The newspaper
reported that the gypsies were successful, attracting large crowds of
Chinese who believed them to have 'the magic of good luck'.
However, problems occurred when the local Chinese Beggars'
Union intervened and complained that the newcomers were erod-
ing their takings. The gypsies were moved on, reportedly heading
to Korea and Japan. The reporter noted their colourful traditional
(i.e. Kalderash) gypsy costume and that 'their bright handkerchiefs
were the envy of every coolie.'[238]

---

237 Advertisement for the Hungaria Club, *North-China Daily News*, June 1940.
238 'Pekin Invaded by Gypsy Band', *Schenectady Gazette*, September 28, 1922.

Demonisation

In the 1920s gypsy music and culture was beginning to permeate the International Settlement's popular entertainment and fashion trends, though Roma themselves in Shanghai were being demonised as criminals. Commenting on a general rise in 'professional beggars' in Shanghai, *The North-China Herald* reported in the summer of 1921: 'At the present time there is a gang of gypsies going around calling themselves Rumanians [*sic*], about 26 in number and residing off the Seward Road [in Hongkew]. On investigation it was found that they were professional beggars and, comparatively speaking, wealthy.'[239] Other professional beggar gangs were noted, including one group from 'the Urals'. In October 1921 the paper also noted that 'a gypsy girl outside a theatre' had helped a man recently escaped from prison to find a lodging house that would take him. Again while no names were mentioned the implication of criminality was clear.[240]

By the later 1920s gypsy beggars were vexing *The North-China Herald* considerably more than a few years earlier. In 1926 *The Herald* reported a new Romany 'family' in Shanghai reputedly using children as beggars importuning businessmen in the International Settlement with 'Pleese. No fadder, no mudder, no eat.' The paper's reporter believed these Roma to be from Russia and to have been in China since the Bolshevik Revolution, moving from city to city targeting the foreign populations as professional beggars. Another gypsy professional begging group was also reported in 1926, about twenty in number and claiming to be 'Galicians'.[241]

Gypsy fashion on the Bubbling Well Road

Still, Romany or gypsy entertainment was popular at the highest levels of Shanghailander society in the 1920s. In March 1923 the celebrated Canadian violinist Kathleen Parlow appeared at the Olympic Theatre on the Bubbling Well Road and performed a

239 'Professional Beggars', *North-China Herald*, July 9, 1921.
240 'Muncie's Wanderings After Escape', *North-China Herald*, October 1, 1921.
241 'Some of our Daily Importunists', *North-China Herald*, September 4, 1926.

number of well received works including the Spanish composer Pablo de Sarasate's *Song of the Spanish Gypsies* to great critical acclaim.[242] Also in 1923 *The North-China Herald's* 'Woman Page' noted that the trend for wearing 'gypsy earrings' had come from London to Shanghai.[243] By the later 1920s, while gypsy beggars were regularly castigated in the pages of the English-language China coast newspapers, gypsy music had become increasingly popular. In November 1926 the local branch of the Alliance Française organised a night of music at the Cercle Sportif Français club[244] attended by a long list of notable French Shanghailanders. The entertainment programme featured Chinese jugglers and a 'modern dancer' performing *Danse de la nymphe des fleurs*. This was followed by dancing and a buffet supper and then finally a recital of gypsy music. The same weekend Miss Alice Bourke married Mr William Rutley Mowll at St Joseph's Church. According to the newspapers, 'The little flower girls were dressed in pale blue pleated georgette and carried silver gypsy baskets from which they strewed rose petals.'[245]

Between a rock and a hard place

The Roma community in Shanghai appears to have been between a rock and a hard place – wanted for their bright fashions and musical skills; demonised as inherently a criminal bunch. The twin attributes popularly given to gypsies in Shanghai – as entertainers and as criminals – was combined in 1922 as *The North-China Herald* noted the arrival in Shanghai of a troupe of Persian gypsy singers who were expected to be popular with local audiences. However, the paper also commented that the troupe had (it was claimed, but there was no actual evidence offered) been expelled from the Japanese treaty port of Yokohama for defrauding shopkeepers,

242 'Miss Parlow's Concert', *North-China Herald*, March 3, 1923.
243 'Triangular Fars', *North-China Herald*, April 28, 1923.
244 Now the Okura Grand Hotel on Maoming South Road.
245 'L'Alliance Français Entertainment' and 'Weddings: Mowll-Bourke', *North-China Herald*, November 27, 1926.

palming change and having stolen 'Yen 15,000'. The paper wrote in an overtly accusatory and mildly racist tone:

> Shanghai is very fond of gypsies. A year or so ago two of them entertained the credulous with whispered fortunes told down dark alleys, and sold marbles in little bags as amulets. And now a new crowd is coming with an entirely fresh line of business. Exactly where the singing comes into operation as an adjunct to the apparently more lucrative form of business is not clear, though it might be that, being discovered in their trickery, they charm the savage breast of the irate shop-keeper with a little ditty. Shanghai shopkeepers who have no particular taste for music in business would be well advised therefore, to count their change before handing it out to anybody who looks like a Romany lass, or even a Romany lad.[246]

In Shanghai there were occasional bouts of anti-Roma sentiment from the rest of the foreign community in the Settlement and Frenchtown. Roma were associated by many with crime, in particular the 'ringing the changes' fraud – a long standing traditional scam whereby shopkeepers or clerks are persuaded to give back more money than they are given by means of confusing them over change. This was a fraud long associated with travelling gypsy gangs across Europe at the time.

There were also quite substantial feuds both between and within Roma clans in Shanghai that did occasionally spill over into public violence involving a large number of people. In general it was believed that the Shanghai Roma community showed no interest in politics and in part was able to remain out of the violent ideological clashes of the period by not taking sides. It was also common, as recounted in Victor Vishnevsky's memoir, for gypsy boys not to attend any formal school. Despite this, Victor, encouraged by his entrepreneur entertainment industry father, did attend school. Most who did go to school attended the Roman

---

246 'Coming Visitors', *North-China Herald*, February 18, 1922.

Catholic St Jeanne d'Arc school, and later a White Russian-run Catholic school, in the French Concession. Vishnevsky maintains in his autobiography that the Kalderash (the Vishnevskys were of the less conservative and traditional Lovari sub-group) never sent their children to school in Shanghai.

Victor's father was more entrepreneurial and settled (a 'modern gypsy') than some other Roma.[247] Victor's sister Lida was not formally educated though became a noted performer herself as a young woman in the family entertainment business. Though regarded as being highly self-contained, many Shanghai Roma did have friends from other communities and those children attending school obviously mixed with the children of other Shanghailanders.

Born in 1938, Victor Vishnevsky recalls English boys and girls, as well as White Russian children, who were his friends and lived on the same streets as he did (Route Père Robert and Route Vallon). Most Roma children were involved in the entertainment industry from a young age and learnt musical instruments and other performing skills when still children (for instance, Victor Vishnevsky was an accomplished accordion player by his early teens).

Though mixing at school it appears that most Roma eventually married other Roma in Shanghai, often within their own sub-group though inter-clan marriages were not unknown. Some Roma, particularly those younger Shanghai-born ones, did marry out, mostly to members of the local White Russian and Eurasian community. While there are reported instances of this leading to trouble it certainly seems to have been common enough and mostly accepted within Shanghai Roma families.

Second-class enemies

Most 'gypsy entertainers' were hired by nightclubs, restaurants or cafés and were effectively self-employed on an engagement-by-engagement basis. However, some prominent members of Shanghai's Roma community did move into business ownership.

---

247 The term 'modern gypsy' appears to have come into use in 1930s France and Spain to refer to Roma who moved into apartments and settled.

Victor Vishnevsky recalls the whole of the Vishnevsky clan as being involved in the entertainment industry, and Victor's father owned and opened his own nightclub called The Black Eyes. He then went on in 1945 to open several successful bars employing the whole extended family and catering to American troops stationed in the newly-liberated Shanghai.

During the Japanese occupation of the Settlement the majority of the Roma community avoided internment. Most had some sort of nationality papers. For instance the Vishnevsky clan, though having come to Shanghai from Russia, had obtained Iranian nationality due to some of the family 'elders' having been born in Iran before moving to Russia. This placed them in the category of 'second-class enemies' and, though they were required to wear a red armband by the Japanese Military Police, they remained at liberty.

However, many Roma were reduced to poverty when the entertainment industry collapsed after the occupation of the Settlement following the Japanese attack on Pearl Harbor in December 1941. Fortunately, unlike in continental Europe where the Nazis held sway, there was no targeting of the Roma community for special persecution by the Japanese forces as long as they were not involved in politics or black-market dealing. Some were caught up in events – one prominent Roma dancer, and friend of the well-known Russian singer, cabaret performer and nightclub entrepreneur

Vertinsky's Gardenia Club

Alexander Vertinsky, was accused of spying for the Russians. Vertinsky often booked gypsy acts at his Badlands nightclub, the Gardenia on the Great Western Road, and performed with them showing a cross-fertilisation of traditional Russian and *Russka Roma* cultures in exile. Similarly the Jewish-Romanian-managed Red Rose nightclub in Hongkew offered 'Russian Gypsy' music nightly, though this appears to have been performed by non-Roma Russian musicians.

Indeed gypsy and non-Roma entertainers intersected in the city's Russian cabarets. *Cabaret Russe* and Vertinsky's Gardenia club were among the best known. This had also been the case in the *Cabarets Russe* of Paris that had, since the mid-1930s, highlighted gypsy bands. As in the West, since the formation of the Quintette du Hot Club de France by Django Reinhardt and Stéphane Grappelli in 1934, non-Roma musicians, such as Grappelli, had been a 'passport' for Roma entertainers and musicians to move up from the *boîtes* and *bal-musettes* and to enter higher-class establishments. It seems Alexander Vertinsky was one nightclub owner in Shanghai who appears to have performed a similar function for gypsy musicians in China.

The demise of Gypsy Shanghai

With the end of the Second World War and the liberation of Shanghai many Roma in Shanghai, like Victor Vishnevsky's father, went into the bar business while gypsy bands changed style to perform songs popular with the American liberation forces in Shanghai. The vogue for Gypsy Jazz, swing and the gypsy style had passed by the mid-1940s. The bar business was profitable, but competitive and rough. Large-scale and frequent fighting between foreign sailors and soldiers led to many of the bars, including the ones owned by Vishnevsky, being designated 'Out of Bounds' by the US Military Police. As the Cold War set in, many Roma-owned establishments and businesses came to be perceived with distrust by the American forces in Shanghai as being pro-Soviet. This led many *Russka Roma* to join the exodus of White Russians in Shanghai to Stalin's USSR – Victor Vishnevsky recalls that most of the Kalderash Roma in Shanghai opted to go to the Soviet Union. In general it seems that life for the Roma returnees in communist Russia was harsh, many were purged or imprisoned in Siberia while their traditional ways of life were highly circumscribed.

However, some seem to have survived and several were reported as having been sent to Moscow to provide entertainment; gypsy music enjoyed something of a renaissance and became fashionable in post-war Russia if not the West. However, traditional Roma lifestyles were severely curtailed by the imposition of the Decree of Nomadic Life Interdiction in 1956, which effectively outlawed nomadism in the Soviet Union.

Shanghai Roma families went to a wide variety of destinations including Hong Kong, Macau, Australia, western Europe and Scandinavia, as well as the United States and various Latin American destinations, primarily Brazil. One large group of Shanghai Lovari, including the Vishnevsky clan, travelled to western China and then crossed into Burma, making a prolonged stay in India before moving on to Tehran and then finally to the United States or Brazil. Along the way they performed their family gypsy music and dance shows to raise funds.

Many other Shanghai Roma remained stateless for many years with a community still awaiting exit visas from Hong Kong, where they were housed in a refugee camp (and later refugee-only hotels) organised by the International Refugee Organisation into the mid-1950s. Conditions in the camp were far from ideal as it was monitored by the police and residents were subject to a midnight curfew. Many of these former Shanghai Roma eventually secured visas to leave for Argentina, Bolivia and Brazil. Both Rio de Janeiro and São Paulo have communities of resettled Shanghai gypsies of both Kalderash and Lovari sub-groups. Some other Russian Roma went to Yokohama in Japan for some time and stayed into the mid-1950s before mostly leaving for the United States.

In the 1930s Shanghai was both in step with, and perhaps slightly ahead of, the international acceptance and adoption of a form of stylised 'gypsy entertainment'. Shanghai had any number of venues across the International Settlement, French Concession and the 'Badlands' that employed, advertised, promoted and in a limited number of cases were owned and managed by Roma. While the interest in gypsy-themed entertainment, or what the journalist Joseph Roth, encountering supposedly gypsy entertainers in France in the 1930s, termed 'balalaika Russians' (romanticised gypsy styles of music performed by non-Roma, invariably Russians, in stylised gypsy costume) was strong, it was indeed also often in Shanghai performed by actual Roma as opposed to non-Roma artistes and performers.[248]

Shanghai's small Roma community was to be largely ignored, sometimes discriminated against and marginalised between the wars. The result has been that the community has been almost totally overlooked by historians of foreign Shanghailander society yet, small as the community was, the Shanghai gypsies were a particularly vibrant part of the city's entertainment scene in the late 1930s and 1940s and deserve to be better remembered.

248 Joseph Roth, *The White Cities: Reports from France, 1925–1939*, (London: Granta Books, 2005).

Bored in the Broadway Mansions:
Penelope Fitzgerald (1977)

'Shanghai is decadent and decrepit.'

A most unlikely inspiration

In 2017 the Spanish director Isabel Coixet released a film version of Penelope Fitzgerald's 1978 novel *The Bookshop,* starring Emily Mortimer, Patricia Clarkson and Bill Nighy, bringing a new generation of fans to the book. Fitzgerald's novel revolves around Florence Green, a middle-aged widow, who decides to open a bookshop in a small English town. Though the book was set in Suffolk (Hardborough, a satirical version of the real town of Aldeburgh) the movie version was filmed in Northern Ireland and Barcelona. *The Bookshop* was Fitzgerald's second novel and is thought by many to be her best.[249]

Nothing very Chinese about any of that. But what most readers, and now cinemagoers, don't know is that *The Bookshop* was largely written in mid-December 1977 in an overheated Shanghai hotel room by a bored and restless Fitzgerald, unable to sleep and already fed up with her long-anticipated trip to China that now seemed never-ending. While, contrary to popular legend, Noël Coward did not write *Private Lives* in Shanghai's Cathay Hotel (he just did a bit of polishing to a second edit while struggling valiantly with influenza[250]), Penelope Fitzgerald really did write most of *The Bookshop* while staying in the Broadway Mansions building with Soochow Creek and the Garden Bridge just outside the window.

Quite where Fitzgerald's initial interest in China came from is hard to pinpoint. Born in Lincoln in 1916, the daughter of a

---

249 Penelope Fitzgerald, *The Bookshop*, (London: Duckworth, 1978).

250 I fully realise that the argument about *Private Lives* and the Cathay Hotel will rage forever more. As a staunch advocate for old Shanghai I wish it were true that Coward wrote the play in a couple of days while laid up with a bad dose of the flu in the Cathay. But the play appears to be the product of stays at several hotels including the Imperial in Tokyo, Raffles in Singapore and the Cathay. Still, Coward himself does state that the final draft was typed while in bed at the Cathay so it's not a total Shanghai urban legend. – Noël Coward, *Present Indicative,* (London: Heinemann, 1937), p. 299.

Broadway Mansions luggage label

one-time editor of *Punch* magazine, she was educated at Somerville College, Oxford and then worked for the BBC during World War Two (a period recalled in her 1980 novel *Human Voices*). During the war she met and married a young lawyer, Desmond Fitzgerald, who had an exciting war, being awarded the Military Cross in Libya during the North Africa Campaign, but came home an alcoholic. They, and their three children, settled down in the literary and well-heeled north London suburb of Hampstead where they established a cultural journal called *World Review*.

Perhaps this was the start of Fitzgerald's China interest? *World Review* was launched in 1951 at a time when most literary and current affairs journals (John Lehmann's *Penguin New Writing*, Cyril Connolly's *Horizon*, etc.) were failing and closing. Perhaps they should have taken more note of that fact. *World Review*, co-edited by Penelope with Desmond, was a short-lived publication. It mixed politics, art, architecture, stories, poems, serialisations and reviews and had colour covers and commissioned cartoons. Among its stated objectives from the start was to cover 'British Relations with China'. And they did, just only once, in July 1952 with an article entitled 'The British in China' by O.M. Green, edited by Fitzgerald herself. The piece was a rather lacklustre defence of the days of the old Canton trade and the treaty port years of Shanghai, finishing with a less than rousing denunciation of the relatively new

Communist government from a man who used to be editor of the staunchly pro-British Shanghai newspaper *The North-China Daily News*. Appointed in 1911, Green had lasted in the editor's chair until 1930. He retired as unwaveringly pro-British as the day he'd got the job. He then had a second career back in England as a professional Old China Hand, reminiscing at Home Counties Women's Institute teas and doing little else except a bit of journalism such as that for the Fitzgeralds.

World Review folded in 1953. Desmond's increasingly heavy drinking led to problems that got him disbarred and threw the Fitzgeralds into poverty. Penelope took a job as a teacher to make ends meet. They lived on a rickety old houseboat on the Thames for a while, until it sank (though the experience provided fodder for one of her best novels, *Offshore*, in 1979). Desmond died in 1976. Quitting teaching, Penelope embarked seriously on a literary career and managed to earn a few advances. With the money she decided to take the holiday she'd always wanted – to China. Writing to her then editor Richard Garnett[251] at Macmillan she told him she was heading east in December saying: 'I've wanted all my life to see the Great Wall under snow'.[252]

To visit China in December 1977 was not all that common. The Cultural Revolution had not long abated, Mao's death was barely a year ago, the fallout from the Gang of Four trial still rumbling on, the Hua Guofeng–Deng Xiaoping power struggle raging, and the Beijing Spring still to come. Despite this, in 1977 Thomson Holidays, the pioneers of the British package holiday, began offering all-inclusive tours to Peking (as they still referred to it) and Shanghai.

Thomson Holidays had been founded by Roy Thomson (later Lord Thomson of Fleet), a Canadian entrepreneur and businessman best known for being a newspaper mogul. By the

251　Among other notable successes as an editor, Garnett had edited the 1954 English translation of the Austrian mountaineer Heinrich Harrer's *Sieben Jahre in Tibet (Seven Years in Tibet)* and arranged for a former Shanghai sojourner and author on China, Peter Fleming, to provide an introduction.

252　Hermione Lee, *Penelope Fitzgerald: A Life*, (London: Chatto & Windus, 2013).

mid-1960s Thomson was at the height of his powers owning *The Times* and *The Sunday Times* as well as *The Scotsman*. Thomson had acquired four tour operators – Skytours, Riviera, Luxitours, Gaytours – and the airline Britannia Airways. In 1965 he merged them all to form the Thomson Travel Group and, in 1971, they became known as simply Thomson Holidays.

Thomson's was the first British mass-market package holiday operator to venture behind the Iron Curtain, offering weekend breaks to Moscow in 1972. At the personal invitation of Premier Zhou Enlai, Thomson made a visit to China in 1972. As a Fleet Street mogul Thomson was able to get things done in China. His deputy editor at *The Times*, Louis Heren, had a son who was partially disabled with polio. Acupuncture seemed to help, but was hard to obtain outside China at the time. Thomson offered to pay for Heren's son to spend six months in China for treatment.[253] Later Philip Morrell, who was organising new package tours for Thomson Holidays, wanted to start tours to China. He asked Lord Thomson for an introduction to Zhou Enlai, but Thomson wasn't interested. Morrell decided to go ahead anyway and found a friendly Chinese chef in London's Chinatown who wrote a letter to the premier of China for him, requesting permission to bring British tour groups to Peking and Shanghai and dropping Thomson's name. Amazingly, Zhou received the letter (it is not recorded exactly what address Morrell wrote to) and replied agreeing. Morrell also reached a deal with Tarom, the Romanian airline that had a weekly service from Bucharest to Peking, and the Thomson package holiday to China was launched. To be fair, Regent Holidays, a Bristol company that had been pioneering holidays behind the Iron Curtain, got to communist China first, offering a package tour via the Trans-Siberian Railway in 1976, but Thomson's was not far behind.[254]

253 'Obituaries: Lord Thomson of Fleet', *Independent*, June 13, 2006.
254 Philip Morrell started his travel industry career as a humble holiday rep in Benidorm, worked for Thomson and then left to form the Voyages Jules Verne travel company, which he later successfully sold to giant travel conglomerate Kuoni. See 'Barnardo's Boy Who Will Float the Queen's Jubilee Boat', *Daily Telegraph*, February 28, 2012.

Penelope Fitzgerald booked one of Thomson's first tours, from the third to the fourteenth of December 1977 – presumably expecting that the Great Wall would be under snow at that time. She got vaccinated against smallpox and cholera as advised, and bought a little red diary (unknowingly suggestive of Chairman Mao's equally little red book) to take with her and record her impressions.

Although marketed by Thomsons as an accessible package holiday, it was still a long flight to Peking on the rather basic Tarom airline, via strictly communist Bucharest, and then to Karachi in Pakistan, a city under martial law. In many ways travel in China was something to be endured rather then enjoyed – IT IS FORBIDDEN TO USE CAMERAS, BINOCULARS OR RADIOS WHILE FLYING OVER THE PEOPLE'S REPUBLIC OF CHINA. Though it was not all communist austerity – China's national airline CAAC flew them into Peking, serving a meal of rice with shrimp, a hardboiled egg, slithers of duck meat, stringbeans and mushroom. Fitzgerald and her fellow tour-group members grudgingly admitted the in-flight meal wasn't too bad at all. However, the plane's intercom still played songs praising Chairman Mao non-stop for the duration of the eight-hour flight.

The Peking Hotel (the former Grand Hôtel de Pékin[255]) was overheated and stuffy; the corridors were dimly lit, towels were rationed, hot water erratic, blown light bulbs went un-replaced, room keys had to be handed in whenever stepping outside of the hotel. Fitzgerald felt, in her own words, slightly self-conscious travelling on her own, an, 'unglamorous widow-lady' with 'shabby luggage' and too hot in her sweaters and trousers (nobody warned the tour group about Peking's suffocating steam heating). Self-deprecating she may have been, but her holiday companions got the same treatment in her China diary: 'dear Miss How, a missionary, with her Primus stove, tea bags and spare bath-plugs'; '"Knightsbridgey" Mrs Handley-Page in a Persian lamb coat'; Mr Hall, a taciturn builder from Norfolk and life-long traveller; Mr Holdford, who constantly shouted 'all aboard' to the consternation of the Chinese tour-bus driver; Mr Ross, a Newcastle factory owner who

255　And now the Beijing Hotel on the corner of Chang'an Avenue and Wangfujing.

drank a little too much rice wine at the nightly, and seemingly endless, banquets. The entire party was united in their loathing of Chinese traditional breakfasts and with their concerns over the cleanliness or otherwise of the shared chopstick jar.[256]

Such were the Brits who booked package holidays to China in 1977. In charge of them all was Madame Sun, who was flabbergasted by the British tourists' ability to buy everything offered to them in the Friendship Stores along the way while also surreptitiously taking advantage of her privileged position to snap up a top-quality padded baby jacket for her grandson. The tourists made their selections and then waved handfuls of yuan at the shop assistants who took as much as was required and never short-changed the foreign innocents. Strange pills appeared for those who had developed colds in Peking's harsh winter air. Salty sodas and endless cups of thin green tea were provided to remove the Gobi grit from the tour party's throats.

Then an itinerary all too familiar to those who have endured a package holiday to China – The Great Wall (which Fitzgerald found to be 'as expected', though no mention as to whether she ever did see it 'under snow'); pandas at the zoo (which she was only forced to coo over for ten minutes); a Chinese opera (very propagandistic and totally flummoxing the translators with lyrics such as 'We dedicate our youth to communism'); the Temple of Heaven (which Fitzgerald found truly impressive); the Forbidden City (which she considered akin to Versailles in atmosphere and 'terrifying'); a people's commune (of little interest) and the children of the Revolutionary Street Committee Kindergarten who gave a performance extolling the recently concluded Eleventh Communist Party of China People's Congress in a most charming fashion. Then finally, in English, the children bade all the 'Mr and Mrs Thomsons' goodbye in a slight translation mix up.

And then Shanghai, a city still seemingly smothered in a dust sheet cast over the once great port in 1949 and left there. Fitzgerald, staying in the Shanghai Mansions (now once again, as it was before

---

256 Extracts from Fitzgerald's China diary are contained in Hermione Lee, *Penelope Fitzgerald: A Life*, (New York: Knopf, 2014).

1949, called the Broadway Mansions), adjacent to Suzhou Creek, wrote that she found the city 'decadent and decrepit'. Red banners ran across the street urging people to UNITE AROUND THE CENTRAL COMMITTEE UNDER CHAIRMAN HUA. After a day or two of yet more sightseeing with the energetic Madame Sun, Fitzgerald was done in, fed up, boiled in steam heating, overwhelmed by children dressed up as turnips dancing to celebrate the success of Maoist agricultural collectivisation, and unsure if curious looks from locals were friendly, indifferent or hostile. She had negotiated enough rivers of weaving cyclists, drunk enough thin green tea, endured enough morning congee and bought more than enough Friendship Store knick-knacks.

Sharing a room in Shanghai with the tea-making missionary Miss How, Fitzgerald woke early unable to sleep. Leaving the Broadway Mansions unescorted was problematic and discouraged so she stayed in her room, quietly writing her China experiences in the small red notebook she had brought from London. She soon found she had nothing left to say about China. At that point she turned her diary upside down and began writing on the back page.

Shanghai Friendship Store, late 1970s

The opening scenes of *The Bookshop* remain in the back of Fitzgerald's China diary almost exactly as they were to appear when the novel was published in 1978 and was swiftly shortlisted for the Booker Prize.

However, there is one change that perhaps reflects Fitzgerald's brief Shanghai time. In the final edit of the novel the opening line is: 'In 1959 Florence Green occasionally passed a night when she was not absolutely sure whether she had slept or not.' In the first draft in her China diary the opening line arguably reflects the early morning winter in her room in the Broadway Mansions:

'Experiences aren't given us to be "got over", otherwise they would hardly be experiences.'

The Last Refuge – How America's Biggest Ever Swindler Ended Up in Shanghai: C.C. Julian & Leonora Levy (1934)

'There is a certain element of truth in the allegation that Shanghai forms a sanctuary for fugitives from justice from all parts of the world.' [257]

257 Editorial, *Shanghai Evening Post and Mercury*, May 3, 1933.

Saturday, February 4th, 1933

The news was all over town – 'The Man Who Made and Lost Five Fortunes was Fleeing Oklahoma Justice'.[258] A nationwide manhunt for 'America's greatest conman' was launched, rewards for apprehension and capture issued, the Canadian border sealed, newspapers across the United States appealed for sightings. Courtney Chauncey ('C.C.') Julian was officially on the run.

Canadian-born Julian had launched Julian Petroleum in 1923. 'Julian Pete', as the firm was known, had struck some oil the previous year in Santa Fe Springs, California. Julian began selling shares in Julian Pete like there was no tomorrow and out of all ratio to the size of his strike. In 1925 the Californian Corporations Commission started investigating him for fraudulent sales promotions. Julian tried to offload the company but an audit revealed that he had issued 4,200,000 unauthorised shares of stock. The Los Angeles Stock Exchange duly suspended Julian Pete, which subsequently collapsed in 1927 amid large-scale fraud, taking with it over US$150 million from 40,000 suckered investors. Company officials were fined and imprisoned, Julian Pete employees arrested and a district attorney sent to jail for taking bribes. In 1931 Julian faced charges of conspiracy to defraud 15,000 investors of over US$3.5 million in the State of Oklahoma. Julian disappeared a day before the trial, forfeited his sizeable $25,000 bail, deserted his wife and two daughters and fled to Vancouver from where he booked a suite on a Japanese ship bound for Shanghai.

For a while plenty of people speculated on why C.C. Julian split America and headed to Shanghai. Surely he could have disappeared somewhere he would never be found, where there were no newspapers, no American embassies or consulates – an African jungle,

---

258 'Hunt Ordered for Oil Man in U.S. Fraud Case', *Pittsburgh Press*, February 4, 1933.

a Dutch East Indies hill station, or a South American logging camp perhaps? But he chose the International Settlement of Shanghai – a city with a thriving press, a sizeable American population, an American court, and hordes of paparazzi crowding the ocean-liner arrival terminals. Shanghai was a city with a seemingly unquenchable thirst for gossip; a town that loved celebrities either good or bad. Quite why Julian chose Shanghai is not clear – but it turned out to be a truly inspired choice.

Some said C.C. Julian had his ill-gotten gains stashed in a Shanghai bank – he hadn't. Other believed he'd always had a fondness for Oriental antiquities – he didn't particularly. The rumours swelled – always with several mistresses in his life, Julian was said to have a lady over there in old Shanghai – but he didn't know anyone in the city. The press speculated he'd done a deal with the Chinese government never to do jail time or be repatriated – no such deal existed, or even needed to.

Of course those that knew Shanghai were not surprised in the least. If you were the biggest conman in the United States – and C.C. Julian undoubtedly held that title in 1933 – and, although you'd bilked a lot of people out of a lot of money but you still needed more, and you wanted somewhere without an extradition treaty back to the United States, and a place where nobody cared too much how your money smelled, then where the hell else would you go but Shanghai? And so arrive in the International Settlement C.C. Julian did ... where the press tailed him relentlessly and he did find a woman, and he did have some schemes left up his sleeve, and he did like the old town of Shanghai plenty. So much so that he never left!

Thursday, March 23rd, 1933

The Dollar Line's *President Jackson* arrived at Shanghai from Seattle after a stop in Yokohama, Japan. A man in his early forties disembarked with a United States passport in the name of Mr T.R. King. He claimed to be of Irish descent. He attracted no particular attention. In fact Mr King was Mr C.C. Julian and he had purchased the forged document in Nuevo Laredo, Mexico a couple of years earlier thinking it might be handy just in case he ever needed to skip the United States in a hurry. That time had come. To C.C. Julian though – regardless of which name he was travelling under and how incognito he wished to be – appearances were important. Mr King had travelled first class, dressed in a freshly pressed white linen suit and with a straw boater. He was accompanied from Yokohama by eighteen-year-old Miss Leonora Levy. She was a temporary employee hired in Yokohama to assist him, hoping to become his permanent secretary, and perhaps much more. Mr King had told her he was planning to open a company seeking to exploit China's mineral reserves. Leonora Levy had been on holiday in Yokohama, but had been born and raised in Shanghai. At the time she met Mr King she was pondering a career move, out of the secretaries' pool at the Metropolitan Film Distribution Corporation of Shanghai and upwards to something better paid and classy, like a personal assistant. She was also hoping to meet Mr Right and just possibly Mr King was Mr Right. Working for him seemed like a move in the right direction for Leonora.

After docking at Woosung the first-class passengers boarded a swift lighter that took them to the customs jetty and disembarkation on the Bund. There, as always when a passenger liner arrived in Shanghai, was a mob of reporters and photographers swarming towards the gangplank. Hoping to arrive anonymously Julian was momentarily alarmed at this welcoming scrum. However he soon realised that the gentlemen, and a few ladies, of the Shanghai press (both Shanghailander and Shanghainese) were there to photograph and interview his fellow passenger Bruce Barton. Barton was at that time perhaps America's best-known adman and the author of the bestselling *The Man Nobody Knows,* a rather strangely conceived modern-day parable wherein Jesus is imagined as a successful business leader building up a huge corporation (Christianity Inc.) with twelve loyal disciples (his board) to market his product (Christianity). Barton's publishing and business success had made his name and his fortune. He was on the cusp of entering politics and running for the Seventeenth District of New York for the House of Representatives. But before that ordeal he opted for a part-sales trip/part-family vacation round the world with his wife and daughter.

And so Mr King and Miss Levy were unnoticed, except by Leonora's brother Ralph who had come to meet her and welcome her back home. Leonora introduced Mr King to her brother as a man with vast experience of the oil business in the United States come to explore opportunities in China and make another fortune in the East, just as he claimed to have already done in the West. There was no immediate reason to disbelieve Mr King's intentions – a first-class cabin, tailor-made suits, the best cigars, some salary in advance to Leonora, and now a suite at Sir Victor Sassoon's luxurious art-deco Metropole Hotel. The Metropole was on the junction of Kiangse Road and Foochow Road, just back from the Bund, not far from the Central Police Station and the American Club. Ralph arranged rickshaws to ferry the arriving businessman's luggage to the hotel and they all strolled to reception together.

Leonora told Ralph that she thought she'd struck lucky meeting Mr King. The Levy brother and sister were both Shanghai-born Jews with Spanish citizenship, due to their Spanish father and British mother. Leonora and her brother Ralph were close after having been orphaned in 1924. Levy was their stepfather's surname and they had both adopted it. Their father, Abraham Goldenberg, a cinema manager, had been brutally clubbed to death and murdered in the lobby of his cinema. After secretarial college, where Leonora acquired skills in typing, shorthand and basic bookkeeping, she had spent some years working as a stenographer with a film-distribution company her deceased father had been associated with.[259] Ralph had stayed in Shanghai and worked for the David Sassoon Company.[260] Leonora saved up enough for a vacation in

259 Details of Leonora's past life and her father's murder from, 'C.C. Julian's Companion', *Shreveport Times*, March 26, 1934.

260 The David Sassoon Company was known generally as 'Old Sassoon' to differentiate it from the Shanghai businesses (over fifty in total) of Sir Victor Sassoon (the Cathay Hotel, Hamilton House, the Metropole Hotel and the Embankment Building, among others around the Settlement and Frenchtown). Old Sassoon was also involved in property, as well as importing cotton yarn from Bombay to Shanghai and to its other branches in Calcutta, Canton, Yokohama, Nagasaki and Hong Kong.

Japan and it was there that she'd met Mr King. They'd become close, somewhat intimate, but she hadn't quite snagged him yet. He'd hired her to help him with his business ambitions in Shanghai, but Leonora thought Mr King, whom she believed to be a widower, might suggest a closer and more permanent arrangement. Mr King checked into the Metropole Hotel alone while Leonora went home with her brother.

Monday, April 10th, 1933

Just across Foochow Road from the Metropole was Hamilton House. Like the Metropole it was a new art-deco style block, only recently finished and part of the large Shanghai property portfolio of Sir Victor Sassoon. Shanghai lawyer Norwood Allman had his offices in Hamilton House. Allman had previously worked for the American Embassy in Peking during World War One and then, in the early 1920s, moved to Shanghai working as the US consul in the Settlement and an assessor (at the time, effectively a co-judge sitting with a Chinese magistrate) on the International Mixed Court that adjudicated legal disputes between foreigners and Chinese in the concessions. By 1933 Allman was one of the best-known characters in Shanghai – a former American consul, the honorary consul for Mexico in Shanghai and with his own successful law firm (Allman, Davies and Kops). On Monday morning April 10th, 1933 Mr King strolled into Allman's office and engaged him in conversation.

In his memoirs Allman claimed that 'Mr King' would regularly wander across the road from the Metropole and up to his Hamilton House office for a chat.[261] Allman claimed that Julian/King had said that he would like to retain him but that he never actually did and probably just wanted a little companionship. Perhaps so. Julian knew nobody in Shanghai apart from Leonora and Ralph Levy. Despite this, Julian did retain a lawyer eventually, a Dr O. Fischer of the firm Musso, Fischer and Wilhelm, but this firm was quite different to Norwood Allman's practice. Musso, Fischer and Wilhelm

261 Norwood F. Allman, *Shanghai Lawyer*, (New York: McGraw-Hill, 1943). There is a reprint of Allman's book now available from Shanghai publisher Earnshaw Books.

was run by 'Commendatore' G.D. Musso, an exceedingly wealthy Italian lawyer who had 'amassed a fortune in mysterious ways'.[262] Actually that fortune had been built over a couple of decades by representing a bewildering array of dodgy clients including the notorious Soviet spies the Noulens and various other pro-Soviet agents in Shanghai[263] as well as Du Yuesheng's Green Gang. Just to balance their interests they also represented various Catholic missions across China from their offices on the Szechuen Road.

Dr Fischer explained to Julian why he was safe in Shanghai. C.C. Julian may have entered the port of Shanghai on a false American passport, but he was in reality a Canadian. That put him under British jurisdiction in Shanghai and so the American and Chinese courts couldn't touch him. The British said the crimes he was accused of were committed on American territory and not under a domain of the British flag. America had no extradition treaty with China or Britain so Julian could remain free in Shanghai. Shanghai's convoluted extraterritoriality ('extrality') laws had once again, as they had so many times over the decades, worked in the favour of nobody but the criminal.[264]

Feeling legally secure, C.C. Julian wasted no time in exploring his new stamping ground – the International Settlement. As a new boy in town he wanted contacts and he wanted to get the lay of the land fast. Grab a drink in any bar, club or hotel lobby in Shanghai and you soon got some advice on how things were done on the Whangpoo. C.C. Julian certainly met J.F. Malone, an American who dealt in tobacco leaf and silver – two very profitable commodities in 1930s Shanghai. Julian, introducing himself still as Mr King, told Malone he was interested in the oil business. Malone

---

262 So said the usually correct judge of character in old Shanghai, J.B. Powell, the editor of the *China Weekly Review* in his memoir *My Twenty Five Years in China,* (New York: Macmillan, 1945).

263 Frederic Wakeman, *Policing Shanghai, 1927–1937,* (Oakland, C.A., Philip E. Lilienthal Books, 1995), p. 149. For more on the Noulens Affair see the chapter 'Red Sojourners at the Zeitgeist Bookstore'.

264 As ever I am indebted to Doug Clarke, the author of the three-volume *Gunboat Justice: British and American Law Courts in China and Japan, 1842–1943* (Shanghai: Earnshaw Books, 2015). C.C. Julian appears in Vol. 3, *Revolution, Resistance and Resurrection, 1927–1943,* pp. 110–111.

told him, quite correctly, that Shanghai was a gold and silver town and not an oil town. Anyone could deal gold or silver, buy and sell bullion and currency, but if you wanted to deal oil then you needed Chinese government contacts, very high-level contacts, and these weren't in Shanghai; they were in Nanking.

'Two Gun' Cohen

Julian concluded that an 'in' with Nanking could help. Quite how Julian met Morris 'Two Gun' Cohen is something of a mystery, but he certainly did, and the two men hit it off. Cohen was a legend in 1933 Shanghai. From the Jewish ghetto of Whitechapel in London's East End he had a rough start. He was arrested for suspected pickpocketing and so his parents shipped him off to Canada in the hope of a fresh start. It didn't totally work – he learnt to shoot and play cards (a lifelong obsession) and sold real estate, worked as a carnival barker, gambler and grifter across Saskatchewan. He got to know the Chinese working on the Canadian Pacific Railway and actually joined the Tongmenhui, Dr Sun Yat-sen's revolutionary anti-Manchu organisation that took power in China in 1911. He fought in World War One and then sailed to Shanghai, eventually becoming Sun Yat-sen's bodyguard. After Dr Sun's death in 1925 he continued to serve various Kuomintang officials and got to know Chiang Kai-shek too. In 1933 Cohen was rather betwixt-and-between – known by his nickname 'Two Guns', billed by the American newspapers as 'the brains' of the Chinese army (he had been a colonel in the Nationalist army and had organised some training) but actually was rather out of the loop in Nanking.

Cohen and Julian became friendly. They both had similar backgrounds, as chancers in Canada and time done selling nefarious schemes, be they Julian's stocks or Cohen's Saskatchewan property deals. Technically Cohen held the rank of brigadier-general in the Nationalist Army, though Chiang Kai-shek had dispensed with his services and he'd found himself sidelined. He mostly sat around in Shanghai, favouring the bar of the Astor House Hotel, getting recognised, signing autographs, giving interviews to visiting pressmen, being bought drinks, winning and losing at cards and seeing if anything interesting presented itself.

Whether he realised it or not Julian had come to a city that was literally chock-a-block with con men and con women, grifters, chancers and fraudsters. True, if any of them knew he was Courtney Chauncey Julian of the Julian Pete con they'd probably stand him a drink, but the chances were he'd not be the only crook at the bar.

Not long after arriving he met Mary Cantorovich who promised to introduce him to some important men-about-town. She claimed to be a Russian countess, born in Moscow but forced into exile in China. Whether Julian believed her or not is unclear; whether she was ever even close to be a countess is also unclear. Mary Cantorovich was probably the former wife of a draper with a store at No. 190 Broadway in Hongkew.[265] This Mr Cantorovich went upmarket after marrying a woman called Mary and opened the Cantorovich Corsetière further along Broadway at No. 28, part of the smart new Broadway Mansions apartment building and close to the Astor House Hotel, across the Garden Bridge from the Bund. Around 1931 the Cantorovichs appear to have split up, though Mary kept the name.[266] Since separating from her husband Mary had been observed in the social pages of the local newspapers being squired around town by various Shanghailander and Chinese gentlemen, all of whom had one thing in common – they were

265 Mary Cantorovich sometimes appears in newspapers and records as 'Contorovich', Contarovich', 'Controvich' and various other variations. It is possible that Julian's Mary Cantorovich, who was initially a draper's wife, is a different Mary Cantorovich, but I think they are one and the same.

266 Whether this was because they never formally divorced or that she just liked the name I'm not sure. For a countess to marry a draper, divorce him and keep his name seems unlikely to me. By obscuring her former surname it is also difficult to delve any deeper into her Russian past.

CANTOROVICH
CORSETIERE

POIRETTE	*NEMO*
BEVOISE	*CAMP BELTS*
MADAME X	*WARNER*

We specialise in Corsettings
Latest models from America & Europe

28 BROADWAY (Astor House Block)

well-heeled. Mary and C.C. hit it off swiftly and she started being seen around town with him, and Leonora, as a threesome.

Mr King was now finding it tricky to walk through the lobby of the Metropole Hotel without the manager or a minion asking him when it might be convenient to settle his bill? He paid some token amounts but begged off paying more, claiming that he just needed to attend to some banking affairs and transfer some cash from the United States.

Thursday, April 27th, 1933

In the meantime Mr King moved hotels – across from Kiangse Road and the Metropole to the Park Hotel on the Bubbling Well Road. When he settled in he decided he liked the Park Hotel better than the Metropole (or at least the Park weren't yet demanding payment as the Metropole were). Just across from the racecourse, it was a great location with a restaurant offering a wonderful view across the city towards Frenchtown. He dined there almost nightly with Leonora; sometimes Mary Cantorovich joined them. Her role is somewhat unclear. They always sat at the same table with a floor-to-ceiling window view over the racecourse and the neon lights of the city beyond and up the broad Bubbling Well Road. A mighty fine view, but the trouble with the Shanghailander village was that sooner or later (as Eugene O'Neill had found out some years previously) you always bumped into someone you knew. One night, dining with Leonora, in the busy Park Hotel rooftop restaurant, Julian bumped into a woman named Winnie St Cyr. She exclaimed for everyone to hear: 'Chauncey Julian, whatever are you doing in Shanghai?' This was serious bad luck for C.C. as Winnie St Cyr had been his mistress back in California, though they'd parted on good terms. She knew his name, his scams, that he was married with daughters . . . and that he'd skipped bail in Oklahoma.

Leonora was confused, and not a little put out, when Winnie St Cyr mischievously asked C.C. to introduce her to his daughter! It went downhill from there. Winnie was not overly discreet, she didn't care who knew she'd once been C.C. Julian's mistress or that the authorities in Los Angeles and Oklahoma were scouring Canada for him. She laughed out loud telling everyone that bail bondsmen were hassling everyone who'd ever known Julian. Just to make matters worse several American newspapermen just happened to be dining at the Park that night and overheard the whole thing. The news was out – Courtney Chauncey Julian was alive, well and living in Shanghai far from the (seemingly not very) long arm of American justice. The local newspapers feasted on the story. If Leonora hadn't known who C.C. Julian was before then the Shanghai newspapers were keen to provide the full story the very next day. The American Consulate began looking into extradition proceedings, though Shanghai's extraterritoriality regulations soon stymied that effort. Mary Cantorovich (a woman who never knowingly let a journalist walk past her without offering a story) claimed that she was assisting Julian in compiling his memoirs for a New York publisher.

But if Leonora was angry at being duped by C.C. she didn't show it. In fact she stood right by her man and helped him pack – too many journalists waiting in ambush in the Park's lobby and management demands for settlement of his rather large bill becoming more vociferous. In good Julian Pete fashion, just when things looked a little sticky, C.C. traded up. He moved into a suite at one of the city's poshest hotels, the Palace, right on the Bund.[267] In Shanghai C.C. Julian was free from the threat of extradition and at liberty to

267 Now the Swatch Art Peace Hotel.

proclaim his innocence of the charges laid against him in Oklahoma to the local press: 'America can go to hell', he told the
Shanghai-based *China Weekly Review*.[268] And if Leonora seemingly
wasn't worried about Mr King being C.C. Julian and the revelations
of his shady past, neither it seems were others in Shanghai.

On April 27th the story broke in Shanghai and a day later,
worldwide – C.C. Julian was back in business. He and General
Morris 'Two Gun' Cohen were working together. Julian was hawk-
ing shares in a fund to raise money to buy the Chinese government
2,500 fighter planes – effectively creating an air force from scratch
for the Nationalists. Julian was to receive commissions on all the
funds raised. Cohen had been in Canton negotiating with Chen
Chitang (Chen Jitang), who had enormous power in southern
China with governing authority over Guangdong province as well
as being commander-in-chief of the Nationalist First Army Group
commanding (at its height) 300,000 troops. Chen seemed like just
the kind of man Julian could do business with. Chen was also
raising funds to transform Canton into a modern city with paved
streets, new buildings, schools and bridges over the Pearl River.
These were not pipe dreams – these improvements were actually
happening. Some called Chen's 'reign' in Canton a golden age and
dubbed him the Celestial King of the South.[269]

Chen was eager to build China's air force up after the 1932
Sino-Japanese War had shown Tokyo's supremacy in the air. The
American journalist Edgar Snow had been down to Canton to visit
Shau Gau Ling, Canton's new military airfield and training centre,
based on the US Army Air Force's Kelly Field in Texas. In April 1933,
China had about ninety fighter planes and a hundred and fifty
trained pilots – the idea of jumping to 2,500 through Julian and
Cohen's investment scheme was appealing to Chen.[270]

268 'Absconding American Oil Promoter Located in Shanghai', *China Weekly
      Review*, April 29, 1933, p. 354.

269 If Chen is not much remembered today or receives any credit for the
      modernisation of Guangzhou (which he does deserve) it is probably because
      in 1950, while serving as governor of Hainan Island, he left for Taiwan where
      he became a 'Strategic Adviser' to Chiang Kai-shek. He died in Taipei in 1954.

270 Edgar Snow, 'China Speed Up Building of Air Forces; Preference Given to
      American Methods', *Dayton Daily News*, April 2, 1933.

But the plan to raise money for the warplanes looked suspiciously similar to the old Julian Pete stock sales – lots of high-powered publicity and ambitious talk of profits to be returned to investors. It was even reported that Julian had sent to the United States for some of his old sales colleagues. Cohen was talking up Julian to the newspapers; they gave the impression the government was on board; Julian even claimed he was thinking of taking Chinese citizenship.[271]

But it all went nowhere. Maybe Chen Chitang realised the investment scheme was being run by a wanted man? Most probably, despite the endorsement of 'Two Gun' Cohen, potential investors had by now read too much about C.C. Julian's past in the Chinese newspapers to trust him. The Nationalist government found funds elsewhere for their fledgling air force and also brought in help from the Italian air force. Julian needed another scam.

Saturday, December 23rd, 1933

With the cat out of the bag why hide your intentions? It seems nobody was willing to trust Julian with building up China's air force so, in December 1933, he went back to what he knew best – it was time to roll out the old dodgy oil stocks game in the Far East. C.C. had found himself some friends and spent months cultivating them – his tobacco and silver-dealing drinking pal J.F. Malone as well as Major Edward Howard, an aeroplane salesman working as the US Commerce Department's Shanghai Representative. Neither seemed too bothered about his purported identity or, when it was revealed, his true identity, or even that he was flat broke. Morris Cohen stayed close to Julian, continuing to lend him some local celebrity endorsement.

Julian got back in the game as the general manager of a venture entitled the Stock and Bond Guarantee Company, a brokerage. Leonora was the company's secretary and they opened offices at the Continental Bank Building on Kiukiang Road in the heart of the Settlement. The business had both Chinese and foreign investors

271 'China Deal Julian Aim', *Los Angeles Times*, April 28, 1933.

and was run by a man called James Dolan who'd been trying desperately to make his fortune one way or another in Shanghai for ages. Julian and his team starting rolling out stocks to Shang-hailanders and local Chinese offering amazing profits – they started taking in amounts of $5,000 (in Chinese dollars) from local inves-tors who sat back and awaited their promised dividend day.

C.C. Julian checked out of the Palace Hotel on the Bund just before Christmas 1933 and checked into the distinctly less salubrious Embassy Hotel on the Settlement's Carter Road. More precisely, he skipped out of the Palace in the wee small hours of the morning when the desk was closed and the night porter snoozing, leaving the staff to discover his room empty and cleaned out.

Alexander MacDonald, an American journalist visiting Shang-hai, stayed at the embassy around the same time: 'The Embassy was like any hotel around New York's Times Square, the Lexington, Taft, the Victoria, Lincoln. Six Chinese dollars a night for a room and an expectant servant at every turn of the elbow. The same mechanical atmosphere and the same gloomy corridors.'[272] At the Embassy, Julian took two adjoining rooms – one he shared with Leonora, who was by now his lover as well as secretary, and another he used as an office and reception room. Mary Cantorovich claimed she visited him there often and that he finally began work (with her assistance) on his long-promised memoirs. However, Mary also claimed he was indulging in excessive weekly drinking bouts and that money was getting tight.

Julian too claimed to be spending his days working on his long rumoured memoirs – *What Price Fugitive? A Refugee from Justice: The Memoirs of C.C. Julian* was to be the title. But it seems that despite his earlier claims there never was an interested New York publisher. Julian corresponded with his old shipmate Bruce Barton, who told him he liked the title. Julian thought he could entice investors into funding the book's printing.

272 'Letter From Japan: Only This One is From Shanghai, Which a Traveling Reporter Finds Not to His Liking. It's Too Hot, Too Noisy and Rather Dissolute', *Honolulu Advertiser*, July 19, 1936. NB: six Chinese dollars was approximately US$2 in 1936.

Wednesday, March 21st, 1934

Things hadn't worked out quite the way C.C. Julian wanted. He resigned from The Stock and Bond Guarantee Company in February 1934 with Leonora following him out the door. James Dolan then wrapped up the business and decided that, rather than stocks and shares, the way to make a fortune was in running mausoleums and set up the Shanghai Casket Company with a shop on the Bubbling Well Road. Ralph Levy later estimated that Julian owed US$25,000 to various Chinese investors he'd promised to 'make rich'. He had also borrowed sums of around 5,000 local Chinese dollars (about US$1700) from various investors, which he was using to fund his lifestyle at the Embassy, reduced as it was. Ralph told the press slightly later that Julian was broke and totally unable to pay any of this money back.[273] The Stock and Bond Guarantee Company was revealed as a fraud.

Julian began to drink heavily during the day, sitting around the Embassy Hotel all day avoiding any overly questioning journalists. He tried to tap friends and acquaintances for more loans he had no hope of ever repaying. He started to withdraw into himself, according to Leonora's later interviews.

Mary Cantorovich arrived at the Embassy Hotel on March 21st around noon. That was roughly when Julian would awake after his previous night's drinking. Julian appeared a little groggy that midday so Cantorovich went to the adjoining room to chat with Leonora. Upon returning to Julian's room she claimed later that she saw him sitting with a razor blade in his hand. There was blood on the carpet and he had slashed one of his wrists. He was about to slash the other. The cuts were not deep, but they were bleeding profusely.

Acting swiftly Cantorovich grabbed the razor blade from him and then proceeded to bandage up his slashed wrist to staunch the blood flow. The hotel manager, Mrs Jessie Cameron and her staff, came, called a doctor and started to clean up the room. Cantorovich told everyone that it was just an accident, that Julian had slipped

Weida Hotel

while shaving. All, it seems, agreed not to say what it obviously was – a suicide attempt.

The next day Jessie Cameron confronted Leonora Levy and told her that she knew they weren't married and that if she did not leave then she would demand that both she and Julian vacate the Embassy. They could not stay there together as an unmarried couple any longer. Leonora and C.C. packed their trunks and moved once again, this time across the border from the Settlement to Frenchtown. By Leonora's own estimate Julian was flat broke but he checked her into the Weida Hotel, part of a smart art-deco block close to Ravinel Park[274] on the Avenue Joffre, the main boulevard of the French Concession. Not wanting a repeat of the the fuss around being an unmarried couple sharing rooms, Julian moved to the Astor House Hotel, where he checked in to Room 300 once again as Mr T.R. King.

274 Now Xiangyang Park. The Weida Hotel and apartments building was sadly demolished a long time ago and a shopping mall built on the site.

Saturday, March 24th, 1934

A first anniversary in Shanghai. A party for C.C. and Leonora at the famous Astor House Grill Room and a chance to announce their engagement. The table was booked for 8 PM Saturday night. Ralph chauffeured them in his Ford from the Weida Hotel on the Avenue Joffre across town to the Astor. Julian was still staying in his suite at the Astor but spending most of his days over at the Weida with Leonora. The Astor House Grill Room was always full with the great and good of wealthy Chinese and Shanghailander society. J.F. Malone was there as was a wealthy local stocks investor Dr C.Y. Whang and his wife. George R. Coleman, vice-president of Elbrook Inc., the largest American wool merchants in China, had also been invited. Julian had met him on the ship that brought him to Shanghai and though Coleman must have known that the seemingly reputable Mr King he met in the stateroom of the *President Jackson* was in fact the distinctly disreputable C.C. Julian he seems to have kept in touch. Mary Cantorovich, festooned in jewellery and with a wealthy Chinese businessman in tow arrived slightly late. They all ate a mixed platter of Chinese and American food. The conversation, the champagne and the wine all flowed. C.C., who was drinking but eating very little according to Leonora,

Astor House dining room

was quite drunk and asked Leonora if she would excuse him for a minute, then he headed out of the Grill Room towards the hotel's lobby.

It was after 9 PM. C.C. had been gone some time. Leonora became worried. She went to C.C.'s suite. Leonora found him lying on the bed, a bottle of amytal sodium sedatives in his hand. He claimed they 'wouldn't hurt a kid'. He asked her to share some with him but she refused, thinking it would be bad for her health. He told her he wanted to make a fresh start, that he had funds coming from America imminently, that he loved her and that they had a 'bright future', Leonora remembered, 'Then he poured the contents of the bottle out into his hands. I knocked about twelve pills from his hands and he swallowed the remainder. I do not know how many. He then told me to call a doctor. He sat down on the bed and I gave him a glass of water. He said that if he kept on drinking water the pills would not affect him.'[275]

They did though. C.C. slumped in a chair, unconscious. The house doctor, Dr Eichengreen, arrived shortly after C.C. passed out, around 10 PM. Eichengreen found Julian fully clothed, lying on the bed in a very deep sleep.[276] His face was blue and he could not be wakened. Leonora showed him the three-quarters-empty bottle. An ambulance was summoned. Leonora and her brother raced behind the ambulance in Ralph's Ford to the Country Hospital on the Great Western Road.[277] There Dr Hall pumped Julian's stomach, but to no avail. C.C. Julian finally expired some time around 1 AM on Sunday March 25th 1934. He was near penniless and did not even have enough to pay his bill to the Astor; they seized his luggage in lieu of the 3,100 Chinese dollars he owned the hotel for his room.

Leonora went from the Country Hospital back to her room at the Weida Hotel. Around 6.30 AM she left the Weida and wandered

---

275 Leonora's version of events from, 'C.C. Julian Inquest', *North-China Herald and Supreme Court & Consular Gazette*, March 30, 1934.

276 There's a discrepancy in the record here between Leonora saying he was slumped unconscious in a chair and Dr Eichengreen finding him unconscious on the bed.

277 Now the Huadeng Hospital, 221 Yan'an Road West.

over to the Bubbling Well Road where the Shanghai Dispensary was just opening for business. She bought a bottle of amytal elixir similar to the barbiturates C.C. had taken though in liquid form, tried to drink it all down and collapsed on the floor of the shop's telephone booth. She too was then raced to the Country Hospital. She survived.

Back at the hospital it was turning into a circus. Journalists, paparazzi, the curious were claiming C.C. had threatened to kill himself before. Leonora swore she never thought C.C. would kill himself – it was all just bar-room bluster. And then, emerging from a loud conversation in the hallway with more news-hungry journalists, Mary Cantorovich demanded to see Julian's body, claiming he was her 'dear friend'. Hospital staff pushed her out of his room telling her that the coroner had forbidden anyone from seeing the corpse.

The Astor House Hotel wasn't saying anything to the press or allowing access to Julian's suite to anyone but the police. They had their own PR worries – for some time the Astor House had been a favoured spot for Shanghailanders to commit suicide – checking in, having one last splurge at the bar or in the Grill Room and then killing themselves in their suite. Naturally this was not a trend the management wished to encourage.[278]

C.C. Julian was forty-eight years of age. He left a widow, Mary, and two daughters in Winnipeg.

---

278 The Astor House Hotel continued to be a favoured spot for suicides (as did the Embassy). The only other building to become a serious focus of suicides in Shanghai was the art-deco wedge-shaped Normandie apartment building on the Avenue Joffre. So many people threw themselves off the roof of the building onto the street below that it became known as 'The Diving Board'. Unlike the Astor House, the Normandie's reputation remained and it continued to be a popular spot for suicides through the 1940s and into the Cultural Revolution. The 1940s Shanghai actress Shangguan Yunzhu (who starred in many much acclaimed Shanghai films including the 1947 *Spring River Flows East* and, one of the best movies to depict late 1940s Shanghai, 1949's *Crows and Sparrows*) threw herself from the Normandie's roof in 1968 after the Red Guards tormented her and declared her films to be 'poisonous weeds'. The more superstitious residents of the Normandie (now renamed the Wukang Building) claim to still be able to smell her perfume in the corridors.

Monday, March 26th, 1934

The first day of the coroner's inquest was held in the drab rooms of the Shanghai Municipal Public Mortuary. Proceedings were overseen by a solicitor working for the British Consular Service in Shanghai as the acting coroner, Mr Idwal Thomas Morris. The first order of business was the identification of the body. By chance a Mr C.E. Van de Verre happened to be staying at the Cathay Hotel and made himself known to the authorities as someone who had known C.C. Julian for over twenty years. He had last seen him the day before his death at the bar of the Palace Hotel on the Bund. Van de Verre verified it was Julian in the mortuary; the proceedings adjourned for the day with the plan being to reopen them the next day at His Majesty's Police Court.

Over the next few days seven witnesses were called to the stand – Dr Eichengreen, the Astor House Hotel's doctor; Dr A.D. Wall from the Country Hospital who had pronounced death; the night floor-boy at the Astor House who brought Dr Eichengreen to Julian's suite; Jessie Cameron from the Embassy Hotel; and Shanghai Municipal Police Detective Sub-Inspector George Hawkin who had attended the Astor on Sunday morning, searched the room and recovered the empty bottle of barbiturates.

Then the witnesses for whom the press in the public gallery had been waiting. First, Mary Cantorovich, described by the newspapers as 'twenty-four years old and attractive'. Cantorovich told her tale of Julian's attempted suicide at the Embassy Hotel on March 21st. However, she also thought he might be coming into some money. Mary had told Leonora that certain people of her acquaintance would pay Julian not to publish his memoirs and that sum would get him out of his various financial fixes around town.

And finally twenty-year-old Leonora Levy took the stand. The newspapers described her as 'a comely Shanghai girl' and a 'striking brunette'. Leonora claimed that C.C. was in a good mood at the Astor House despite his business worries, that he had proposed to her, stated that he was going to make a new start, that he had US$25,000 stashed in a safety deposit box in the United States that a colleague was going to bring to him in Shanghai. Leonora told the inquest that Julian called General Cohen and told him to come over to the hotel to meet his fiancée (Leonora). Leonora did admit that she knew Julian medicated with amytal, but that he had told her they were not that strong and when he had tried to swallow them all she had tried to knock them out of his hands, fearing that he was taking them on an empty stomach. But still she maintained he had not meant to kill himself – 'Why, he had everything in the world to live for. We were engaged to be married'.[279]

The inquest closed on March 30th with a verdict from Idwal Thomas Morris that C.C. Julian died of 'narcotic poisoning, self-administered'.

Why did C.C. Julian decide the long road of his adventurous trickster life had come to an end that night in the Astor House? He was certainly down on his uppers, out of cash, out of assets, and business was a bust. It was also the case that, in Washington DC, President Roosevelt had just signed a bill authorising the extradition of American fugitives from places where the United States exercised extraterritoriality rights.[280] Though Julian was Canadian some lawyers in Shanghai had thought the new law could be used to extradite him back to Oklahoma to face justice.

Friday, May 11th, 1934

C.C. Julian was buried at the Hungjao Road Cemetery on May 11th. For seven weeks since his death Julian's body had been held at the International Funeral Director's private chapel on Kiachow Road on the orders of the British Consulate. Julian's sister, Violet Greenhow, wanted the body shipped to Los Angeles for burial there; his wife Mary in Winnipeg said he should be buried in Shanghai. Eventually the dispute was sorted out; Shanghai was decided on as C.C. Julian's final resting place. The Reverend Emory

279 Inquest details largely from 'C.C. Julian Inquest', *North-China Herald and Supreme Court & Consular Gazette*, March 30, 1934.

280 A law that would, several years later, be used to extradite the fugitive from Oklahoma State Penitentiary and 'Slots King' of Shanghai, Jack T. Riley, back to a prison sentence in the United States – see my book *City of Devils: A Shanghai Noir* (Beijing: Penguin North Asia, 2018).

Luccock of the Shanghai American Community Church conducted the service at graveside; a dozen 'friends' of C.C.'s attended;
twice as many journalists turned up. Wreaths arrived from C.C.'s
brother and sister in Los Angeles, Mary Julian in Winnipeg and
Jessie Cameron and the staff of the Embassy Hotel. The British
Consulate paid for the service and the simple pine coffin. Despite
speculation around town, C.C. Julian really was broke. The grave
was unmarked.

Postscript

It seems Julian's memoirs, *What Price Fugitive?* did exist. Mary
Cantorovich claimed he completed them with her help. One
newspaper report says a local newspaperman (unnamed) cleaned
up the manuscript for Julian. C.C. himself claimed to have mailed
it to a New York publisher and that no copy remained in Shanghai.
One Julian biographer, Jules Tygiel, wrote that the Hollywood actor
George Hamilton later purchased the only copy and was trying to
turn the manuscript into a movie.[281]

Mary Cantorovich applied for American citizenship the following year, got it, and then her trail goes cold.

But it's Leonora Levy who is the real heart of this tale. It's hard
not to feel that, whatever she knew about C.C. and hoped for from
their relationship, that she was treated shabbily. Her father had been
murdered when she was barely ten years old; she worked in a dreary
office; C.C. must have at least seemed exciting and a way out of
that routine life. But he wasn't the man she thought – he wasn't an
honest businessman, nor a millionaire. He wasn't interested in ever
going straight but only in working out more long-cons. He may
well have proposed to her but any marriage in Shanghai would still
have been bigamy. He never made her rich, he never lived up to
any of his big promises and not long after proposing to her he left
her in the shabby Weida Hotel, moved to the smart Astor House

---

281 Jules Tygiel, *The Great Los Angeles Swindle: Oil, Stocks and Scandal During
     the Roaring Twenties*, (Oxford: Oxford University Press, 1994).

and killed himself. He left her nothing – not a penny. How distraught all this must have left her.

But Leonora recovered and, as far as I can work out, went back to being a secretary. She moved jobs a lot in the late 1930s. In 1936 a Miss L. Levy was working for De La Rue Co., a British supplier of stamps to the Chinese post office they manufactured in a factory in the French Concession. With the fall of France in June 1940 Frenchtown fell into the hands of Vichy and so De La Rue moved its China operations to Rangoon in British-controlled Burma. Miss Levy did not move with them but got a secretarial post with Walter G. Berger, an exporter. After that, I found no trace of her.

Shanghai forgot about C.C. Julian in a heartbeat. Conmen had passed through town before and would again. Business still needed to be attended to; the next ocean liner brought fresh interesting characters and new sojourners. Suite 300 at the Astor House Hotel was cleaned up and a new guest checked in.

Appendix

Placenames, old and new

Shanghai roads

Old	New
Astor Road	Jinshan Road
Blood Alley	*See* Rue Chu Pao San
Boundary Road	Tianmu Road East
Rue Bourgeat	Changle Road
Broadway	Daming Road
Bubbling Well Road	Nanjing Road West
Bund	Zhongshan No. 1 Road
Carter Road	Shimen No. 1 Road
Rue Chu Pao San	Xikou Road
Columbia Road	Panyu Road
Dalny Road	Dalian Road
Boulevard des Deux Républiques	Renmin Road
Avenue Eddy	*See* Avenue Edward VII
Edinburgh Road	Jiangsu Road
Avenue Edward VII	Yan'an Road
Fearon Road	Jiulong Road
Foochow Road	Fuzhou Road
Route Frelupt	Jianguo Road West
Garden Bridge	Waibaidu
Route Francis Garnier	Dongping Road
Great Western Road	Yan'an Road West
Avenue Haig	Huashan Road
Hankow Road	Hankou Road
Route Herve de Sieyes	Yongjia Road
Hungjao Road	Hongqiao Road
Avenue Joffre	Huai Hai Road Middle
Kelmscott Gardens	A lane off Avenue du Roi Albert
Kiangse Road	Jiangxi Road

Kiaochow Road	Jiaozhou Road
Kiukiang Road	Jiujiang Road
Rue Lafayette	Fuxing Road Middle
Love Lane	Wujiang Road
McBain Road	Fengxian Road
Medhurst Road	Taixing Road
Mohawk Road	Huangpi Road North
Muirhead Road	Haimen Road
Nanking Road	Nanjing Road East
Ningpo Road	Ningbo Road
Route Père Robert	Ruijin No. 2 Road
Quai de France	Zhongshang No. 2 Road
Range Road	Wujin Road
Avenue du Roi Albert	Shaanxi Road South
Scott Road	Shanyang Road & Shande Road
Seward Road	Dongdaming Road
Singapore Road	Yuyao Road
Soochow Road South	Suzhou South Road
Swatow Road	Shantou Road
Szechuen Road	Sichuan Road
Thibet Road	Xizang Road
Thibet Road North	Xizang Road North
Route Vallon	Nanchang East Road
Ward Road	Changyang Road
Wayside Road	Huoshan Road
Woosung Road	Wusong Road
Yu Yuen Road	Yuyuan Road
Ziang Teh Road	Shanyin Road

Shanghai districts

Old	New
Chapei	Zhabei
Hongkew	Hongkou
Hungjao	Hongqiao
Kiangwan	Jiangwan
Paoshan	Baoshan

Pootung	Pudong
Siccawei (Zikawei)	Xujiahui
Soochow Creek	Suzhou Creek
Whangpoo River	Huangpu River
Woosung	Wusong
Yangtszepoo (Y'Poo)	Yangpu

Cities

Old	New
Canton	Guangzhou
Chungking	Chongqing
Dairen	Dalian
Hankow	Hankou
Kalgan	Zhangjiakou
Mukden	Shenyang
Peking	Beijing
Soochow	Suzhou
Tientsin	Tianjin
Tsingtao	Qingdao
Yunnan-fu	Kunming

Acknowledgements

In general I'd like to acknowledge everyone who has read, commented, emailed me or got in touch one way or another relating to posts on my blog *China Rhyming* since I started it in September 2008. Over 4,000 posts later it seemed time to take some of the most interesting characters who'd appeared in various posts and give them their own book. My special thanks to Dan Washburn who has hosted this blog for me for many years, helped me when I forgot the passwords, and ensured it's never crashed in over a decade.

The bulk of the chapter on Aleister Crowley was written while staying in Morocco. Crowley did visit Morocco (Tangier, to be precise) not long after his brief Shanghai sojourn in 1907, with his friend George Montagu Bennett, the Earl of Tankerville. They visited to recuperate from their cocaine addiction. He visited again the following year, this time with his lover the English occultist and poet Victor Neuberg. I stayed in the southern Atlantic coastal city of Essaouira (formerly Mogador) at the excellent Villa Maroc. I should also extend thanks to Ned Kelly, long-time Shanghai sojourner, who shares my interest in The Beast and his wicked ways.

The chapter on Elly Widler was originally published in a slightly different form in *That's Shanghai* magazine. I must thank J.A.S. Cunningham, a descendant of Elly's who generously provided family photographs and information. When I first wrote about Elly's exploits I was delighted that the Consulate General of Switzerland in Shanghai took an interest. My thanks to Erwin Lüthi, the then Swiss deputy consul general, who dug around in their archives to see what his predecessors had made of Elly.

Lily Flohr has been a minor obsession of mine for many years. Indeed I cannot now recall how I first heard of her. Perhaps it was simply seeing an advert for her cabaret at the Elite Bar in a 1941 *China Weekly Review* that brought her to my attention. She's slumbered in the back of my mind for so long, occasionally nudging me to recall her, that during the intervening years I actually had cause (for reasons non-Lily related) to visit Vienna, Berlin, Frankfurt (home of the Deutsches Filminstitut) and Bucharest to grab chances to pull at the various threads of Lily's life. However, the chapter was largely written in an old apartment of mine on Shanghai's Dalian Road, which lies on the eastern edge of what was the former Jewish ghetto and is the border between the districts of Tilanqiao and Yangpu. I like to think Lily strolled along the street occasionally back in the day. A good many details of Lily's life later came to me via email conversations with Sophie Fetthauer at the Institut für Historisch Musikwissenschaft at the University of Frankfurt. I'd especially like to thank long-time Shanghai resident and documentary filmmaker Lothar Spree (who sadly passed away in 2013) for his help in tracking down Lily all those years ago.

Irene Weitemeyer remains pretty elusive, as does much of what went on in and around the Zeitgeist Bookshop. We may never know the truth about Roger Hollis in China, or the identity of the 'Fifth Man'. I must acknowledge the work done on Irene Weitemeyer by Thomas Kampen at the University of Heidelberg's Institut für Sinologie.

Murder in the Shanghai Trenches first appeared in the UK Crime Writers' Association 2015 real crime anthology *Truly Criminal* (London: The History Press). My thanks to the CWA (who were kind enough to award me one of their prestigious Daggers for *Midnight in Peking* in 2013) and particularly the book's editor Martin Edwards for comments on the manuscript. Additionally to Professor Robert Bickers of Bristol University and Doug Clarke, the author of the *Gunboat Justice* trilogy (available from Earnshaw Books of Shanghai), in Hong Kong for their informed comments on the case.

Thanks to Jo Lusby, Patrizia van Daalen, Lena Petzke and Anya Goncharova at Penguin-Random House North Asia in Beijing who commissioned my Penguin China Special, *Bloody Saturday: Shanghai's Darkest Day* (2017) about the tragic events in the International Settlement and Frenchtown on August 14th, 1937. Terese Rudolph came to me out of that research, but space annoyingly kept her out of the final book. I'm delighted to have found a home for her story finally.

André Malraux's *La Condition Humaine* (*Man's Fate*) remains a favourite book of mine. The chapter on *Man's Fate* and Malraux originated as a speech given at a series of lunches in China in 2010 to commemorate the fifth anniversary of Penguin books in China. Thanks once again to Jo Lusby for suggesting the events. And also thanks to Michelle Garnaut at Shanghai's M on the Bund and Alex Pearson of the Beijing Bookworm for hosting those lunches.

Thanks to author and managing editor of the *Los Angeles Review of Books China Channel* Alec Ash for permission to reprint a version of my articles for them on Arthur Ransome's Shanghai sojourn and also on Penelope Fitzgerald's 1970s package holiday to China.

My thanks to Doug Clarke and Tess Johnston for helping track down some details on the Shanghai life of Leonora Levy and the suicide of C.C. Julian.

The article on the Roma of Shanghai was first published in a slightly different form in the *Journal of the Royal Asiatic Society China*, Vol. 75, No. 1, 2013, as 'Gypsies of Shanghai: The Roma Community of Late 1930s and 1940s Shanghai and Their Role in the City's Entertainment Industry'. This version is only slightly changed. My thanks to the RAS Shanghai for permission to republish.

I've talked Asia books with Pete Spurrier of Blacksmith Books in Hong Kong over beers for many years. I'm glad we finally got to do a China book together. Alan Sargent in Hong Kong did the final edit and text layout for Blacksmith. Regionally-based independent small publishers are the lifeblood of publishing in Asia and I'm eternally grateful to everything they publish that would not other-wise perhaps see the light of day.

Anne Witchard diligently read, commented and edited all of these pieces (several times in some cases) invariably turning them from my rather floating whimsies into more readable, tight and scholarly articles.

Paul French
Email – paul@chinarhyming.com
Blog – www.chinarhyming.com
Twitter – @chinarhyming
Instagram – OldShanghaiPaul
WeChat – paul_french

Image credits

p 14. Map – from John Pal, *Shanghai Saga* (London: Jarrolds, 1963)

p.15. Alice Boughton Collection, Library of Congress Prints and Photographs Division

p.31. Carl Van Vechten Collection, Library of Congress

p.45. *Cincinnati Enquirer*, December 14, 1928

p.52. Mai Mai Sze, 1945

p.55. Library of Congress Prints and Photographs Division

p.57. *Photoplay*, April 1932

p.68. City of Vancouver Archives

p.71. Louis L'Amour Enterprises Inc.

p.73. Louis L'Amour Enterprises Inc.

p.99. Twentieth Century Fox

p.105. British Film Institute

p.109. Twentieth Century Fox

p.110. *Honolulu Advertiser*, February 27, 1936

p.115. Carl Van Vechten Collection, Library of Congress

p.116. Buck Clayton Collection, LaBudde Special Collections Department, Miller Nichols Library, University of Missouri – Kansas City

p.123. Roy G. Butler Collection, Chicago Public Library

p.125. *Maui News*, May 5, 1922

p.127. *Honolulu Star Bulletin*, April 1, 1933

p.135. *Star Press* (Muncie, Indiana), February 8, 1931

p.141. Library of Congress Prints and Photographs Division/IMDB

p.142. *Brooklyn Daily Eagle*, July 30, 1935

p.144. *Philadelphia Inquirer*, March 13, 1938

p.147. Originally published in *The Equinox*, vol.1, issue 10 (1913)

p.161. The Arthur Ransome Society

p.171. Arizona State University Library

p.177. Agnes Smedley – Arizona State University Library

p.177. Hotsumi Ozaki– MIPictorial History of Modern Japan Vol.12, Sanseido Publishing

p.178. MI5

p.185. AKG-Images/Ullstein Bild

p.187. *Guangzhou Republic Daily* (*Guangzhou Minguo Ribao*),
   November 28, 1936

p.196 *China Weekly Review*, July 3, 1941

p.208. *Shanghai Echo*, August 15, 1940

p.231. Museum of Applied Arts and Sciences, Sydney

p.233. Powerhouse Museum, Sydney

p.234 Powerhouse Museum, Sydney

p.236. Museum of Applied Arts and Sciences, Sydney

p.238. *The Morning News* (Wilmington, Delaware), July 22, 1926

p.239. *Bonham Daily Favorite* (Bonham, Texas), July 26, 1913

p.241. Agence de Presse Meurisse

p.251. Courtesy of JAS Cunningham

p.252. *China Weekly Review*, November 16, 1940

p.255. Courtesy of JAS Cunningham

p.259. Courtesy of JAS Cunningham

p.260. *China Weekly Review*, November 30, 1940

p.263. *Santa Cruz Evening News*, August 21, 1937

p.273. *The San Francisco Examiner*, September 16, 1937

p.274. *Reading Times* (Pennsylvania), October 13, 1937

p.276. The United States Pro-Skating Historical Foundation

p.282. *The China Press*, June 8, 1940

p.288. courtesy of Katya Knyazeva

p.293. Fourth Estate

p.303. *New York Daily News*, September 11, 1933

p.310. *The Salt Lake Tribune*, April 2, 1933

p.312. *The China Press*, July 8, 1930

p.318. courtesy of Virtual Shanghai

p. 23, 41, 61,67, 78, 80, 90, 95, 107, 158, 159, 164, 168, 173, 193, 199,
   201, 211, 248, 277, 295, 300, 319. author's collection

front cover photo: Waterfront at Shanghai, c1931. Library of
   Congress Prints and Photographs Division

back cover postcard: courtesy of the personal collection of Anne
   Witchard

Forthcoming: *DESTINATION PEKING*

by PAUL FRENCH

Including:

The Peonies and the Ponies – Harold Acton & his Peiping
　　Characters (1941)
Finding Mr Moto in Peking – J.P. Marquand & Adeleine Hooker
　　(1934)
The Madonna of Peking – Bertha Lum (1930)
The Peking Aesthete's Aesthete – Desmond Parsons & Robert
　　Byron (1937)
On Tour With The Quaints – John Mills & Hayley Bell (1930)
From the Trenches to the Hutongs – Ellen La Motte (1919)
'Peking is Like Paris' – Isamu Noguchi (1930)
Life in The Camel's Bell – Helen Burton (1928)
The Other 'Grand Hotel' – The Lost World of the Grand Hotel
　　des Wagons Lits (1905)
An 'American Girl' in Peking – Mona Monteith (1901)
The Nazis of Peiping – Charley Schmidt and Adelbert Schulze (1947)
The Great Bibliophile of the *Grand Hôtel de Pekin* – Henri Vetch (1930)
Making a Pulp out of Peking – L. Ron Hubbard (1927)
From Tientsin to Hollywood – Sari Maritza (1910)
Lev Karakhan – Peking's First Bolshevik (1923)

EXPLORE ASIA WITH BLACKSMITH BOOKS

From retailers around the world or from *www.blacksmithbooks.com*